INTRODUCTION TO CRITICAL LEGAL THEORY

Second Edition

Cavendish
Publishing
Limited

London • Sydney • Portland, Oregon

INTRODUCTION TO CRITICAL LEGAL THEORY

Second Edition

Ian Ward
BA, LLM, PhD, Professor of Law
University of Newcastle upon Tyne

Cavendish
Publishing
Limited

London • Sydney • Portland, Oregon

Second edition first published in Great Britain 2004 by
Cavendish Publishing Limited, The Glass House,
Wharton Street, London WC1X 9PX, United Kingdom
Telephone: + 44 (0)20 7278 8000   Facsimile: + 44 (0)20 7278 8080
Email: info@cavendishpublishing.com
Website: www.cavendishpublishing.com

Published in the United States by Cavendish Publishing
c/o International Specialized Book Services,
5824 NE Hassalo Street, Portland,
Oregon 97213-3644, USA

Published in Australia by Cavendish Publishing (Australia) Pty Ltd
45 Beach Street, Coogee, NSW 2034, Australia
Telephone: + 61 (2)9664 0909   Facsimile: + 61 (2)9664 5420
Email: info@cavendishpublishing.com.au
Website: www.cavendishpublishing.com.au

© Ward, I	2004
First edition	1998
Second edition	2004

British Library Cataloguing in Publication Data
Ward, Ian, 1963–
Introduction to critical legal theory – 2nd ed
1 Law – Philosophy
I Title
340.1

Library of Congress Cataloguing in Publication Data
Data available

ISBN 1-85941-928-3

1 3 5 7 9 10 8 6 4 2

Printed and bound in Great Britain by
Biddles Ltd., King's Lynn, Norfolk

PREFACE

In some ways nothing has really changed since July 1998. Or at least nothing fundamental has changed in my own approach to the study of legal theory. I am just as convinced that the age of positive jurisprudence has passed, and that this is a good thing. I am every bit as persuaded by the intellectually liberating potential of interdisciplinarity. To this extent, the tone of this second edition has not changed. Of course, there are certain substantive alternations which aim to chronicle recent intellectual contributions to the study of legal theory. The most interesting of these tend to relate to the emergent challenges of globalisation and the 'new' world order within which we live. At various stages in this new edition we will encounter jurisprudential attempts to account for these particular challenges: the revival of a Kantian 'law of peoples', a Benthamite 'general' jurisprudence, a Derridean cosmopolitan 'politics of friendship', and so on. There has also been a marked evolution in narrative theories of law and justice, and the collateral idea of a new legal 'humanism'. The thought that questions of law and justice should be understood in terms of an exchange of 'stories' seems ever more compelling. This new edition of *An Introduction to Critical Legal Theory* is one such story. Whether it promotes a vigorous exchange depends entirely on you.

Ian Ward
May 2004

CONTENTS

CHAPTER 1

IDENTIFYING MODERNISM

THE CLASSICAL TRADITION

The search for meaning

This book is premised upon the need to identify modernism, in order then to describe the various critical legal theories which have sought to revise an original model. Of course, the unavoidable paradox here is that there is no universally regarded model of modernism – just as there is no universally accorded critical tradition. There are various modernisms and various critical traditions, a number of which we will encounter in subsequent chapters. However, in order to establish a sufficient basis for our critical project, we must attempt to excavate certain theories of law and politics which are often alleged to be representative of modernity, and thus, in this first chapter, we will revisit the classical tradition of Plato and Aristotle, as well as later medieval theological variants, before finally addressing the survival of contemporary ideas of natural law and natural rights. By the end of this chapter, we will already have encountered a number of revisionist and critical theories of law. Indeed, by the time we leave Plato, we will have made critical concessions, for, as we shall shortly see, Aristotle was Plato's greatest critic, and just as modernism is often traced back 2000 years, so too are the origins of critical legal thinking.

The earliest recorded legal code is that of Hammurabi of Babylon, who ruled from 2067–25 BC. Greek legend records lawgivers such as Solon and Dracon drafting legislation around 700 BC. An interest in legal theory is just as ancient. For centuries, law has been justified in philosophical terms: in terms of an intrinsic rationality. Law is rational, and because of that, justified. In making this claim, philosophers have necessarily aligned law with the truth. In other words, they have justified law in terms of its foundation in some sort of supreme truth. As we shall see in this chapter, for Plato, it will be a truth in natural order, whilst for Aristotle, it will be a truth in moral virtue, and for Aquinas, a truth in God. Classical Greek philosophy could not accept that life had no meaning. The very earliest civilisations tended to found their social laws and customs in forms of divinity and associated fertility cults. The first organised churches, established by the Orphics, were devoted to the cult of the Thracian god, Bacchus. For them, the only meaning in life was pleasure, and more particularly sex.

The search for 'essence' intensified with the pre-Socratics. It was they who first wondered whether there might not be more to life than sex. Thales of Miletus, alive during the 6th century BC, was convinced that everything was made of water. Another Miletian, Anaximander, can be termed the first legal philosopher, in that he decided that justice was the essential intellectual concept, and could be proved in natural order. Still another, Anaximenes, decided that everything was made of air, and spent most of his life trying to prove that the world was shaped like a round table. The evolution of pre-Socratic ideas tended to progress in this way – mixing the perceptive insight with the bizarrely improbable. Heraclitus of Ephesus concentrated on death and struggle, and concluded that the essential experience of life lies in exterminating someone else. Such pessimism finally led him to declare that 'The cosmos, at best, is like a rubbish heap scattered at random'. Parmenides decided to the contrary that nothing ever changes; we are always stabilised by our history, and should always organise our social institutions in such a way as to prevent innovation.

It is only with the Athenians that we encounter a more immediate concern with legal and political philosophy. It is often asserted that the Athens of around the 3rd and 4th centuries BC was the first to experience democracy, as it was also the first political State to define itself in terms of laws (Kelly, 1992, p 10). This is only partly true. Democracy is a relative concept, and in the democracy founded by Pericles of Athens, there were 230,000 slaves. Pericles's democracy extended participatory power to a select number of essentially aristocratic citizenry, and no further, and it is Pericles's Athens which provides the immediate historical context for both Plato and Aristotle. In 429 BC Pericles died and was succeeded by radical democrats, and a period of intermittent civil disorder. It was amidst this political chaos that Plato's great mentor and teacher, Socrates, was executed, and the recorded accounts of his trial and death provide the immediate perspective for Plato's *Republic* and *The Laws*. Socrates was condemned to death in 399 BC, on charges of introducing new gods and corrupting the youth. His defence was based on the idea that reason could describe truth. It was intrinsically right to articulate the truth and, being necessary for the good order of society, could never be unjust (Plato, 1969, pp 51–52, 60–64). Socrates's death is as important as his trial. Following his refusal to seek mitigation and his determination to ensure his own capital sentence, Socrates then stolidly refused to escape, even though the nature of imprisonment was such as to encourage it. He decided to die in the cause of his philosophy. It was a matter of integrity, and to have run away and avoid death would have been to admit that philosophical principle was not of ultimate importance. Preservation of the body is a mere distraction, when compared with the preservation of truth. Moreover, it would also break his agreement with the society in which he lived. If Socrates had evaded the law, he would have been conceding that the individual interest could sometimes come above that of the State. To have evaded the law would indeed have rendered him guilty as a corrupter of young minds (Plato, 1969, pp 89–95).

Law and order in Plato's *Republic*

Plato's *Republic*, written around 375 BC, was composed as a paean to Socratic moral and political philosophy, and at its heart could be found the concept of order. It was an immediately jurisprudential gesture, for it is 'justice' which assures order (Grayling, 2003, pp 24–25). Good order is just and disorder is unjust. There are three essential themes in *Republic*: the construction of the ideal commonwealth; the role of education; and the role and definition of philosophy. Moreover, each book of *Republic* contributes to the description of a utopian society. Every philosophy aspires to describe a utopia. Philosophy founds politics, and it is crucial that this order is not reversed. Indeed, this notion of ideal form, which we then aspire to emulate in reality, was Plato's core philosophical tenet, and presented as a counter to the suggestion that justice is simply a matter of dealing with each situation as it arises. For Plato, there are supreme rules which can and must be used in the resolution of every situation. This 'theory of forms' is founded on his distinction between knowledge and opinion. Knowledge simply is, and is quite apart from our perception or sensation of it. Our sensation of knowledge is opinion. Ideas, accordingly, simply are. Our perceptions of ideas are our approximations of them, founded upon opinion. This basic thesis is described by a series of metaphors, of which the Cave metaphor is perhaps the most famous. Plato describes a situation where a number of primitive cave dwellers are bound together facing a wall upon which a series of shadows play. The shadows are, of course, merely illusions or approximations of the real forms from which the shadows are cast. The light which casts the shadows represents the idea or truth, and the more advanced society is one which models itself upon the light and ideal, rather illusion and shadow (Plato, 1987, pp 316–21; cf MacIntyre, 1967, pp 44–45).

Plato's ideal society is fashioned with this philosophical model in mind. At the same time, there is an essential congruence between society and self. The ideal society is constituted by ideal individuals. We aspire to be good as individuals because that is how we can contribute to the good of society, and we will do so because we will be educated in an understanding of reason. We can then aspire to excellence, which is, indeed, the duty of the good person. For Plato, then, justice lies in the perfectly ordered society, populated by perfectly ordered individuals, and the interest of the self and of society are as one. The ideal commonwealth is determined by its good order, and this order is natural and metaphysical, which means it exists external to the individual. The metaphysical world and its order exist, whether or not you and I do, and anything in accordance with this order is just. Understood in this sense, justice is the 'highest category' of good to 'which everyone who is to be happy' must aspire (Plato, 1987, pp 75, 103). And because we are all rational beings, we must necessarily share this aspiration. Justice has nothing to do with equality or fairness. Neither, accordingly, do just laws. Just laws constitute good order, mirroring, or attempting to mirror, the ideals of natural order.

This basic idea underpins the various constituents of the ideal republic which Plato proceeds to describe. Most importantly, there are three kinds of citizen: artisans, who provide basic material needs and constitute the commoners; soldiers, who defend society; and rulers, who administer society. These three kinds mirror the three divisions of the soul. The first of these is the rational, and it is the rulers who are supremely rational. The second is the spiritual or agent, and it is the soldiers who act as agents of the State. The third is the appetitive, and it is the artisan who all too often abandons all reason and indulges in wild desires. The class of each individual is determined by which part of the soul is dominant, and it is therefore very necessary that political power rests with the rulers, whose souls are dominated by reason, 'the reflective element in the mind'. Just as justice in the ideal individual would be a perfect balance between each, so too is justice in the ideal republic (Plato, 1987, pp 208–21). In real terms, therefore, justice is everyone 'minding one's own business' and doing the task best allotted to them in terms of the natural disposition of the soul. In this way, there will also be perfect harmony between ruler and ruled, State and society, so 'the individual man is just in the same way as the State is just' (Plato, 1987, pp 204, 218). At all times, then, Plato is describing a society defined by order. Sex, for example, should be harmonic, perfect in form, and in the service of the State. In the ideal society, only the most distinguished and rational should be encouraged to copulate and procreate; that is, those who appreciate the importance of order. Moreover, in case parental relations intrude upon an appreciation that everyone's first duty is to the State, children should be removed from their families and reared by the State. Inferior or crippled children, plainly lacking in perfect form, are to be banished (Plato, 1987, pp 237–41).

The idea of education is essential, necessary for the purpose of training the mind in the relation of reason, justice and harmony. As Socrates suggested, 'rhythm and harmony penetrate deeply into the mind and take a most powerful hold on it'. It is education, not law, which will produce good citizens. Such education will be conducted primarily through music and gymnastics. Only the musician who appreciates harmony can play beautifully, and only the gymnast who appreciates perfect form will avoid perpetually falling over (Plato, 1987, pp 157–68). Aside from music and gymnastics, the ideal citizen is to be inculcated in the virtues of gravity, decorum and courage, and most certainly discouraged from laughter. Nothing can be more disruptive to natural harmony than jollity. Poets and artists who so indulge are to be banished from the ideal society (Plato, 1987, pp 132–39). Of course, it is only reasonable to expect the citizenry to be educated. It is not necessary for anyone else. Indeed, philosophy is 'impossible among the common people'. Education is essential for the guardian class, and Plato's ultimate ideal is for a philosopher-king – someone supremely capable of rule, precisely because he is supremely educated in the intrinsic relation of justice and harmony.

Realising this ideal is essential, because 'the society we have described can never grow into a reality' until 'philosophers become kings in the world'. Such kings are like 'king bees in a hive ... better and more fully educated than the rest and better qualified to combine the practice of philosophy and politics'. It is they who will legislate for the benefit of the 'society as a whole', using 'persuasion or compulsion to unite all citizens and make them share together the benefits which each individually can confer on the community'. Moreover, 'its purpose in fostering this attitude is not to leave everyone to please himself, but to make each man a link in the unity of the whole' (Plato, 1987, pp 263, 289, 323–24). Such a ruler, Plato calculates, will be precisely 729 times happier than a tyrant. His subjects will also be considerably happier that those who live in 'imperfect societies', of which tyranny and democracy are the two prime examples. Democracy is a form of anarchy, in which various political interests dedicate themselves to the extermination of all others, and such polities are characterised by a lack of principle, order and justice (Plato, 1987, pp 377–91, 415).

Plato's *Laws* have been described as something of a 'postscript' to *Republic* (MacIntyre, 1967, pp 51–56). To a considerable extent this is true. Once again, Plato describes a utopia, and the philosophical model presented in *Republic* – the theory of forms – again provides the foundation. In this utopia, which Plato calls 'Magnesia', there are precisely 5,040 citizens, together with as many slaves as necessary, all of whom enjoy a sunny climate, good water supply and a happy disposition. There is a comprehensive State religion, and all property is inalienable, staying within the family. This way, no one should squabble about theological matters, possessions or climactic disadvantage. The threat of wealth and property is particularly acute. 'Virtue and great wealth', Plato assures us, 'are quite incompatible' (Plato, 1970, pp 212–13, 350–53). This sense of community is enhanced by State supported drinking parties and communal feasts. Such parties are all part of the education of the good citizen. So, once again, is music. The great mistake in Egyptian society, Plato confidently advises, is a failure to educate people in the importance of musical harmony (Plato, 1970, pp 63, 91–92, 116). Sex is again paramount, and Plato enhances the various ways of ensuring ideal procreation advanced in *Republic*, adding a series of insights, including the importance of prohibiting copulation whilst drunk (so by implication much of the time in Magnesia). Chastity is not in the best interests of the community, and anyone who has failed to marry by 35, and who is sufficiently reputable as to be likely to produce good citizens, is to be fined annually. The onus of responsibility lies with the men. Women tend to chastity, and are naturally less inclined to virtue in the wider sense of contributing to the good of the community. Female officials are to be employed to travel round ensuring that people are copulating and doing so properly, and are particularly trained to detect intransigent women who remain deviously chaste (Plato, 1970, pp 250–63).

Plato's concern with procreation is founded on the central belief that man is defined by life in communities. Man has a natural inclination to live in communities, and therefore man has a natural inclination to good order, only disrupted by wealth or poverty, but not presumably by inebriation or indigestion, or loud music. Man does not simply wish to 'survive', but to 'become as virtuous as possible'. He can only do so in a just (meaning well ordered) society, for it is only 'when a single people speaks the same language and observes the same laws' that 'you get a certain feeling of community'. There was no room for multiculturalism in Plato's utopia, and certainly not migrants. Nothing was more likely to disrupt good order than a foreigner (Plato, 1970, pp 122, 162–63). Furthermore, the good citizen will appreciate the role of law in preserving justice. Deviants, unwelcome guests and poor musicians will enjoy a punishment inspired by a common revulsion and 'righteous indignation' (Plato, 1970, pp 188–95).

Finally, the role of the philosopher-king is once again paramount, and his laws play a crucial role in fashioning society. At 'every stage', Plato suggests, the lawgiver 'should supervise his people' and use laws as instruments for the 'proper distribution of praise and blame' (Plato, 1970, p 55). For the practical political world, Plato advances related principles of the rule of law and the balance of powers, both of which are cast as a defence against anarchy or tyranny. It is for the ruler, who naturally exists aloof from the rule of law, to maintain perfect harmony and a balance of power. Such a ruler, Plato readily admits, is a 'dictator', but being educated in the virtues of reason, should be a fairly benign one. History suggests, Plato assures us, that malignant dictators have not come across his philosophy before, and so might be excused the more regrettable examples of their tyranny. Once the virtues of natural order are properly understood by the educated ruler, such tyrannies will disappear from history. Certainly, absolute monarchy is the best hope there is, for if the ruler fails, the society will be cast into the horrors of democracy, where everyone does pretty much what they want, pursuing their own interest regardless of that of the wider community. Such a form of government Plato dismisses as 'voluntary slavery'. Fortunately, those of a democratic disposition can be spotted by their failure to appreciate harmonious music and their predilection for poetry and theatre (Plato, 1970, pp 140–42, 167–74).

Aristotle and the ethics of virtue

Born in 384 BC, Aristotle is the first, and most important, critic of Plato. The basis of Aristotle's critique is founded on the need to make philosophy practical. Rather than devoting himself to the tricky business of metaphysics, he concentrated on the application of philosophical principles to the sciences of politics, law and economics. Whereas Plato started from the question 'what is man?', and progressed to a definition which required the congruence of man and society, Aristotle immediately concentrates on that society, assuming that it is impossible to conceive of man external to society. Unlike Plato, who was happy to write a philosophy in the form of a series of often rather whimsical dialogues, Aristotle determined to systematise. Rigour, not rhetoric, was the key to understanding. Law and politics is not just a philosophy, it is a philosophy of science. Moreover, it is a science because man is rational, and it is the possession of reason which ensures that both man, and the world in which he lives and which defines him, can be fully rationalised. Aristotle's certainty that science could discover the foundation and meaning of everything, through the power of reason, remains hugely influential. The systematisation of philosophy is one of Aristotle's great contributions, and matters of ethics and politics, of justice and law, are part of this great overarching system. Where meta-ethics is the science of pure rationality, ethics, which is the concern of Aristotle's greatest work, *The Ethics*, is the science of political rationality and political philosophy.

The essential theme of Aristotle's *Ethics* is established with the initial question, 'What is the object of life?'. In the very first lines of *The Ethics* he suggests: 'Every art and every investigation, and similarly every action and pursuit, is considered to aim at some good' (Aristotle, 1976, p 63). The presence of a *telos*, or ultimate good, is taken from Plato as the centrepiece of Aristotle's ethics. The ultimate good in Aristotle's ethical world is happiness, and that happiness can only be attained through virtue and the performance of good actions. The 'doing' element is important. Citizens are active, and define themselves through their active participation in society. Therefore good must be done, not merely imagined (Aristotle, 1976, pp 66, 73–76, 97–98). The central concept in *The Ethics* is 'virtue', of which there are two types: intellectual, which can be taught and learned; and moral, which is inculcated by legislators in the form of 'habit'. *The Ethics*, as a manual for good citizenship, is accordingly part of the educative process. Aristotle, like Plato, intends to teach virtue to the intellectual elite. It is not addressed to anyone else. The commoners and labourers are stupid by definition, otherwise they would not be commoners and labourers, and they cannot be expected to do good, at least not to the extent that the aristocracy and citizenry can. The need to effect political and social constraints to ensure their doing good will be all the greater. The aristocrat can be more trusted to appreciate the virtue of virtue. It is important to remember that virtue is relative to the individual and his situation (Aristotle, 1976, pp 91–93). Here, of course, the influence of Plato's theory of forms is also apparent. The form is one thing: the practical political substance is another. Virtue, like everything, has a perfect form, as an idea, but its substance can vary from one political circumstance to another. It is for this very reason that government should lie with the virtuous, and those who have been educated in virtue. The science of government is an intellectual virtue, which can be learned and practised in accordance with the rules that the science lays down. That is why nature prescribes some to rule and some to be ruled (Aristotle, 1976, pp 209–13).

At the same time, virtue lies in the mean, which means that it lies between extremes in a position relative to our particular political situation. Thus a virtuous man is not poor, but not rich, not prodigal, but not mean, and so on. Justice, undoubtedly a virtue, is precisely such a mean. As we have just noted, what is important is that Aristotle relativises the mean. In other words, he suggests that what is virtuous, or moderate, for one citizen, might not be so for another (Aristotle, 1976, pp 101–02, 107–08). Thus what counts as excessive wealth depends on what the person is accustomed to, or deserves. Accordingly, it is natural that aristocrats should be wealthy, because they are more virtuous. Similarly, what is just in the treatment of one man may not be just in the treatment of another. Thus slaves can be treated justly, and so can women, even if their treatment would not be just for a free, male, Athenian citizen. Power rightly rests with the virtuous, which, given that it is in part constituted by education, necessarily vests in the educated aristocratic elite. At the same time, contemplation of the good was not, of course, itself sufficient. Good, as we have seen, must be done.

Man is first and foremost a 'political animal', and an ethical philosophy is immediately a matter of politics and law. In the very first book of *The Ethics*, Aristotle emphasises that the 'science that studies the supreme Good for man is politics'. Man lives in a community, and defines himself politically in relation to this community. As a matter of ethics, and virtue, therefore, the interest of the community and common good enjoys priority over that of the individual. Aristotle affirms that:

> For even if the good of the community coincides with that of the individual, it is clearly a greater and more perfect thing to achieve and preserve that of a community; for while it is desirable to secure what is good in the case of an individual, to do so in the case of a people or a State is something finer and more sublime (Aristotle, 1976, p 64).

Relatedly, of all the social virtues, 'friendliness' is the most important. It is certainly the 'most necessary for living', and its value must be inculcated by society's teachers and philosophers. This recommendation of sociability exemplified Aristotle's determination to emphasise the responsibility of each citizen to contribute to the wellbeing of his community. Unlike Socrates and Plato, who liked a good drink, Aristotle was the first of the puritans, decidedly unimpressed by the unsociable potential of drinking parties. Temperance and self-control were far more respectable, if less fun, for temperance represented the mean of personal behaviour. Over-eating was unsociable, and so was too much sex. For the same reasons, he was quick to condemn too much cooking with spices. People who liked spicy food were clearly not moderate in taste, and should not be trusted with political responsibility (Aristotle, 1976, pp 131–41, 163–64, 258–78). We shall revisit the Aristotelian politics of 'friendship' at the end of this chapter.

Aristotelian jurisprudence

The idea that the philosophy of law could be somehow distinguishable from the very idea of philosophy itself would have made absolutely no sense to Aristotle. In order for there to be justice, people must act justly in everything they do. To act justly is to act rationally, in the best interest of both the self and, most importantly, the community. In turn, the 'virtuous' community is precisely defined as the just community. The unjust act, accordingly, is irrational by definition. This can lead to some interesting conclusions. Adultery, for example, is not unjust. Adulterers, Aristotle suggests, are driven by passion not reason, and so act neither rationally nor irrationally. Neither do they act unjustly, even if they certainly do not act in the wider interest. The same analogy applies to all acts which are the result of provocation (Aristotle, 1976, pp 187, 193). In simple terms, justice is the exercise of virtue, and is, moreover, the sovereign virtue. Justice 'is not a part of virtue but the whole of it' (Aristotle, 1976, p 174). It is not a concept simply invoked in a court of law, or for resolving distinctly legal issues, but is the idea at the very core of our ethical existence.

The political context of man's existence is pivotal. The virtue of justice only has meaning in the political context. Like all virtues it exists in the mean, and justice must enact what is moderate or fair, as an accommodation of extremes and extreme interests. Thus, as a matter of political ethics, justice is 'complete virtue ... not unqualified but in relation to somebody else' (Aristotle, 1976, p 173). Justice is the exercise of virtue in the real political situation. It is the recognition that the common interest is always superior to the individual interest. It is for this reason that Aristotle emphasises that suicide is unjust, because it is an action against the community, rather than just against the self (Aristotle, 1976, pp 200–01). Understood in this political context, justice exists both in a universal sense, as an idea in Platonic terms, but also in the particular. Substantive justice varies from situation to situation, and so does law (Aristotle, 1976, pp 174–76).

There are two forms of substantive or 'particular' justice, distributive and rectificatory, and the virtuous community will employ both. Distributive justice describes the basic principle of justice in the public sphere, whilst rectificatory justice addresses the private. Distributive justice, as its name suggests, looks to distribute the goods of society in order to effect the wellbeing of that society. Once again, it is a justice that observes the mean, working out what is the just distribution of goods in accordance with the particular situation of each individual. As Aristotle suggests, it is 'a sort of proportion' (Aristotle, 1976, pp 177–78). It is certainly not equality. Indeed, enforced equality would be unjust, because it would refuse to recognise the particularity of virtue in the political situation, whilst denying the fundamental truth that man is a 'political animal'. Rectificatory justice again acknowledges particularity by addressing the question of justice in transactions or relations between private citizens. As a principle, it ensures fair dealings, so that, in a commercial transaction, for example, no one individual should enjoy too great a gain or suffer too great a loss. Rectificatory justice ensures the mean between private parties, and thus prescribes an innate fairness in their relations (Aristotle, 1976, pp 179–83).

Law plays a key role in encouraging a virtuous life. This is particularly the case, Aristotle observes, with the young, who have a propensity to be 'intemperate' and to eat too much. Civil law should particularly address itself to the problems of youth (Aristotle, 1976, pp 337–38). Such pragmatism follows inexorably from Aristotle's premise that justice is a concept of political philosophy as opposed to pure metaphysics. It only has meaning in the political situation. Such justice is termed 'political justice', and 'is only found among those whose mutual relations are controlled by law' (Aristotle, 1976, p 188). This is the science of law which complements the philosophy of justice; a critical concession which goes a considerable way to distinguishing a modern jurisprudential tradition. Political justice is constituted by principles of natural law and is realised as civil law. In these terms, civil law is written to reflect the guiding principles of natural law, which direct us to act virtuously towards one another. Although natural law is a constant, civil law can vary from one particular to another; as, of course, does justice. Indeed, the definition of civil law is its mutability. If it did not change, it would not be civil law but natural law (Aristotle, 1976, pp 189–90). At the same time, law is simply a means, not an end. Law is not an absolute good. It is justice which is an absolute good, and justice has priority. This distinction establishes the genus of natural law. It is also the reason for Aristotle's introduction of a principle of 'equity'. Equity 'corrects the deficiencies' of law as it is applied in the particular situation, and, as such, ensures justice in all situations (Aristotle, 1976, pp 198–200).

Aristotle's subsequent work *The Politics* is composed of a multitude of various conclusions as to how a society should be best composed and governed, drawn from a series of empirical observations and studies of comparative politics. Having established the ethical foundations for good government, Aristotle then turned to the science of constitutional jurisprudence. Empirical observation reveals three forms of good government and three of bad. The three forms of good government are monarchy, aristocracy and constitutional government or 'polity'. Monarchy is a good form of government, because it is most likely to effect good order. Aristocracy is also a good form of government, because, as was emphasised in *The Ethics*, aristocrats are necessarily the most virtuous and contemplative of citizens. Better still is constitutional government, which is constituted by both monarch and aristocracy, and, moreover, which is distinguished by a rule of law. The subjection of kings to the law is a valuable check against corruption and the temptations of tyranny, although, Aristotle adds, a supremely virtuous monarch should be allowed to rule absolutely. A government constituted by monarch, aristocracy and citizenry, but governed by monarch and aristocracy, is the best form of government, because it is 'mixed' or 'middle' government. In other words, it is government of the mean (Aristotle, 1981, pp 230, 265–69).

The three forms of bad government are tyranny, oligarchy and democracy. Each is bad because it is the government of a particular section of the community in the interest of that section. The identification of bad government is again very much along the lines of that suggested by Plato. Oligarchy, for example, is identified as the interest of a wealthy elite. Democracy is identified as the commoner interest, and any government induced by such factional interests is bad. Of course, there are degrees of undesirability. Thus agrarian democracy is the least bad form of democracy, because farmers are unlikely to accumulate much wealth or power, and are anyway too indolent to participate much in government or become too tempted to tyranny. Likewise, moderate oligarchies and moderate tyrants are far preferable to extremes of either (Aristotle, 1981, pp 191–92, 368–79). The great danger of democracy, and other bad forms of government, lies in their instability. Certainly, as we have seen, Aristotle was reconciled to the inevitability of change. But change is not the same as instability. Good government effects ordered change. Bad government, in contrast, leads to civil unrest and revolution. History has shown that the bad forms of government tend to breed from one another, with each birth accompanied by violent change. Thus oligarchies give rise to democracy, as the poor resent the wealth of the few, which then give rise to tyrannies, as the idiot commoners are gulled by demagogues into assigning power to the least virtuous (Aristotle, 1981, pp 223, 245–50). Change may indeed define the 'political animal', but Aristotle remains vehemently opposed to change which is destabilising or otherwise counter to the common interest.

We shall return to Aristotle in Chapter 3 in order to develop further this idea of the political community. As is always the case with the most influential figures, such as Aristotle, there is much that is relevant to more than one particular intellectual discipline. Aristotle had much to say of importance with regard to philosophy, politics, economics and so on, and the influence of Aristotelian ethical and political philosophies can never be entirely distinguished. As we move to another identifiable development in modernist theories of natural law and order, political theology, we do so aware that we have established the essential foundations of our particular jurisprudential tradition. To the extent to which there is a readily identifiable modernist tradition of jurisprudence, it is that prescribed by Plato and his pupil, and first critic, Aristotle. Each theory of law which we will encounter in the subsequent pages of this book will, to various extents, be written as a critique of this foundational model, and the subsequent varieties of natural law and rights, to which we will now turn, are no exception.

NATURAL LAW AND POLITICAL THEOLOGY

The foundations of Christian political theology

The presence of a Christian God at the very centre of its philosophy is the critical and distinguishing feature of medieval legal and political theory. Whereas the Greeks had accommodated gods within their philosophy, Christian thinkers recast philosophy itself as a theology. In doing so, of course, they made a critical adjustment, subjugating the faculty of human reason to the ordinances of divinity (Grayling, 2003, p 85). The task, taken up by later theologians, most notably St Thomas Aquinas, was to make this accommodation as seamless as possible, to reinvest the Aristotelian tradition, with all its emphasis on reason and order, virtue and community, whilst also impressing the authority, not just of God, but of God's lieutenants on earth, His priests and kings.

The political context within which these medieval theologians worked was determined by the emergence of political States as a direct response to the perceived disorders of the dark ages. In spiritual terms, St Augustine composed his *City of God* in order to present a model of heavenly community and divine justice which could provide an intellectual alternative to political chaos. Humanity must seek spiritual salvation in God rather than worry about imperfections in its civil condition. Only God, it was clearly implied, could restore order to Europe and beyond, and political order must be recast in the image of the Christian State and, crucially, under the authority of the Roman church. The Christian challenge was directed very much at the nascent idea of the medieval political State. In *Romans 13:1–7*, St Paul had asserted that all 'authority comes from God only, and all authorities that hold sway are of his ordinance'. Any civil magistrate is merely 'God's minister'. By suggesting that law was not simply divine revelation, Paul challenged the doctrine of the 'old' law, the Mosaic law of the 10 commandments. Law was also a matter of practical rationality, and thus enjoyed a distinct, if derivative, secular form (MacIntyre, 1988, pp 150–52). It was to the Greeks that Paul turned to found his Christian politics. The book of Isaiah was translated so that Plato's cave became the valley of the shadow of death. Mankind was saved by 'a great light', and that light was Plato, albeit in the guise of Jesus.

If early Christian theology, particularly Augustinian, had tended towards Plato and pessimism, Aristotelianism and its more optimistic vision of civil life was taken up by Islam. In his *Confessions*, Augustine mused at great length on his own and everyone else's sinfulness, and embraced the barbarism of the dark ages together with the increasing popularity of poetry as clear evidence that we are all destined to suffer endless misery. Whilst Christian Europe spent much of its energy, and most of its money, despatching wave after wave of crusades to the Middle East, each of which was sooner or later annihilated by various Arab armies, Islam, in contrast, built libraries, spread knowledge and sought to build a social philosophy on the foundations of virtue and justice found in Aristotle. The re-emergence of Aristotelianism at the beginning of the 12th century, undoubtedly the most significant intellectual event of what Petrarch later termed the 'middle' ages, was largely facilitated by the writings of three Arabic philosophers in particular, Avicenna, Averroes and Maimonides.

In terms of legal philosophy the most important was undoubtedly Maimonides, who wrote *The Guide for the Perplexed* and in it provided the foundations for an Aristotelian political theology (Marenbon, 1991, pp 59–107; Roberts, 1991, pp 63–102). The model of reason and revelation presented in *Guide* would be taken, lock, stock and barrel, by Aquinas and reproduced at the very heart of his *Summa Theologica*. In Book One of *The Guide*, Maimonides described a complementary relation between revelation and reason; what he termed the two 'planes of cognition'. Revelation, the first plane, is that law revealed by God. It is law that is recognised by us, as a matter of 'truth' and 'falsehood'. Reason, the second plane, is law that is the product of our own experiences. It is law that is cognised by us, and judged as a matter of 'fine' and 'bad'. The authority for this system lay with the story of the creation. We are empowered with reason, and thus left to muse on matters 'fine' and 'bad' because we are fallen from our perfect condition. This perfect condition, prior to Adam's lapse, left us in a perfect intellectual ignorance, so we were not 'perplexed' by the demands of judgment and the responsibility for deciding things for ourselves. In our fallen and 'perplexed' state, we must pursue two forms of perfection, that of our spirit and that of our political and ethical existence. The 'guide' for the former is the Mosaic law; the 'guide' for the latter is Aristotle (Ward, 1992).

It was left to Aquinas to fashion the supersession of Augustine's acute pessimism with the emerging enlightenment of later medieval Europe and the re-emergence of Aristotelianism. Humanity, Aquinas suggested, was necessarily imperfect, but it did not have to live a life of utter misery, and could do something to realise a greater degree of spiritual fulfilment whilst on earth. The ideal to which it could aspire in its fallen state was that established by Aristotle, the 'community' of the 'common good'. Whereas Augustine mused on the decadence of Babylon and the fallen condition of the sinner, Aquinas looked to the enlightenment of classical Greece and the redemptive potential of a virtuous community. Two great tracts dominate Aquinas's work. The first is *Summa Contra Gentiles*, which was written as a counter to the heresies of Islam and Judaism. The second, *Summa Theologica*, was written as a student manual, and is our more immediate concern. In theological terms, Aquinas's reputation largely hangs on his five 'proofs' of the existence of God, presented in *Summa Theologica*; none of which, of course, proves anything, least of all the existence of God. Paradoxically, of course, Aquinas never intended to prove the existence of God. To prove God would necessarily entail the founding of God in some way, and that sort of suggestion could lead to excommunication, accusations of heresy, and all sorts of unpleasant ways of dying. Instead of proving anything, Aquinas presented an elaborate metaphysical structure, designed by God and at the apex of which sat God. God was part of a structure designed by Him. Our appreciation of his 'existence' could then be proved, because God provided it. But God himself was certainly not proved as such. *Summa Contra Gentiles* concentrated on establishing this essential 'truth' of Christian theology. The ultimate end, or *telos*, of the universe was knowledge, not of God, but in God. Necessarily, this knowledge established the limitations of all other knowledge, including human knowledge.

Aquinas and the law of the *Summa*

Summa Theologica is composed in the customary scholastic form of questions or *summaes*, each of which is devoted to accommodating this undoubted 'truth' of God with the challenge of human reason. This accommodation of God's revelation with Aristotelian reason represents the great and enduring contribution of Aquinas to legal philosophy, ultimately pointing the way beyond purely theological theories of natural law to later secular variants (Crossan, 1988). At the same time, it must be noted that the use of Aristotle was not unreservedly popular in early 13th century Christendom. In 1215, Aristotle was banned in Paris University. If men could reason, then they could reason about God. Yet, God was not to be reasoned about. God just was. This was the essential dilemma which faced Aquinas and which he resolved by affirming that man could reason, but that this reason was purely in the gift of God. Thus, where Aristotle concentrated on the 'essence' of things, Aquinas evaded the obvious heresy of questioning the 'essence' of God, and instead recast theology in terms of affirming the 'existence' of God. It was, once again, knowledge *in* God, not *of* God.

According to Aquinas, there are two distinct spheres of knowledge: reason and revelation. As Maimonides had suggested, revelation is beyond reason and beyond question, whilst reason itself is addressed to matters of ethics and politics. God laid down the former, Aristotle the latter. There are therefore no innate principles in the mind. The mind in its original form is a blank, which is then filled by our experiences of things as humans. Such an experientialism finds room for reason, and our perfection of ethical and political matters, without challenging revelation. Reason deals with political particulars, whilst the universal remains the domain of God. In this sense, then, God is 'known' through our experiences, most obviously of nature and natural order. The way things happen, as we come to appreciate, is not by action, but by grand, indeed divine, design. Philosophy, accordingly, begins with human experience, followed by reflection upon it, and ends with our coming to 'know' God spiritually. Of course, just as Aristotle affirmed that only aristocrats can contemplate virtue properly, so theologians alone can reflect upon matters spiritual. This is why it was so necessary that everyone should be encouraged to donate vast sums of money to maintain monasteries full of deeply contemplative monks. This is the realm of reason, and its limitations. But it is revelation, of course, which reserves the final confirmation of the 'truth' of God. Revelation deals with our intuitive knowledge of God, whilst reason concerns itself with our social existences and defines social goods. In this way, there is perfect harmony. Reason and revelation are complementary, working together to ensure that our life on earth is virtuous, and then followed by our final spiritual redemption or 'eternal blessedness'. The perfection of the human condition mirrored the perfection of the spiritual. Leprosy was a spiritual as much as a physical contagion, whilst people with soft skin were considered to be more spiritual than those whose skin was covered by callouses (Aquinas, 1991, p 1, Question 85; Coplestone, 1955, pp 28–66).

Aquinas addresses the philosophy of law in Questions 90–97 of the second part of *Summa Theologica*. In the following Questions, 98–108, he then undertakes a close examination of the status and veracity of the Old Laws. Aquinas does not reject the Mosaic law, but he does, following Maimonides and Paul, admit the need for supplementary civil laws themselves founded on natural law. The Mosaic law, he concludes in Question 98, 'was good indeed, but imperfect'. Question 90 establishes the basic philosophical determination of law. According to Aquinas, 'the essence of law' is 'nothing else than an ordinance of reason for the common good, made by Him who has care of the community and promulgated'. The 'essence', which for Plato lay in justice as order, and for Aristotle lay in justice as virtue, for Aquinas, lies in Him. The law may be comprehensible as rational, and promulgated in the cause of the 'common good', but metaphysical authority is divine, even if the philosophical authority, as Aquinas explicitly acknowledges, is Aristotle.

In Question 91, Aquinas then establishes four kinds of law. The first is eternal law, which is fleshed out in Question 93. Eternal law provides the gear for the entire system. In simple terms, it represents an appreciation that the following three kinds of law are all part of a whole designed by God. All law is derived from eternal law. The second kind of law is natural law, which is then developed in Question 94. Natural law is simply 'participation in the eternal law by rational creatures'. In other words, natural law is the order by which we lead our lives if we are rational, and do so rationally. Natural law is 'a norm of right conduct and equally well known to all'. The influence here of Aristotle's idea of natural inclinations is considerable. These inclinations are threefold. We have a natural inclination to aspire to the good, to appreciate the 'truth' of God, and to live in a community. In Question 90, Aquinas had taken pains to confirm this and to emphasise that its authority is divine. Natural law 'is promulgated by the very fact that God instilled it into man's mind so as to be known by him naturally'. This source of authority is crucial, because it denies any notion of natural rights. Individuals are gifted natural law by God. There is no question of rights held against God, or God's civil or spiritual magistrates. Indeed, there are no rights, natural or civil, in Aquinas's philosophy of law.

The third kind of law is human law, which is simply the rational comprehension of eternal law. In other words, as Aquinas develops in Questions 95–97, it is that law established by civil magistrates as their best approximation of natural law. The presence of human laws reflects the pervasive need for order in a community, so that each individual can aspire to the distinctly Aristotelian *telos* of goodness. Of course, as Maimonides had emphasised, reason empowers man to both good and evil, but natural law will ensure that goodness will out. Indeed, the very existence of evil merely proves our natural inclination to overcome it. Natural and human law, then, constitute those laws cognisable by reason. They are laws which the common horde can appreciate, or at least their sovereigns can. In Aristotelian terms – and Aquinas adopts precisely the same concepts – these are laws geared to virtue and to assisting our natural aspiration to live virtuously. The fourth kind of law established by Aquinas is divine law. This is the law which Maimonides described as 'recognisable'. This divine law, which is concentrated in the Mosaic commandments, is revealed. It is not thought about, and it is not for us to understand. Divine law, like God, just is. Just as human law aids man's aspiration to live the good life, it is the presence of divine law which saves man's spiritual soul and ensures that he is 'destined to an end of eternal blessedness'. As Aquinas affirms in Question 91:

> ... because man is destined to an end of eternal blessedness, and this exceeds what is proportionate to natural human faculties ... it was necessary that he should be directed to this end not merely by natural and human life, but also by divinely given law.

Law, politics and the Christian community

Although clearly subservient to the overarching nature of 'eternal' law, the definition of a distinct sphere of human or civil law, within which the civil sovereign enjoys power untrammelled by any civil authority, represented a crucial concession to the emerging power of the political State in later medieval Europe. The Papacy saw itself as much a political as a spiritual actor in medieval Europe, and matters of politics were of at least as much importance to the medieval church as were questions of theological philosophy. We have already seen the extent to which Aquinas's philosophical model borrowed from Aristotle, and this indebtedness is at least as great in his more immediately political essays. As *Summa* emphasised, Aquinas shared Aristotle's primary belief that man had a natural civil inclination. As he stressed in the *Commentary on the Ethics*, the 'fact that man is by nature a social animal ... has as a consequence the fact that man is destined by nature to form part of a community which makes a full and complete life possible for him' (D'Entreves, 1959, p 96). Political communities were part of the wider natural order. Necessarily, he also shared Aristotle's belief that there was a natural affinity between law and the common good. The intrinsic relation of man and community, taken from Aristotle, was the very keystone of medieval political theology. The *respublica Christiana* that Aquinas, and the Roman church, was so keen to prescribe, was to be established as an Aristotelian community founded on a concept of Christian duty. At the same time, given the reality of the emergent political State, Aquinas was keen to constitute the *respublica* in the form of a series of 'free communities' which were sovereign in political terms but voluntarily subject to the spiritual authority of Rome (D'Entreves, 1959, pp xxiv–xxxi).

Aquinas's major political treatise, *On Princely Government*, confirmed the influence of Aristotle. Two concepts are essential to a Christian politics. First is the 'common good', and the extent to which Aquinas accepted the Aristotelian model of the political community can be seen at the very beginning of the essay: 'When we consider all that is necessary to human life, however, it becomes clear that man is naturally a social and political animal, destined more than other animals to live in community.' Nature, furthermore, has 'destined' man 'to live in society' so that his own interest can be furthered by contributing to the improvement of all. The fact that man can speak, and does not bark, is conclusive proof that he should live in a community. Though our 'particular interests' may differ, it is 'the common good which unites the community' (D'Entreves, 1959, pp 2–4).

The second essential concept is a strong government effected by a strong king. Only three things can prevent man living a life of virtue, and attaining 'blessedness': 'perversity of will'; invasion by barbarians; and death. The latter was unavoidable, whilst the first two could be evaded through the good offices of a virtuous sovereign (D'Entreves, 1959, pp 40–42). Human laws are promulgated, as Aquinas had affirmed in Questions 90 and 94 of *Summa*, by sovereigns. Sovereigns were chosen by God to exercise their practical reason in the interest of the 'common good'. This did not just mean exercising a constitutional function, as legislator or judge. It also meant that the godly sovereign had to suppress the Jews, whilst also, like the Socratic philosopher-king, ensuring that everyone was well fed and enjoyed the benefits of a measured climate (D'Entreves, 1959, pp 34–48). In such terms, sovereigns were natural, and no natural polity could do without one. In the more precise matter of constitutions, Aquinas followed Aristotle in asserting that mixed government, between sovereign, aristocracy and citizenry, is the 'best form of government' (D'Entreves, 1959, pp 4–5).

The godly sovereign, however, had further duties, which required his position above the law. The sovereign is subject to the law of God and, crucially, his 'priests' (D'Entreves, 1959, pp 38–39). He is not, however, as Aquinas stressed in Question 96 of *Summa*, subject to the constraining power of the civil law. In part, the reason for this was practical. In a fallen world, government must be strong. As St Isidore emphasised, civil authorities did God's work by terrorising their subjects, for 'if all men were free of fear, who would keep anyone from wickedness?'. A sovereign who could not enforce law, as Aquinas acknowledged, was no sort of sovereign at all. The king is the source of all civil authority, and so can hardly be subject to any. Rather, the godly sovereign respects law as a matter of conscience and moral duty. The chances of a sovereign failing to fulfil Aquinas's expectations were, of course, remote. As he affirmed in *Summa Contra Gentiles*, nature assures that 'men of outstanding intelligence naturally take command' (D'Entreves, 1959, p 51). Corruption was unlikely because nature prescribed who the sovereign should be, and the virtuous natural sovereign would appreciate that his ultimate rewards lay in heaven, not in earthly property. The sovereign who properly 'fosters the common good with all care' will be rewarded with 'blessedness' and the 'love' of his subjects, and is unlikely to want anything more (D'Entreves, 1959, pp 22–29).

Of course, history had revealed that there were tyrants – invariably barbarians, heretics or Jews – who refused to rule in accordance with the eternal or natural law. Yet, though they could be excommunicated by the Papacy, it was not sensible in the delicate politics of medieval Europe for Catholic theologians to be justifying a general right of rebellion against secular authorities, no matter how tyrannical they might be. In Questions 92 and 93 of *Summa*, Aquinas carefully fudged the problem by suggesting that tyrants' laws were not real laws, but rather a 'perversion' of law. But it was still law, and so obedience to it was rational. In Question 96, Aquinas confirmed that there can be such a thing as 'unjust' law. Following Aristotle, the matter of justice, as a virtue, is extricated from the of law, which is simply a matter of particular politics. The just law, of course, is law which furthers the 'common good', and so the unjust law is that which militates against the community. However, only those laws which can be discerned as being contrary to divine law can be wilfully disobeyed. Indeed, they *must* be disobeyed. Of course, only theologians – those who are intellectually capable of spiritual 'reflection' – can discern which laws are to be disobeyed. It is not for ordinary folk to try to decide which laws are unnatural, unjust, or against the will of divine law. As we have already noted, there are no natural rights in Aquinas's thought, least of all rights of rebellion. Besides, the uninformed, incapable of proper reflection, invariably rebel against the wrong sovereigns. Nature prescribes the good order of the community, and that is not served by popular insurrection against sovereigns, no matter how tyrannical they might be. Moreover, history further showed that rebellion merely makes tyrants more tyrannical (D'Entreves, 1959, pp 15–17). Accordingly, it is far better to leave it to priests to decide which laws should be obeyed, and which can be disobeyed.

Hooker, the English constitution and the godly commonwealth

There is a tendency to consign medieval political theology to the realm of historical anecdote. Modern jurisprudence places rather less importance on theories cast in terms of eternal or divine law. Yet, it would be a mistake to diminish the enduring influence of theologians such as Aquinas. In the final part of this chapter, we will see the extent to which political theology provided an essential conduit for modern theories of natural law. Moreover, in Chapter 3, we will also revisit Aristotelian ideas of political community, and their particular influence on contemporary communitarian political thought.

More immediately, however, Thomist jurisprudence played a critical role in the fashioning of an equally distinctive English constitutional jurisprudence, again founded on the collateral ideas of natural law and the 'good' community or commonwealth. During the 16th and 17th centuries, the emergent English nation-state, and its constitution, was securely founded on a peculiar elision of sovereign, church and commonwealth, and it has remained ever since. The critical intellectual figure in this particular prescription was Richard Hooker, whose *Of the Laws of Ecclesiastical Polity* was written in the attempt to legitimate the Elizabethan settlement in the late 16th century. In his *Laws*, Hooker described a discrete order which included both world and heaven, humans and angels, and which bore striking similarity to Aquinas's. Most importantly, given the desire to legitimate the sovereign authority over any countervailing notions of natural right, Hooker emphasised that civil authority is derived directly from divine law, such that 'of law there can be no less acknowledged than that her seat is the bosom of God, her voice the harmony of the world' (Hooker, 1989, p 127).

The role of the sovereign, as head of both civil and spiritual jurisdiction, was absolutely pivotal, and the continuing importance of theories of sovereignty in our constitutional jurisprudence can be traced directly to Hooker's settlement. According to Hooker, when:

> ... Christian kings are said to have spiritual dominion or supreme power in ecclesiastical affairs and causes, the meaning is that within their own precincts and territories they have an authority and power to command even in matters of Christian religion, and that there is no higher nor greater that can in those cases overcommand them, where they are placed to command as kings.

The intellectual authority for this was taken directly from Aquinas's political theology, even if the 'precinct' was determined by the reformation settlement. By reasserting the theological authority of the political sovereign, Hooker could effect the translation of medieval Thomist providentialism into Tudor constitutional thought. God moves through 'natural agents' who are his 'anointed' civil magistrates (Hooker, 1989, pp 69, 117–18). As Aquinas had suggested, the monarch, as God's anointed, was answerable only to God and punishable only by God. It was this doctrine of obedience which gave providentialism its immediate political edge. There could be no theological facility for civil disobedience.

The holistic idea of the constitution of a godly 'commonwealth', a nation described by a king and 'church' of England, was central to Hooker's thesis, and was shared by a number of near contemporaries such as John Selden and Sir Robert Filmer. It also represented a crucial concession to classicism. Hooker consciously aligns his theology with Aristotle's fundamental assertion that man is naturally inclined to 'goodness'. Moreover, goodness is 'seen with the eye of understanding' which is 'reason'. It is the primary duty of God's magistrates to prescribe the proper use of reason. At the same time, with regard to politics, Hooker's communal model is again overtly Aristotelian, and the co-determinative church-State relation is founded on the assumption that the community is the 'natural' unit of politics (Hooker, 1989, pp 66–80). By founding his idea of politics on the community, Hooker immediately refines his idea of kingship. No longer is the sovereign merely God's anointed, the conduit of natural law. In the English commonwealth, the sovereign is the essential link between church and people, the force that binds the community itself together. A 'commonwealth' is defined by the immanent relation of church and community, and the distinction between church and State, Hooker affirms, is the mark of 'heathen' societies. In these terms, therefore, to rebel against a sovereign is to will the 'inevitable destruction' of the community (Hooker, 1989, pp 130–33, 139).

The only justification for civil law is to effect the 'greater good' of the community and to bind it together. This is the 'law of the commonwealth, the very soul of a politic body, the parts whereof are by law animated, held together, and set on work in such actions as the common good requireth' (Hooker, 1989, p 87). Hooker's ambition was to settle a commonwealth, and by founding the English commonwealth on a classical model of community, he necessarily moderated the idea of divine right providentialism, as indeed had Aquinas and earlier medieval English jurists such as Bracton. The king is God's lieutenant, but with regard to civil matters remains bound by His laws as interpreted through natural law. In an ideal commonwealth, king and law are in perfect harmony, 'like an harp or melodious instrument' (Hooker, 1989, pp 140–42, 146–47). The 'natural subject of power civil all men confess' is not the person of the sovereign, but the 'body of the commonwealth' (Hooker, 1989, p 179). It was such a redetermination of the godly commonwealth which led John Locke to appraise the 'judicious' Hooker as the founder of a distinct English liberal constitutionalism (Hooker, 1989, pp xxv–xxvi).

Locke's praise is striking, not least because it speaks to the malleability of Hooker's, and Aquinas's, jurisprudence. On the one hand, the idea of the godly 'commonwealth' could be found at the heart of most absolutist theories of law and State, such as Sir Robert Filmer's *Patriarcha*, composed in the years immediately preceding the English civil wars. For Filmer, as for many of his generation, medieval Christian jurisprudence provided the intellectual authority for the 'divine right' of kings to rule. More precisely, the ultimate authority enjoyed by Stuart monarchs, such as Charles I, was rooted in the 'Adamic succession'. Charles was, Filmer suggested, by means of a somewhat tortuous genealogy, descended from Adam himself. A proper study of scriptural text, Filmer continued, revealed that there 'were' kings long before there were any laws. And, moreover, it followed that there could 'be no laws without a supreme power to command or make them', and that power must be vested in God's chosen lieutenant, the king (Filmer, 1991, pp 35–44).

At the same time, rather different invocations of the godly 'commonwealth' could also be found in overtly republican treatises, such as James Harrington's *Oceana* and Algernon Sidney's *Discourses Concerning Government*, both of which we shall encounter in Chapter 3. Indeed, the idea of a godly English 'commonwealth' was a mainstay of radical republican thought in mid 17th century England. It founded, for example, John Milton's two great defences of the English republic, his *Tenure of Kings and Magistrates* and *A Defence of the People of England*. Citing *Romans 13* and *Deuteronomy 17*, Milton affirmed that the scripture invested in all such commonwealths the power, indeed an incumbent duty, to preserve the 'good' of the community over and against any putative despot. 'God', Milton affirmed, 'has decided that the form of a commonwealth' is determined not by the whimsy of kings, but in terms of the 'greater benefit' of its people. And the heart of this 'benefit' can be found in the principles of natural law, the very 'fountain of justice' originally described, as Milton explicitly affirmed in Chapter Five of his *Defence*, by Aristotle. If need be, in short, the collateral Aristotelian ideas of natural justice and the 'common good' vest in the English the authority to behead their kings (Milton, 1991, pp 13–14, 80–87, 149–51).

Alongside Milton's defence of the English commonwealth could be placed Richard Baxter's rather more authoritarian *A Holy Commonwealth*, first published in 1659 at the very end of the English republic. Here Baxter prescribed an ideal godly commonwealth, the sovereignty of which rested in God alone, and the 'communion' of the godly 'saints'. At the same time, Baxter's commonwealth resisted any democratic impulses and denied the possibility of legal or natural rights. Indeed, government could only be exercised by the godly 'saints' of the presbyteries (Baxter, 1994, pp 3–14, 55). As a committed Calvinist, Baxter maintained that the godly were predetermined both to be spiritually saved and civilly empowered to govern. The theology of Baxter is less important, at least for our purposes, than the extent to which he adhered, like Hooker and Aquinas, to an Aristotelian model of government. Man, by both 'necessity and inclination', militates towards society, and political order is prescribed by nature (Baxter, 1994, pp 55, 63–64). With the aid of God's providence, man can rationalise the forms of civil government most appropriate for the pursuit of spiritual and political harmony. Moreover, again echoing Aristotle, and in striking anticipation of later communitarian theses, Baxter affirmed that a godly commonwealth is constituted by a multitude of localised commonwealths (Baxter, 1994, p 64).

It was this degree of decentralisation which distinguished Baxter's political theory from Hooker's settlement. Yet, both were securely established on the same theological foundations prescribed by classical and then Thomist theories of natural political order. Baxter consciously followed medieval theology in his assertion that natural law was the foundation for any godly commonwealth. Indeed, it is the authority of divine law which proscribes any notion of democratic government. God 'elects' governors, and the good of the community is always better recognised by God and his 'saints' than it is by self-interested individuals (Baxter, 1994, pp 69–70, 79–84). Likewise, divine providence will effect any necessary changes in civil magistrates, and so, whilst there is no general right of civil disobedience, individuals do have a duty to obey providential signals which demand the removal of tyrants. It was in this sense that the deposition and execution of Charles I could be legitimated (Baxter, 1994, p 117). As we shall see in Chapter 4, it was in the same decade that Thomas Hobbes published his *Leviathan* and suggested the metaphor of a social contract. The intellectual authority for the idea of covenanted or contracted sovereignty lay in reformist, and particularly Calvinist, theology. Unsurprisingly, it provided the keystone for Baxter's particular commonwealth. Although men may have contracted with a civil sovereign, the godly had a superior 'covenant' of 'conscience' with God, and it was this covenant which could authorise rebellion in order to preserve the spiritual integrity of the commonwealth (Baxter, 1994, pp 117–19).

In one sense, Baxter's *Commonwealth* may seem to be a somewhat arcane, even tangential, text in English jurisprudence. Yet, as is the case with Hooker's *Laws* or Milton's *Defence*, such a conclusion would be mistaken. Each prescribed a commonwealth in terms of both spiritual and constitutional authority, and moreover, both did so in distinctly nationalist tones. The peculiarity of a constitutional settlement founded upon the elision of theological and political authority, the ideal prescribed by

Aquinas, was realised in a peculiarly English setting. The commonwealths of Hooker and Baxter expressed a national political consciousness (Baxter, 1994, pp 160, 217). It was for this reason that, a century and a half later, Edmund Burke would attempt to counter the destabilising influences of the French revolution in terms of an identifiably English constitutional settlement. Burke's *Reflections* emphasised the apparent virtues of a constitution which was founded on both a common law and a theological settlement. Burke was fervently against the involvement of the church in matters of government, and certainly could not be aligned with any theological form of natural law. Yet, he remained convinced that any community, and particularly an English one, was founded on a particular theological morality. As we shall see shortly, it is an attitude which has been more recently, and more notoriously, revisited by Lord Devlin. The idea of 'civil society' Burke confirmed is one given by God as a 'necessary means' to the 'perfection' of 'our virtue', and protestant theology fashions a necessary 'impression' on the 'mind' of every Englishman. It is not a matter for metaphysical debate, but rather a simple assertion of historical fact (Burke, 1986, pp 188–89, 196–98).

NATURAL LAW REVISITED

Law and morality: Hart and Fuller

The rise and rise of the secular State has increasingly marginalised theological theories of law and, whilst Hooker's constitutional settlement may continue to enjoy a certain contemporary relevance, the notion of a godly commonwealth has largely disappeared from modern political discourse. Indeed, in the words of one contemporary commentator, Christian theological arguments in support of particular political moralities are so incredible that it is both 'surprising' and 'saddening' to find some 'educated people still invoking' them (Grayling, 2003, pp 80–81). However, as we shall see in the following two chapters, the idea of a secular commonwealth founded on some sort of contingent political morality remains influential. Moreover, it would be a mistake to abandon natural law with Aquinas or Hooker, for ideas of natural law and natural rights have continued to attract their adherents. This enduring influence is attested to by two famous 'law and morality' debates, both of which involved a leading legal positivist, Herbert Hart. We will consider legal positivism in Chapter 4, but for our present purposes, it can be said that positivists, such as Hart, adhere to an idea that law should be understood as a social or political, rather than natural, entity. Against philosophical speculation, positivism posits the rigour of scientific analysis. Its origins, as we shall see, lie in the anti-metaphysical scepticism of the late 17th and 18th centuries, represented by the likes of John Locke and David Hume.

Although, as we shall see in Chapter 4, Hart's particular idea of positive law enjoys certain characteristics which distinguish it from such a generalised summary, the extent to which he rejected naturalist speculation could be seen in his essay *Positivism and the separation of law and morals* which triggered the first of these 'law and morality' debates. In the essay, Hart clung rigidly to the basic positivist idea that we must 'distinguish, firmly and with the maximum of clarity, law as it is from law as it ought to be' (Hart, 1958, p 594). Positivist theory seeks to analyse the legitimacy of law by locating sources of constitutional legitimacy and sovereign authority. At the heart of Hart's argument could be found a commentary on one German legal theorist, Gustav Radbruch, whose philosophy of law appeared to change shape quite dramatically as a result of his own personal experience of life in Nazi Germany. Hart referred to Radbruch's 'positivist' sympathies prior to 1933 and the arrival in power of Adolf Hitler, and then took note of Radbruch's 'recantation' after 1945 and his turn to natural law theory. Law, Radbruch suggested after the experience of Hitler, must be more than simply rules and commands. According to Hart, this was strikingly 'naive', and merely served to confuse the issue. Because a law is immoral, it does not make it any less a law. It simply becomes a bad law. But the qualities of command, effective enforcement and sanction are all present, and it does nobody any good, in the real world, to wax lyrically about the immorality of laws. It certainly made no difference in the real experience of Nazi Germany. Expressions of morality are not laws; they only become laws if a recognisable sovereign authority can enforce them (Hart, 1958, pp 615–21). Two points should be noted here. First, as we shall see in the next chapter, Radbruch fiercely rejected the suggestion that he was either a positivist or a natural lawyer. Secondly, such a critique can be accommodated by the likes of Aquinas or Hooker, and the kind of stringently metaphysical idea of natural law which Hart attacked has never really been advocated by anyone, certainly not since Plato.

The second of these points was emphasised by the American jurist, Lon Fuller, in his reply to Hart, entitled 'Positivism and fidelity to law – a reply to Professor Hart'. Fuller countered that the crucial issue was indeed that of 'fidelity'; how can the law secure its legitimacy? In contrast with Hart, for whom legitimacy remained bound up more with clarity and effectiveness, for Fuller, it is dependent upon popular support. This idea of popular support is resonant of a theory common to secular natural law, that of popular sovereignty, articulated most strongly by Enlightenment *philosophes* such as Jean-Jacques Rousseau whose ideas we will encounter in the next chapter. Sovereign authority lies, ultimately, with the people, and not with constitutional orders, and therefore, law is legitimated by the people, and not with regard to constitutional technicalities. Legal orders must enjoy 'moral foundations'. Most importantly, in such terms, law must be about so much more than simply rules. In these immediately political terms, law is always about matters of political morality. Accordingly, the example of Nazi Germany was prescient, for such was the perversion of justice experienced under Nazi law that it could not properly be termed law. As a matter of political morality, Nazi Germany had failed to legitimate its legal order. Moreover, it would be wrong for legal theorists now to ascribe a spurious legitimacy to such laws just because they were effected under such a perverse political and constitutional order. It was the realisation of this potential error which, according to Fuller, underlay the turn of certain German jurists, such as Radbruch, towards natural law. To deny that certain rules can be so immoral as to be denied moral and popular legitimacy would be to permit a degree of relativism which could legitimate any 'legislative monstrosity'. The future of Germany, as Radbruch appreciated, demanded an appreciation of the distinction between 'the demands of order, on the one hand, and those of good order, on the other' (Fuller, 1958, pp 651–57).

Such a response reflected Fuller's broader idea of natural law, as articulated in his *The Morality of Law* and *Principles of Social Order*. Fuller rejected both Aquinas's theological foundations, and, indeed, the subsequent Kantian alternative of natural and rationally constructed rights. Instead, he expressed a greater affinity with Aristotle, and the natural law which he presents bears striking similarity to that which can be found in Aristotle, as well as in the more political writings of Aquinas. In the final part of this chapter, we will find John Finnis taking the same approach. Fuller suggested that all natural law theories share a common foundation in the political desire to establish 'principles' of social order. Moreover, we share a 'morality of aspiration', which means that we lead our lives purposively. However, in contrast to Aristotle and, most particularly, Plato, we do not know precisely at what end our efforts are directed, whilst, in even sharper contrast, such ends that relate to matters of purely individual morality must not be prescribed by law or government. Such principles, he added, are 'deliberative' principles. In other words, they are resolved by our communication with one another. Accordingly, much of Fuller's developed theory concentrates on procedural mechanisms of law and government (Fuller, 1969). In these terms, law and morality, being both products of this form of deliberative political process, are intrinsically related. Moral and ethical questions cannot be divorced from legal and political questions. It is worth bearing in mind Fuller's revised theory of natural law, for its similarities to Kantian constructivist and communitarian variants, which we will encounter in the following two chapters, are striking. There is much in Fuller which is echoed in the theories of such as Rawls, Unger or Habermas.

Law and morality again: Hart and Devlin

In a series of lectures given during the late 1950s and early 1960s, Lord Devlin suggested that law has a duty to enforce certain moral standards. It was not an explicitly natural law thesis. Indeed, Devlin expressed an essentially positivist sympathy with regard to the legitimacy of laws enacted in accordance with due constitutional procedures. However, his lectures presented one of the clearest recent articulations of a distinctly Christian and theological foundation for English jurisprudence. The immediate trigger for Devlin's lectures was the Wolfenden Committee Report of 1958, which recommended the decriminalisation of homosexual acts between consenting adults in private. There was, the Committee resolved, an area of 'private morality and immorality' which is 'not the law's business'. There can be no doubt that Devlin shared a number of opinions on private sexuality which served to place him firmly within a particular intellectual and historical context. He described homosexuality to be 'a miserable way of life' and one from which it is the 'duty of society' to try to save people, whilst rampant sexual activity, particularly outside monogamous marriage, could only lead to the 'degradation' of men and women (Devlin, 1965, p v).

According to Devlin, the morality of English jurisprudence is described by a political theology, and questions of morals, religion and law are 'inextricably joined', such that 'without the help of Christian teaching the law will fail'. Moreover, as it is impossible to delineate 'crime' from 'sin', so too criminal law, which is an emanation of public law, must assume a public interest defined by a conception of public good. In such matters, relating to sexual relations and conduct, there can be no attempted demarcation of a private sphere of morality. For reasons of both law and political theology, sexual relations are a matter of immediate relevance to the public good (Devlin, 1965, pp 4–6, 23–25). In his analysis of community, and its foundations upon a conception of public good, Devlin revealed an acute awareness of the historical nature of a political morality. Morality is not frozen in time, and neither should be the laws of morality (Devlin, 1965, p 100). Accordingly, contemporary laws and morals relating to sexuality are not set in place simply because of Christian theology, but because that theology has entered the community's soul. Our political morality, for good or bad, cannot be distinguished from the theological impulses which originally established it and which have served to refine it over the centuries. It is, therefore, a morality which is political as well as theological, accepted by Christians and non-Christians alike, and the reason why thousands of non-churchgoers still seek Christian baptism and aspire to Christian marriage ceremonies.

The extent to which Devlin sought to legitimate the 'enforcement' of morals through the law in terms of an established political community and its morals is immediately resonant of political theology and the idea of a godly commonwealth. A society is always a 'community of ideas', one in which there is a rational political morality defined in terms of the 'right-minded person'. Thus, what the 'lawmaker has to ascertain is not the true belief but the common belief'. It was such a vision of social construction that led Devlin to assert that marriage was a public as much as a private institution, one which should be encouraged by society as an alternative against extra-marital relations. Marriage may not now be a 'sacrament', but it does represent a 'sacred' commitment, made by individuals not just to each other but to their community. Thus, although there was no metaphysical necessity for natural law, as a matter of historical reality, English law must be understood in the context of its particular, distinctly theological jurisprudence. Moreover, as no society can exist without such a historically determined political morality, the duty of a judge lies in enforcing the law as determined in the light of such moral principles (Devlin, 1965, pp 9–10, 15, 77–83, 94). The fact that society has the 'right to make a judgment' about certain moral issues is the 'price' of living in communities. A common morality, founded on theological precepts, or indeed any other, fashions a 'common agreement about the way we should go' (Devlin, 1965, p 120). Approving Cicero, he acknowledged that 'we are all slaves to the law, for that is the condition of our freedom', for 'each have rights over the whole' and 'therefore the rights of each must be curtailed so as to ensure as far as possible that the essential needs of each are safeguarded' (Devlin, 1965, pp 12–16, 101).

A central part of the Hart-Devlin debate oscillated around John Stuart Mill's 'harm' principle. According to Mill, a society is only entitled to infringe individual freedom in the case of threatened physical harm to another member of the community (Mill, 1985, pp 68–69). Against such a negative idea of freedom, Devlin countered with a positive conception which redefined freedom in terms of rights to contribute to and reform society. To a considerable extent, Hart's response concentrated on reaffirming Mill's classical liberal defence of private rights. Hart suggested that the question was not one of whether or not modern society enjoys moral foundations, for undoubtedly it does, but whether the law is entitled to enforce certain interpretations of this morality, and to do so on the premise that there is an identifiable community interest which can trump individual autonomy. According to Hart, Devlin's lectures articulated a revived 'legal moralism' in English society, and a concomitant crisis in liberal ideology. In a contemporary case, *Shaw v DPP* [1961] 2 All ER 446, the House of Lords had resurrected the common law offence of a 'conspiracy to corrupt public morals', last used in the 18th century, in order to suppress a magazine advertising the services of prostitutes. In doing so, the House had failed to appreciate that the morality of the 18th century no longer described that of the 20th. As such, Hart did not deny political morality, but he did deny the House of Lords' ahistorical appreciation of its constitution (Hart, 1968, pp vii, 4–11, 17–22). Both Hart and Devlin accepted that 'some shared morality is essential to the existence of any society'. However, a proper historical understanding of political morality must recognise its constructive, and fluid, constitution. In founding his society on one particular moral vision, Devlin had in fact rooted it to some essentially imaginary ideal of a moral determined community, a revived godly commonwealth (Hart, 1968, pp 28–29, 38, 63).

The Hart-Devlin debate is not, of course, the only modern reassessment of 'law and morality'. Another recent, and challenging, contribution has been made by Ronald Dworkin, whose ideas we will investigate in greater depth in the next chapter. In his *Life's Dominion*, Dworkin has attempted to reinvest contemporary 'law and morality' debates with a distinctive philosophical import, whilst not denying their inevitably political impact. Like Devlin, Dworkin acknowledges that a community is always founded on a particular morality which, in western society, is a distinct moral theology. It is this which constitutes the political morality which provides principled supports to the constitution (Dworkin, 1993). As we shall see, Dworkin's idea of moral principles is cast in a distinctive Kantian, rather than consciously theological, mould. Yet this reorientation of contemporary approaches to questions of law and morality should not detract from the enduring influence of classical and theological ideas of natural law. Aside from its intrinsic jurisprudential import, the Hart-Devlin debate is instructive because it underlines the extent to which issues of natural law and political theology, which might at first glance seem to be rather arcane, are in fact immediately relevant. Sexuality is still closely prescribed in modern English law, and, indeed, in every other modern legal system. Laws prescribe both permissible sexual activity and expressions of it, and the reason for such prescription lies in the historical morality which continues to underpin our jurisprudential morality. Just as our constitutional order is still founded on Hooker's commonwealth, so too our attitude to questions of law and morality is still determined in relation to our particular historical and political morality.

The return to classicism

The fate of natural law theory has, since Aristotle, largely risen and fallen in line with the oscillating reputation of his rather grander theories of moral and political philosophy. In this context, the Thomist sequestration has proved to be less then helpful. We live in a determinedly secular age, and the shadow of sceptics such as Friedrich Nietzsche, whose fiercely anti-Christian sentiments will be revisited in the final chapter, hangs heavy. As AC Grayling has recently asserted, in his polemical dismissal of theological appropriations of Socratic philosophy, the age of 'superstition' has passed, and in its wake must come a reinvested humanist ethics:

> From classical antiquity to modern philosophy the fundamental idea has been that people possess reason, and that by using it they can choose lives worth living for themselves and respectful of their fellows. The contrast between a humanist ethics of freedom and a transcendentalist claim that man's good lies in submission to an external authority – the authority of a supposed divine power or transcendent order; which in concrete terms means the teachings of a priesthood or tradition – is therefore a sharp one. Where humanism premises autonomy as the basis of the good life, religion premises heteronomy. In humanist ethics the individual is responsible for achieving the good as a free member of a community of free agents; in religious ethics

he achieves the good by obedience to an authority that tells him what his goals are and how he should live (Grayling, 2003, pp 218–19).

The disjuncture is stark: the liberty of humanism against the tryanny of theology.

It is for this reason, perhaps, that the most compelling modern defences of natural law theory tend to shy away from the more overtly theological tone. Perhaps the most influential of these defences is John Finnis's *Natural Law and Natural Rights*. At its heart can be found the overarching ambition to reinvest jurisprudence with a concept of the 'good'. The classical tradition, Finnis argues, has been first distracted by the temptations of theology and then smothered by centuries of scepticism and positivism. The classical humanist tradition, founded on reason, community and good, rather than the theological, which depends upon an acceptance of a more metaphysical authority, can counter this scepticism and reinvest an ethical theory of law. Classical natural law does not need or even countenance moral force, because its political morality is founded, not on metaphysics, but on practical reason. Natural law is a 'set of principles of practical reasonableness in ordering human life and human community' (Finnis, 1980, pp 3–18, 280–81, 378–92, 409–10). Thus, although Finnis alludes to Aquinas, it is to Aristotle that he returns in order to restate principles of natural law and rights, and most particularly the idea that such principles can be approximated through the medium of practical reason. A modern natural law, according to Finnis, is one which can 'identify conditions and principles of practical right-mindedness, of good and proper order among men and in individual conduct' (Finnis, 1980, p 18). It does not deny the possibility of theological belief, but neither does it prescribe or require it. Indeed, as Finnis rightly notes, the recourse to practical reason in order to legitimate civil laws was central to Aquinas's political theory (Finnis, 1980, pp 34–37).

Thus, rather than shrouding the determination of this good in metaphysics or theology, Finnis suggests that 'goods', which include life, knowledge, play, aesthetic experience, friendship, practical reasonableness itself and the 'origins of cosmic order' and 'religion', are self-evident or 'intrinsic'. They are goods which provide the premises for the application of practical reason in political communities. Two points should be noted here. First, these are Finnis's goods and cannot be universally justified. Finnis suggests that they all 'enrich' our lives (Finnis, 1980, pp 81–90); but not everyone would agree that the 'origins of cosmic order' are necessary in any list of goods, or that religion enriches our lives. Indeed, not everyone would agree that such a list is anyway necessary. Secondly, necessarily there is a certain circularity in such an approach to identifying goods. The good of order prescribes itself, and then founds the other goods of which it is a part. Such an internal ambiguity is perhaps unavoidable in any theory of natural order which declines metaphysical authority, and it is, of course, precisely the concession recognised by Aristotle. It is here, too, that we can detect the same translation of a theory of law into an expression of political practical reason. These are goods which can only be secured by political institutions, and the object of legal theory is first to 'identify' these tools in order then to legitimate the exercise of law (Finnis, 1980, pp 3–4).

Classical theories of natural order and practical reason provide 'rational foundations for moral judgment' (Finnis, 1980, p 25). Natural law is something which provides for all of us to act justly in relation with one another. It is a model of practical reason for use in any community, ancient or modern. The foundations of Finnis's theory closely proceed along the lines Aristotle prescribes. Most importantly, the participation of citizens, the active doing of good, is what defines the good and harmoniously ordered community. Such action, in turn, depends upon our ability to exercise this moral judgment. The political morality of a community is the product of its collective practical reason and exercise of moral judgment (Finnis, 1980, pp 29–36, 111, 119–27). The model of an Aristotelian community is the pivot in Finnis's thesis. It is the essential 'unifying relationship between humans', and law can only be legitimated if it seeks to preserve the 'unity of common action' which any rational community pursues in order to attain its goods. Legal rights, in turn, are only legitimate insofar as they facilitate the individual pursuit of the 'common good' within an identifiable political community (Finnis, 1980, pp 134–56, 206–08). Once again, there is an immediate resonance, not just with Aristotle, but also with Fuller. Similarly, the 'elements of justice' which Finnis identifies, each of which centres on the idea of duties to others with a community and the preservation of equality as a balance between individuals, are also taken directly from the classical tradition. Thus the idea of justice itself only has meaning in terms of a common good. It is the 'object of all justice' (Finnis, 1980, pp 161–64, 168).

Accordingly, it can be suggested that Finnis's modern theory of classical natural law, like Aristotle's, is premised upon a communitarian theory of justice, and it is worth noting again, as we did with Fuller, the extent to which there is an immediate affinity between ideas of natural law and order and communitarianism. It is this which commends Finnis's theory of natural law and rights. At the heart of the classical tradition of natural order lies a presumption that this order is at once philosophical and political. Order only makes sense in a community situation, whilst justice can only be located in an order which seeks to promote the 'common good' (Finnis, 1980, pp 152–56, 168–73). In a very real sense, then, Finnis's return to the classical tradition furnishes a neat circularity to the rise and fall, and perhaps rise again, of natural law theory. Critical legal theories are all directed at the assertion of metaphysical foundations which seek to legitimate the exercise of law in real political conditions. In some ways, the kind of political theologies of Aquinas or Hooker provide the easiest target, even in contemporary societies which subscribe, both constitutionally and socially, to a theological morality. At the same time, it must be stressed that part of the strength of the Aristotelian thesis lies in its concession to political expediency, and in the following two chapters we will address theories of law and politics which are themselves critical, in the sense that they seek to redetermine a non-metaphysical foundation in ideas of the moral self or the moral community. Of course, such a non-metaphysical foundation can be criticised for being precisely foundational, and so the argument becomes reductive to some degree, and we shall, in subsequent chapters, encounter some of these more radical anti-foundational critiques. But, regardless of its merits, the original classical tradition, filtered through political theology and then recast during the 20th century by the likes of Fuller and Finnis, can furnish us with an identifiable modernist theory of law; one which inheres, and is perhaps even defined by, its own critical potential.

A jurisprudence of compassion

Whilst Finnis's *Natural Law and Natural Rights* remains the most compelling restatement of classical natural law in recent years, it is not the only one. One of the most striking recent developments in moral and political philosophy has been the reassertion of a distinctively humanist politics, and jurisprudence, of friendship and compassion; one, moreover, that seems rather more willing to flirt with Christian theology. A starting point here, perhaps, is St Paul's injunction, in *Romans 13:8*, 'Owe to no man anything, but to love one another: for he that loveth another hath fulfilled the law'. This particular injuction had a huge impact upon Renaissance and then Enlightenment jurists. In his essay *On Friendship*, Montaigne declared that 'friendship is the peak' of the 'perfect of society', and upon the very highest peak of all could be found pure 'love' (Montaigne, 1993, pp 91–93, 97–98). The 17th century Dutch jurist Johannes Althusius similarly affirmed that the 'common law' of a commonwealth is 'nothing other than the general theory and practice of love, both for God and for one's neighbour' (Althusius, 1995, pp 12–22, 70–71, 80–81, 139–43).

But it found perhaps its most striking expression in the writings of the Hanoverian philosopher Gottfried Wilhelm Leibniz. Writing in the wake of the ruinous religious wars of the late 17th century, Leibniz mused wistfully on a lost 'age of gold', one in which the Word of God had, he rather credulously supposed, for centuries secured peace across Europe (Riley, 1996, p 243). At the heart of this age, Leibniz alleged, could be found a distinctive 'universal jurisprudence', derived principally from Aristotle, and Paul's intepretation of Aristotle. It was a jurisprudence founded on 'charity' and the 'love of peace, which is so recommended by Jesus Christ', a 'universal benevolence, which the wise man carries into execution in conformity with the measures of reason, to the end of obtaining the greatest good' (Riley, 1996, pp 58–60, 236). In his short treatise, *On Piety*, Leibniz argued that those who prefer a jurisprudence of mere rules 'fail altogether to understand that one cannot be just without being benevolent', whilst in his rather grander *Codex Iuris Gentium*, he opined that a 'universal jurisprudence' of 'charity' should focus on this innately human capacity for 'benevolence', being a 'habit of loving and of willing the good' (Leibniz, 1988, pp 19, 171, 195–96).

The critical passage, for the likes of Leibniz and Althusius, aside from *Romans 13*, was Aristotle's commentary on friendship in the *Ethics*:

> Between friends there is no need for justice, but people who are just still need the quality of friendship; and indeed friendliness is considered to be justice in the fullest sense. It is not only a necessary thing but a splendid one. We praise those who love their friends, and the possession of many friends is held to be one of the fine things of life. What is more, people think that good men and friends are the same (Aristotle, 1976, pp 258–59).

In essays such as 'The common concept of justice' and 'Opinions on the principles of Pufendorf', Leibniz placed this idea of friendship at the centre of his 'universal jurisprudence'. In the latter, for example, he declared that:

> Aristotelian philosophy bases all of the virtues splendidly on universal justice; and we owe it not only to ourselves, but also to society, above all to that in which we find ourselves with God, by the natural law written in our hearts, that we have a soul imbued with free thoughts, and a will which tends constantly towards the just (Leibniz, 1988, p 69).

During the 19th century the German school of Higher Criticism, whose ideas were introduced to a wider audience by the novelist George Eliot, sought to reinvest the Leibnizian idea of a compassionate politics in their particular interpretation of scriptural texts. Ludwig Feuerbach's *Essence of Christianity*, for example, oscillated around the idea that a politics of love and compassion should concentrate on facilitating the 'direct promptings of the sympathetic feeling' (Eliot, 1990, p 462). And the same essential aspiration can be detected in a number of more contemporary commentaries on justice in the modern, perhaps even postmodern, world. Three such commentaries are illustrative.

Two, those presented by Archbishop Desmond Tutu and the former Czech President Vaclav Havel, were generated within particular and immediate political contexts. For Tutu this context was the inauguration of a Truth and Reconciliation Commission in post-Apartheid South Africa. We shall revisit this Commission in greater depth in Chapter 3. According to Tutu, who chaired the Commission, the focus was not upon assigning blame, but 'the healing of breaches, the redressing of imbalances, the restoration of broken relationships'. In doing so, the Commission executed a very different jurisprudence; an alternative, as the first President of the post-Apartheid Supreme Court, Arthur Chaskalson, observed, to the 'impoverished' formalism of positive jurisprudence (Dyzenhaus, 1998, p 81). Much was made of the need to speak and listen, to deal in terms of respect and forgiveness, rather than blame and punishment. For Tutu it was a jurisprudence that owed everything to shared native Ubuntu and Christian doctrines of confession and atonement (Tutu, 1999, pp 34–35, 51–52, 86–87).

For Havel, the context was set by the need to reinvest a broadly liberal democratic public philosophy in his newly liberated Czech republic; a public philosophy which, he hoped, would also be infused by what he held to be a definitively European humanism. At the end of one of the most brutal of centuries, Havel suggests, it was more than ever apparent that the 'salvation of this human world lies nowhere else than in the human heart, in the human power to reflect, in human modesty, and in human responsibility' (Havel, 1998, pp 18–19). Admitting its irreducibly 'metaphysical' tenor, Havel has repeatedly invoked the 'miracle of Being' as the core conceptual component of any revived humanism, and more particularly of a humanism that might serve to overcome the alienation which is otherwise produced by the often bewildering effects of globalisation. In a particularly resonant passage in his *Art of the Impossible*, Havel confirms that:

> It is my belief that, if there is a bond uniting the diverse religious and cultural worlds that make up our civilization today, it can only be their unwavering certainty that the key to solid human coexistence, and to a life that does not become hell on earth, lies in respect for what I call the miracle of Being. True goodness, true responsibility, true justice, a true sense of things – all these grow from roots that go much deeper than the world of transitory earthly schemes. This is the message that speaks to us from the very heart of human religiosity (Havel, 1998, pp 240–42).

Religiosity, a sense of some deeper metaphysical meaning to life, is not the same as an adherence to one specific religious dogma, such as Christianity or Islam. But its conceptual roots are, to a certain degree, shared.

And the same essential religiosity roots, the third of these contemporary commentaries, Raimond Gaita's *A Common Humanity*. There is, as Gaita readily acknowleges, a danger that a jurisprudence of compassion might seem to be somehow 'sentimental or soft-headed'. As we shall see in subsequent chapters, modern legal thought, particularly of the positivist and realist variety, makes little concession to sentimentality. But this should not lead us to neglect some of the defining traits of humanity and the classical conception of the 'good life'. According to Gaita:

> Were it not for the many ways human beings genuinely love one another – from sexual love to the impartial love of saints – I do not believe we would have a sense of the sacredness of individuals, or of their inalienable rights or dignity. Working together, sometimes harmoniously, sometimes in tension, our ways of loving create and are also formed by a language of love in which we record and explore the ways we matter to one another (Gaita, 2000, p 5).

It is in this context that Gaita goes on to argue that a meaningful culture of 'rights' must be founded upon a bedrock of 'love and respect' for one another. Rights should be received, indeed, as a 'spontaneous expression of human fellowship'. We cannot, ultimately, 'detach' our understanding of 'justice' from our capacity for 'sympathy' (Gaita, 2000, pp 26, 48–49, 72, 267).

There is much here that should intrigue us, whether or not we share a more sceptical approach to certain aspects of natural law theory. The idea of a politics, and a jurisprudence, that is based on compassion and friendship has taken a broader hold across various sections of the academy. In the final chapter we will find postmodernists such as Jacques Derrida likewise returning to Aristotle in order to retrieve an identifiable 'politics of friendship'. And as another modern sceptic, Richard Rorty, concedes, whilst the more literal claims of classical scripture might seem to be rather too incredible today, that does not in any way diminish the 'inspirational value' of St Paul's injunction. We can, he argues, 'skip lightly past' the more dubious 'predictions' that are scattered about both testaments, and instead 'concentrate on the expressions of hope' (Rorty, 1999, pp 204–05).

CHAPTER 2

THE CRITIQUE OF MODERNITY

THE MORAL SELF

Enlightenment

In the previous chapter, we explored a particular line in legal theory which stretched from classical Greece, through medieval and early modern Europe, to modern theories of natural law. In doing so, we established a model of modernity, defined by an adherence to the idea of law as an expression of natural or divine order. At the same time, we also noted the immanent potential for critique. In this chapter, we are going to investigate another intellectual tradition which is founded on a notion of order, Kantianism. At the same time, we will also be engaged in a distinctly critical legal theory, for it was Immanuel Kant, perhaps more than any other single figure in western philosophy, who challenged the received traditions of classical metaphysics. Natural order, Kant concluded, is not pervasive, and reason is limited by the creative power of the individual enlightened rationalist within the rationally constructive political community. By the time we complete our study of Kant and contemporary Kantians, such as John Rawls and Ronald Dworkin, we will have encountered modernism's most concerted attempt to re-establish a rational justification for law, but we will also have made a critical switch, from a foundation in nature or God to one in a presumed rational moral self.

In a book entitled *Religion Within the Limits of Reason Alone*, Kant suggested that, as we cannot reason about God, matters of theology are best left to theologians to worry about. Governing individuals, in contrast, is the preserve of individuals, and it was this that was the matter for political philosophy. Such was the attitude of the 18th century Enlightenment, the essence of which lay in redetermining the power of reason and relocating it within the individual. To a certain degree, therefore, it represented a return to the spirit of classical Greece, but whereas classical philosophy looked to a form of reason governed by metaphysics, by natural or civic harmony, the Enlightenment sought to situate reason purely within the moral self. It should not be supposed that the Enlightenment, or indeed Kant himself, was atheistic. Indeed, Kant was an active member of an extreme puritan sect of Lutheran Pietists. In fact, as Herbert Marcuse noted, it was the empowerment of the individual conscience facilitated by the Lutheran reformation which provided the intellectual foundation for Kantian theories of the moral self. According to Marcuse, it was Kant who provided a 'secularised' protestant theology (Marcuse, 1972, pp 56–94). At the same time, the rise of the political State, which had forced Aquinas and Hooker to fashion distinct political theologies, reached its epitome towards the end of the 18th century, by which time it could fairly be said that ideals of godly commonwealth and *respublica Christiana* only existed in the poetry of Milton or Blake. In reality, the rise of Protestantism, particularly in northern Europe, signalled the end of a unified church, and in the place of institutionalised Catholicism, a multitude of different protestant sects advised the possibility of the individual's direct communion with God. The mediation of God's 'vicar on earth', the Pope, no longer secured salvation, and in its place was the conscience of the individual moral self.

At the same time, the intellectual dynamic behind the Enlightenment was largely sceptical. Rene Descartes, often thought of as the father of modern philosophy, suggested that the only thing of which we can be sure is the thinking self. Everything else might be illusion, but we know that we exist, at least in so far as we think. Thus, he could famously conclude, 'I think, therefore I am'. Again, the concentration lay upon the individual moral rational thinking self. The most immediate sceptical influence on Kant was, however, David Hume, one of the British empiricists who, as we shall see in Chapter 4, vigorously asserted that there are no innate ideas. In other words, our minds are blanks upon which various experiences make impressions. Everyone's mind evolves as a 'bundle of perceptions'. The liberalism which emerged during the later 17th century, and which gained momentum during the 18th, articulated a political theory of scepticism and, if the philosophical essence lay with the moral self, concluded that so too must the centre of politics. A second, and in many ways conflicting, influence was Jean-Jacques Rousseau, who articulated a distinctly romantic desire to return man to the condition of the 'noble savage', before the oppression of gods, kings and States. In his *Discourse on Inequality*, Rousseau suggested that the political State was the primary cause of social inequality and misfortune in Europe, and that the return to nature and to inner 'nobility' would only be achieved by the destruction of both State and property. Though he did not share such radical inclinations, Kant was hugely influenced by Rousseau's commitment to the idea that man could determine his own political fate and need not be subjected to any supposed metaphysical truths.

Rousseau refused to wear a watch, because he thought that time was a constraint on individual freedom. Kant, too, declined a watch, but, just as a precaution, organised his daily life so that he did everything in precisely the same way every day at precisely the same time. Indeed, the populace of Koenigsberg, where Kant lived, are reputed to have set their own clocks by his daily movements. Not for him the romanticism of the unconstrained 'noble savage'. Everything in Kant's personal context, throughout his life, was geared to self-control and self-discipline. Whereas Rousseau wished to return man to his primitive state, Kant shared the wider Enlightenment confidence in common progress towards a state of individual freedom that was not a romantic anarchy, but rather one governed by the power of reason. The emancipation of modern humanity would be achieved by human reason.

The Critique of Reason

This emancipation was charted in a series of three *Critiques, of Pure Reason, of Practical Reason*, and *of Judgment*. Prior to this 'critical' project, Kant had been engaged in exploring the limits of science and knowledge. In the *Critiques*, he concluded that knowledge was limited only by the reason of the self. In 1770, he suggested that a 'great light' had 'dawned' upon him; that the realms of reason and sense were quite distinct. Thus, against Hume's assertion that the mind was simply a sponge for experiences and sensibilities, Kant suggested that there was a realm of immanent reason. But, unlike Plato, Aristotle or Aquinas, who had situated this realm within some sort of metaphysical system, natural, political or theological, Kant situated it in the self. There is a core part of every individual which remains pure, apart from experience, and which is not subsumed in metaphysics. Accordingly, Kant confidently proclaimed that the individual was never determined by his utility, as a means, but represented an 'absolute end in itself', an absolute good. Indeed, as he was to suggest in *The Critique of Judgment*, man is the only 'end': 'without man ... the whole of creation would be a mere wilderness, a thing in vain, and have no final end' (Kant, 1991a, p 108).

In 1781, Kant published *The Critique of Pure Reason*, and situated the idea of freedom, the essential intellectual concern of the Enlightenment, in the moral self. The only moral rules to which we are subject are our own. We alone enjoy pure practical moral reason, and so we alone can self-govern, self-create and self-determine. Accordingly, we create our own understanding. This is the essential 'critique' of reason. Metaphysics is reconstituted through individual reason. At the same time as enjoying this core of immanent morality, the self is also subject to experience, as indeed sceptics such as Hume had emphasised. It is this duality, of immanent reason and experience, which constitutes Kant's 'synthetic' model. On the one hand, there are the ideas of pure reason, fashioned by immanent reason; on the other, there are the concepts or reflective representations of these ideas, fashioned by experience. Thus everything has an idea and a concept, an ideal and an experiential approximation of it. The resemblance between this model, and the Aristotelian idea of form and substance, was not, of course, coincidental. Most importantly, therefore, Kant had reserved this crucial realm of the moral self, within which was situated a realm of pure rational freedom apart from any experiential realm of political freedom. In *Groundwork to the Metaphysics of Morals*, Kant sought to develop further this duality of freedom by prescribing a series of 'maxims' or duties which were expressions of both immanent reason and experience. The link was crucial, because it meant that duties, of morality and political behaviour, could not be drawn solely from experience. It was, he suggested, 'absolutely impossible' to derive a 'maxim of action' from experience. Indeed, quite the reverse is true, for the moral individual has an absolute duty to act in accordance with the dictates of his or her own moral reason, rather than be ruled by perceptions of what others do. In doing so, the moral self exercises 'practical reason' (Kant, 1964, pp 74–80).

It was in *Groundwork* that Kant formulated the generic idea of the 'categorical imperative'. This imperative expressed the rule of the moral individual, stated by Kant as, 'I ought never to act except in such a way that I can also will that my maxim should become a universal law' (Kant, 1964, p 70). In a crude sense, the imperative, as the only fundamental rule of the moral self, suggests that we should only act in such a way as we would have others act towards us. It is a maxim of common and reciprocal respect. Above all, it is a maxim of non-contradiction, demanding that every individual act in such a way as not to contradict himself. Thus, in later political essays, Kant would suggest that suicide was wrong because it was a gesture of self-contradiction. Likewise, breaking a contract would be irrational and wrong, because it would contradict a former expression of the self (Kant, 1991b, pp 93–95). Most importantly, it is a maxim for political activity founded upon a philosophy centred on the self, rather than on a God or nature. The 'categorical imperative' was a completely political idea, based entirely upon individual interaction. At the same time, as an imperative of 'universal' application, it was a metaphysics. The individual 'will' remained subject to certain laws which, even if drawn from the moral self, were justified by reference to a form of universalism.

The Critique of Practical Reason was dedicated to fleshing out this idea of the moral self, defined by a freedom itself constrained only by the 'categorical imperative'. It is the conclusion to the second *Critique* which is most instructive. Here, Kant articulated perhaps his most famous observation: 'Two things fill the mind with ever new and increasing admiration and awe, the oftener and more steadily they are reflected on: the starry heavens above me and the moral law within me.' The 'starry heavens' may not be fathomable, but the moral law could be. The individual is subject only to those moral 'laws that he gives himself through reason'. Thus the individual is bounded purely by the self, and will act in accordance with 'free will'. Such a 'will' provides for a good that is intrinsically moral, rather than experiential and contingent. Significantly, as the *Critique* concluded, it concentrated on the matter of practical politics. As we have noted, the whole idea of the 'categorical imperative', and thus the idea of the moral self, was intrinsically political, concerned with the relation between the self and other selves. The final 'end' of the 'moral self', Kant concluded, was political 'community'.

Politics and judgment

The politics of the 'critical' project was given a striking twist in Kant's third *Critique, of Judgment*, published in 1790. The essential theme of the third *Critique* is contingency, and signals Kant's own conversion to matters of practical political philosophy. But rather than concentrating purely on matters of political morality, Kant turns to the 'faculty' of 'judgment' as an aesthetic faculty, one which appreciates that everything is judged on its particular merits. The whole tenor of this *Critique* becomes one of reflection rather than truth, 'thinking the particular' rather than universals (Kant, 1991a, p 407). Whilst the realm of reason, as derived from within the moral self, accounted for the immanent, there was still the constitutive role of experience to be accounted for. Moral duties could be accessed by pure practical reason, but the practical world of politics is one of experience, reflection and judgment. This is the second realm of the basic synthetic model.

There are two parts to *The Critique of Judgment*. The first part addresses the development of the 'aesthetic', thus providing a means of approaching political questions without having to worry about universal values. The second addresses the 'teleological', stressing the historical and purposeful situation of mankind, together with the fundamental truth that humanity is an 'absolute end'. Humanity has an existential dimension within history, reflecting upon this history and directing itself accordingly towards the highest good (Kant, 1991a, p 111). In both senses, humanity is contingently situated and acknowledges this. All moral questions are thus thought in the particular situation. In other words, all moral questions are understood only as applied moral questions. Political issues, those encountered by an individual's relation to others, are resolved as questions of judgment, of the substantive application of duties to particular situations. This is an 'aesthetic' experience, enjoyed by the immanently moral self. The desire to wed the immanent moral self to the contingencies of 'aesthetic' experience is finally realised in Kant's most immediately jurisprudential essay, *The Metaphysics of Morals*.

The most pertinent sections of *The Critique of Judgment* are numbers 21 and 40, in which Kant addresses the idea of communicative rationality, or, as he terms it, the *'sensus communis'*. This is the reason constituted by the interaction of the moral selves which make up the community. It is not an absolute rationality, but is, rather, a rationality fashioned by the community. In other words, it is reason constructed by people as they live together. Because all the communicating selves are moral selves, then the form or idea of the reason can be universal, but the substance – what they actually decide – is contingent or relative to the political situation. The distinction was, of course, precisely that made by Aristotle. Accordingly, it is the 'critical faculty which in its reflective act takes account of the mode of reflection of every one else' (Kant, 1991a, p 151). In these terms, then, judgment is an expressly anti-metaphysical faculty. As we shall see shortly, various theories of 'constructive rationality' have been fashioned around sections 21 and 40, and they remain Kant's most important bequest to critical legal theory, as well as providing the intellectual foundation for *The Metaphysics of Morals*.

Following *The Critique of Judgment*, Kant concentrated almost exclusively on more immediate matters of government and politics, determined to realise a long held ambition to emulate Plato's ideal model of government. Like Plato – and, of course, Aristotle, Aquinas and Hooker – Kant was acutely aware of his own context and the immediate political constraints within which he worked. The Prussian State was not given to disobedience or sedition. Yet despite this authoritarianism, or perhaps because of it, Kant greatly admired Prussia and all things Prussian; not just its discipline, but also its newness. The two political events which most impressed him were the American and French revolutions, which, like the rise of the Prussian State, seemed to complement, indeed prescribe, the demise of the *ancien regimes* of the old order. Kant saw the Prussian State as expressing the 'spirit' of its people, just as the two revolutions, of 1776 and 1789, represented the essential political 'spirit' of the American and French peoples. As Rousseau had intimated, the French Revolution expressed the popular sovereignty of the French people. Each of the three political transformations testified to the teleological evolution of the political world, towards a more refined politics which expressed the 'freedom' of the self and was represented by forms of government asserted as expressions of the 'moral' self. The discipline imposed by the Prussian State was, thus, a self-discipline imposed by the Prussian people. Political events seemed to vindicate Kant's teleological account of human politics, as well as his fundamental philosophical belief in the ideas of autonomy and self-assertion. These were events which encapsulated the spirit of the Enlightenment, revolutions of reason against the old orders of tyranny and absolutism. He referred to the French Revolution as an 'occurrence' which 'proves the moral tendency of the human race' and the essential correctness of his own political philosophy (Reiss, 1991, p 182).

This process of intellectual enlightenment, then, complemented the political enlightenment being experienced in the 'new' world of Prussia, France and America; the experience of progress rather than the futile inactive yearning for a 'golden age' which had characterised the Holy Roman Empire, British colonial rule in America, and the *ancien regime* of France. The Enlightenment was more than a form of consciousness. It was a real, and irresistible, political force, sweeping away the dogmas of classical and theological metaphysics. The power of reason could fashion, not merely an improved understanding of the nature of the self, but also an improved understanding of politics. Indeed, the two ambitions could not be separated. Applying the *sensus communis* model of sections 21 and 40 of the third *Critique*, Kant affirmed that the 'highest good cannot be achieved merely by the exertions of the single individual toward his own moral perfection, but instead requires a union of such individuals into a whole working towards the same end', being the 'highest moral good'. In a series of political essays written during the late 1780s and 1790s, Kant applied his own methodology, prescribing political concepts as practical applications and descriptions of ideas of moral philosophy. In an essay entitled 'What is orientation in thinking?', he affirmed that the ambition of the political philosopher must be to take ideas and provide concepts 'suitable for use in the experiential world', adding, 'To think for oneself means to look within oneself (that is, in one's own reason) for the supreme touchstone of truth; and the maxim of thinking for oneself at all times is enlightenment' (Reiss, 1991, pp 237, 249). The Enlightenment was, thus, both a political and philosophical experience, and represented 'man's emergence from his self-incurred immaturity', meaning 'the inability to use one's own understanding without the guidance of another' (Reiss, 1991, p 54).

The Metaphysics of Morals

The Metaphysics of Morals was published at the end of Kant's life, in 1797. It realised a long held ambition to present a comprehensive critical legal and political theory, whilst articulating, in coherent form, the varied political expressions contained in the three Critiques. Central is the systematic relation between ideas and concepts, most particularly between the idea of freedom, as found within the moral self, and the concept, as experienced by the Enlightenment. Such a 'metaphysics' is found 'within' each and 'every man'. The 'metaphysics of morals', therefore, lies solely within the moral self (Kant, 1991b, pp 44–45). The substantive part of the Metaphysics is divided into two 'doctrines', of 'right' and of 'virtue'. The two are quite separate realms, but are united in the sense that they represent the two 'practical' applications of critical moral philosophy. Both define complementary realms of freedom. The first 'doctrine', that of 'right', is devoted to the 'just ordering of society', in other words, the constraints demanded by the existence of individuals in the ethical community. Crucially, unlike natural rights theorists, who located the justification for such constraints in the natural world or theology, Kant located his in the moral self. At once, therefore, this is a 'right' of freedom and equality. The 'principle of innate freedom', or the free will, inheres an 'innate equality, that is, independence from being bound by others to more than one can in turn bind them' (Kant, 1991b, p 63). This is the applied political expression of the 'categorical imperative'.

As he suggested in the Groundwork and the Critique of Practical Reason, the idea of right is defined by 'duties'. Like rights, these 'duties' are immanent to the moral self, and the ultimate duty is the 'categorical imperative'. Indeed, the 'categorical imperative' is the keystone to the entire political structure. As an idea of reason, it provides a universal consistency, which can then be applied to test the validity of every particular law in the real political situation. A law is good and rational if it approximates the ideal of the 'categorical imperative'. If it does not, then it is not a rational or good law (Kant, 1991b, p 51). Likewise, rights are ideas of reason, and this idea of right is the pivot of Kant's political and legal theory. Of course, the idea is founded on the essential philosophical notion that the moral self is an 'absolute end', not a means measured by utility (Kant, 1991b, pp 189, 195–96). Because the moral self is the 'essence' of Kant's moral philosophy, the idea of individual 'right', which attaches to this self, enjoys a similar essentiality in the political philosophy. For Kant, the 'right' belongs to the individual in the political situation, and is not simply the grant of some constitutional sovereign. As a concept of practical political application, there can be a whole array of particular rights established by 'civil act'. Accordingly, the validity of each right will not depend upon its particular substance, whether it seems to be fair or not, but rather will depend upon its rational form. A conceptual right is valid if it approximates the formal idea of right.

There are two constituent doctrines of right, of 'public' and 'private' right, and Kant applies the synthetic model to both spheres. Thus, in the sphere of 'public' right, an irrational 'right' would be a right to harm the community to an extent that oneself was then harmed. Disobeying a sovereign is thus irrational, because the sovereign is defined by the 'social contract' effected, in an analogical sense, between the community and that sovereign. This is the central theme of the 'doctrine of public right'. The idea of a 'social contract' founded on the moral self was central to Kant's thesis. The self contracted with all the other selves, to vest power in a sovereign. The contract is not a document of State, but an expression of practical reason. The idea was developed from Rousseau, who suggested that the 'contract' could be an expression of 'popular sovereignty', and more originally from Thomas Hobbes, whose version we will encounter in Chapter 4. It should be noted that the very idea of a social contract is an expression of the constructively rational political community, a concession to the reality of political philosophy as a matter of interrelation between various selves in a community. As ever, the validity of the 'social contract' is not determined by its particular substantive political relations, but by the extent to which it is rational and coherent in form. The sovereign can therefore be a monarch, an aristocracy or a democratic body, but the rational 'contract' cannot seek to destroy any of the contracting parties. Likewise, at the same time, to be an expression of practical political reason, it must preserve lawful freedom, and civil equality and autonomy (Kant, 1991b, pp 123–28).

Given the nature of 'public right', as defined by the relation between self and community, it is unsurprising to find that Kant's idea of private right is similarly circumscribed by the overriding concern for the reciprocal interest of self and other selves. There is, for example, no absolute right to possession. However, there is a political right defined by the need for good social order. But the right to possess property is always limited by the community interest, for nothing is free by nature in a community. The possession of everything is subject to the interest of others because it seeks to justify its removal from others, and this removal is only justified if it is in the interest of others. In other words, it is only justified because the same principle allows others to remove things from you (Kant, 1991b, pp 69–74). Precisely the same principle applies to private contracts, the legitimacy of which depends upon formal rationality and not substantive content. A contract is the acquisition of someone else's promise, and thus a constraint upon that person's choice, and justifiable only in terms of the rationality of the relation between contractors. Once the self has made a private contract, then, as with the public contract, the moral self has a rational duty to obey the contract and thus obey the self (Kant, 1991b, pp 93–95).

The 'doctrine of right', as we noted before, is only one, albeit the most important, part of the 'metaphysics of morals'. There is also the 'doctrine of virtue'. Virtue, as we saw with Aristotle, has been traditionally associated with matters of justice. Indeed, for Aristotle, 'virtue' defined the philosophy of law. For Kant, it enjoys a more restricted role, devoted to the refinement of ethical matters, but quite apart from questions of legal philosophy. The matter of external 'right' is separate from that of internal 'virtue', and the two are most certainly not synonymous. Kant's critical addition to Aristotelian metaphysics is precisely to contribute a rationally defensible 'idea' of right, founded in moral philosophy, in the moral self. The 'maxims' of 'virtue' present guides to ethical behaviour, a series of ideas for enhancing social relations. Being nice to one another is a 'virtue', a moral duty or 'maxim'; it is not a matter of 'right', and cannot be compelled. However, 'rights' which seek to approximate 'virtues', in the synthetic model, should look to 'perfect' both one's own 'happiness' and that of 'others'. Happiness, and niceness, should be encouraged by good laws. But the laws or 'rights' themselves will address more particular matters (Kant, 1991b, pp 190–97). In this distinction can be detected a certain affinity with legal positivism. However, Kant is all too often aligned with a rigidly formal and positivistic theory of law, and whilst such an interpretation is valid to a certain degree, it is important to note also that Kant remained acutely aware of the distinction between the intellectual rigour of critical philosophy and the compelling need to prescribe practical theories of law and politics. The latter, moreover, was always described in terms of a constructive political community, of which right is only one constituent.

NEO-KANTIANISM

Pluralism and formalism

Contemporary neo-Kantian legal theory owes its influence, in large part, to Kant's first biographer, Ernst Cassirer. Adopting Kant's own historicist critique, Cassirer recognised that the Enlightenment represented a particular philosophical method, which was the application of a critical reason. According to Cassirer, Kant's bequest to modern philosophy was to insist upon a 'critical' approach, and a denial of any metaphysical truths which could not be founded in the autonomy of individual reason. It was only in this way that Kant could retrieve a theory of immanent individual right from the intellectual challenge of a deeper scepticism (Cassirer, 1951, pp 197–201). The determination to address all questions in this way, by contextualising them within a particular historical and intellectual tradition, announced an 'age of criticism' and, according to Cassirer, all intellectual enquiry after Kant is 'liberating' precisely because it is critical. The appreciation that all thought is ultimately contingent and historical liberates modern man by empowering the political potential of individual rationality (Cassirer, 1951, pp 18–19; 1981, pp 220–27, 238–41).

Cassirer's neo-Kantian 'pluralism' stressed the possibility of purely rational ideas and form, whilst admitting the indeterminacy of concept and substance. It was distinguished by its particular emphasis on potential political malleability, and the justification for this concentration through the employment of the third *Critique*. What it meant in practice was that Kantianism could maintain its intellectual integrity as a moral philosophy, whilst admitting a variety of substantively different political philosophies. According to Cassirer, Kant's third *Critique* represented a natural political conclusion to the entire critical project, and was not, as a number of Kantians had suggested, something which should be consigned to matters of art and aesthetics alone. The entire *Critique*, he suggested, was dedicated to a 'striving' for individual political autonomy. It sought to liberate by demanding the active participation in the fashioning of a political narrative by rational moral selves (Cassirer, 1951, pp 325, 333; 1981, pp 272–83, 312, 350–52). In his later study of Nazism, *The Myth of the State*, he concluded that the jurisprudence of a modern liberal community must be founded on the belief that 'the law we obey' is 'not imposed from without', but rather 'that the moral subject gives the law to itself' (Cassirer, 1946, p 287).

At the same time, having admitted the reality of a critical approach to matters of substantive political morality, Cassirer was determined to establish the rationality of political and legal form. If the process of communication within the political community admitted a substantive indeterminacy, this process could also be founded by its rational form. In his *Language and Myth*, Cassirer stressed that modes of political communication created their own immanent rationality, and that the creative capacity of the individual operated within this rationality. It is rational form which preserves the possibility for individual freedom, and in this way Cassirer could emphasise the unity of experience and reason in language (Cassirer, 1953, pp 136–37). This turn to language, though rooted in the third *Critique*, certainly took Cassirer beyond the traditional tenets of Kantianism. Indeed, in many ways it presaged the kind of constructive and communicative rationality that has characterised so much critical legal theory, from the Kantianism of Rawls and Dworkin, both of whom we shall consider shortly, to the communitarianism of Habermas and Nussbaum, and even to the postmodernism of such as Richard Rorty. Though often forgotten in Anglo-American histories of legal thought, Cassirer's development of the third *Critique*, into a distinguishable theory of constructive formalism, played a pivotal role, not just in the evolution of Kantianism, but in the wider critical legal project.

In contemporary jurisprudential guise, Cassirer's neo-Kantianism has been reasserted as 'legal formalism'. Whereas many jurists have concentrated on the ethical substance of Kantian legal philosophy, the most influential formalist, Ernest Weinrib, concentrates instead on the 'idea' or 'form' of Kantianism. The admission of substantive indeterminacy must not detract from the rationality of the 'form' of the Kantian model. In terms of its 'form', law enjoys an immanent rationality. In other words, as a matter of abstract theory, as an 'idea', law is entirely rational regardless of any irrationality or indeterminacy of substance. The substance and morality of a law is a 'matter to be settled by an argument outside rather than inside the law' (Weinrib, 1988, p 955). This 'immanent rationality' is effected by maintaining an integrity of juridical relationships. Thus, Weinrib advocates the rationality of corrective justice, which is concerned simply with effecting fairness and equality between actors in direct relation with each other, rather than distributive justice, which is dependent upon some ideological conception of what is in the public interest. Immanent rationality, accordingly, centres the idea of justice on the moral individual, rather than making any metaphysical claim to universality (Weinrib, 1988, pp 997–98).

Being 'immanently rational', law enjoys an 'internal' aspect, meaning that it is rational regardless of any external factors, such as politics, economics, language and so on. Law, Weinrib suggests, can be 'assumed to be intelligible from within' (Weinrib, 1988, p 962). Law must make sense on its own terms. In other words, it must be consistent and must not contradict itself. But, in substance, it can prescribe pretty much anything. So it could, for example, prescribe that all dark haired people pay extra taxes. This may seen substantively unfair, but so long as there is no contradictory law, which prohibits dark haired people from paying any taxes at all, then it is 'formally' rational. Weinrib emphasises that 'nothing about formalism precludes indeterminacy'. Rather, he continues, the 'forms of justice are both determinate and indeterminate'. They 'are indeterminate in that they do not predetermine exhaustively the particular results they govern'. Yet, they 'are determinate in that they establish the bounds of coherence for the particulars that fall under them, thus making these particulars intelligible as sorts of things that they are'. In essence, he concludes, in its 'governance of juridical relationships, formalism is universality with a variable content' (Weinrib, 1988, p 1011). The separation of the form of law from its content is, then, the centrepiece of legal 'formalism'. It does not deny the importance of content, or the possibility of indeterminacy of content. Indeed, Weinrib recognises that social 'interaction takes place in a world of shared vocabularies and understandings' so that the 'conceptualism of Kantian right is compatible with cultural diversity'. What 'formalism' does deny is the futile 'rummaging around within the law in search of a content' (Weinrib, 1987a, pp 504–05; 1987b, p 67).

Relativism

Cassirer's 'pluralism' was enormously influential upon a generation of contemporary legal philosophers, foremost of whom was Gustav Radbruch, the jurist over whose soul, as we saw in the previous chapter, Fuller and Hart did battle. In his 'Legal philosophy', Radbruch took Cassirer's 'pluralism' and recast it as a distinctive jurisprudential 'relativism'. Once again, the purpose was to preserve the need for rationality and coherence in the idea or form of law, whilst admitting the possibility of variations in substance. Adapting the critical distinction between what law 'is' and what law 'should' be, Radbruch suggested that law 'is' rational, but 'could' be many things in terms of substance. The 'science' of law, he suggested, addresses the form of law, but the 'philosophy' of law looks to its content. Despite the subsequent attempts, of Fuller and Hart, to suggest that this represented an affinity with natural law theory, Radbruch was quite explicit in his denial. To stress the distinction between the 'is' and the 'ought' of law is to adopt an explicitly Kantian approach to legal thought, whether or not it might also appear to align with similar positivist statements. The 'is' and the 'ought' must not be confused, but neither can a coherent theory of law be designed upon one without consideration of the other. For Radbruch, as for Kant, the moral philosophy lay within the moral individual, and any jurisprudence which denied this ethical constituent was necessarily incomplete (Radbruch, 1950, pp 53, 85).

Substantive legal indeterminacy, then, does not undermine a Kantian philosophy of law. Radbruch had 'no fear' of 'irreconcilable antimonies', suggesting that 'to decide for oneself is to live'. Indeed, it is this flexibility which encourages the development of substantive justice within real legal systems. As both Kant and Cassirer had emphasised, it is the indeterminacy of law which preserves its liberating potential. For Radbruch, engaged in the increasingly desperate attempt to preserve the Weimar Republic, in which he served as Minister of Justice, it was also this substantive indeterminacy which preserved the idea of democracy. The great virtue of legal relativism, he asserted, lay in its facilitating the 'free and tolerant exchange of thought, and therefore a democratic form of life' (Radbruch, 1950, p 121). Radbruch's legal thinking was always coloured by immediate political necessity. Abstract jurisprudence was useless if it failed to effect social improvement and preserve constitutional democracy against the threat of moral and political totalitarianism.

Political purpose is the vital component of any critical jurisprudence, 'able to fill the abstract thought of justice with the effective fire of individual life' (Radbruch, 1950, p 136).

Radbruch's 'Legal philosophy' was premised upon this practicality. Explicitly acknowledging the politics of law and legal thought, Radbruch asserted that society is reformed, indeed can only be reformed, through the 'power of ideas' and, moreover, the most important of these ideas are legal ideas. More than any other constituent of a community, lawyers and legal theorists are best equipped to fashion social and political change. A lawyer who merely applies rules, without regard to the deeper demands of justice, is a lawyer who fails properly to appreciate the critical political perspective of any 'system' of laws. In a poetic passage, he emphasised the innate virtue of a critical 'philosophy of law', in which 'ideas do not fight the struggle of the interests all over again in the clouds like the Valkyries above the battle', but 'rather, like Homeric gods, they descend to the battlefield and fight, powerful forces themselves side by side with other forces'. Accordingly, he could conclude, with a flourish, that, 'All great political changes were prepared or accompanied by legal philosophy' for in 'the beginning was legal philosophy; at the end, there was revolution' (Radbruch, 1950, p 55). Social change is dependent upon a proper critical appreciation that law is a tool for the reform of society, and not an expression of any abstract morality or merely a formal rule to be applied without regard to its immediate political or social context. The form of law, its 'science', is 'helpless' when 'faced with a collision of norms', and it is in the world of norms that the real political individual lives. Accordingly, the formal 'idea' of law should never be allowed to suppress the demands of real political justice within individual communities (Radbruch, 1950, pp 73, 113).

The desire to fashion some sort of ultimate jurisprudence, coherent in substance as well as form, is a natural human 'urge', but a futile one. According to Radbruch, 'relativism cannot help rejecting the pretended universality of any such attempt', of which Nazism was only the most recent, 'and demonstrating its ties to very definite basic assumptions of world outlook' (Radbruch, 1950, p 69). The need to embrace indeterminacy was central to Radbruch's understanding of a genuine Kantian critical jurisprudence. He repeatedly cited Goethe's observation, 'I understand again ... that the different ways of thought are founded upon the differences of men, and that for this very reason a general uniform conviction is impossible' (Radbruch, 1950, p 57). Radbruch himself used the metaphor of a cathedral 'in which the masses support each other by pressing against each other', and concluded: 'How suspect would be a philosophy that did not consider the world a purposeful creation of reason and yet resolved it into a rational system with no contradiction' (Radbruch, 1950, p 112). Critical reason, he emphasised, is merely a methodology, and not itself a moral or political ideology. It is 'not an arsenal of finished theoretical cognitions' but 'rather the mere power to arrive at such cognitions'. A Kantian theory of law is immediately critical, 'not a complex of answers, but rather one of questions', and such cognitions 'which are definite in content are never produced by pure reason, but always only by its application to something definitely given' (Radbruch, 1950, p 60). Radbruch's particular Kantianism was clearly aligned with the critical legal project, and against the aridity of legal positivism as much as the abstraction of classical and theological metaphysics.

Constructive rationality

Kantianism returned to prominence in Anglo-American jurisprudence with the publication of John Rawls's *A Theory of Justice* in 1971. The evolution of Rawls's Kantian legal theory, from 1971 until his recent death, provides a striking mirror for the development of Kant's own thoughts, moving from an interest in the possibility of moral foundations to a more ready acceptance of substantive ethical indeterminacy, grounded only by the political reality of constructively rational processes of deliberative judgment. The keystone of Rawls's thesis in *A Theory of Justice* is the principle of justice as fairness, which is fashioned in a real political situation around the two fundamental concepts in Kantian moral philosophy – freedom and equality. Ultimately, these two concepts define what Rawls terms 'justice', something which, as a matter of form as opposed to substance, must lie at the heart of any 'well ordered' society. In terms of substance, as Kant appreciated, particular conceptions of justice may be various. Even at this relatively early stage in his development, Rawls was committed to the idea of 'reflective equilibrium' as a process of reaching a consensus of judgment. *A Theory of Justice* posits an 'original position' of 'ignorance', which is itself premised on the validity of the Kantian model of the moral self, and which provides a constraint against the 'arbitrary contingencies or the relative balances of social forces'. In this way, the only constraints on the political community are constraints internal to the moral self (Rawls, 1971, pp 3–20, 120–21, 140–49).

The necessary accommodation of interests, founded only on the twin principles of freedom and equality which define the moral self, is confirmed in political terms by a 'social contract' which is therefore 'constructive'. In other words, the members of the reflective community construct the terms and conditions for their own political contract, and do so only constrained by the two principles of freedom and equality. The deeply critical nature of Rawls's project is emphasised in the final sections of *A Theory of Justice*. All principles of substantive justice are determined by and fashioned within the 'basic structures of well ordered societies'. The community thus 'shapes' a particular 'sense' of justice, and its morality is founded upon a 'common allegiance to justice'. At the same time, because of the creative role of the individual in constructing that morality, it becomes a 'morality of self-command'. Substantive principles of justice thus evolve experientially, as the means of determining 'relations' between members of that community, precisely the purpose of the metaphorical contract (Rawls, 1971, pp 457–58, 472–79, 495–96). In a striking echo of Kant's third *Critique*, Rawls emphasised that the community develops a shared conception of 'judgment', through the creative activity of individuals who are always 'historical beings' operating within a particular historical context. Ultimately, a group of rational moral selves effects a theory of law which is an expression of its 'community sense' (Rawls, 1971, pp 523–29, 561–65).

Rawls's later work concentrated on further developing this process of construction. Most importantly, it affirmed that this process is an irreducibly communicative or dialogic one. The reflective conditions for a political society are reached by conversation and dialogue. It is this turn to language and communication which led a number of commentators to sequester Rawls, as either a communitarian or perhaps, as Richard Rorty suggested, a postmodern liberal. In 1980, searching for a more 'practicable' theory of law, Rawls published 'Kantian constructivism in moral theory'. This series of essays signalled a sharper turn in his thinking, from a philosophy of ethics to a politics of justice. Instead of fashioning universal formulae for justice, Rawls concentrated on 'basic institutions within democratic society', institutions which can facilitate the dialogic process of 'construction'. Such a model of constructivism concerned itself only with morality 'understood in terms of a suitably constructed social point of view that all can accept'. Indeed, apart from 'the procedure of constructing the principles of justice, there are no moral facts' (Rawls, 1980, pp 516–19).

Here Rawls also stressed the procedural nature of this construction, abandoning any notion of universal or foundational reason, and replacing it with a constructive rationalism. To abandon the illusion of absolute truths is not 'skepticism or indifference'. It is just an inevitability of history. It is also, as Radbruch emphasised, to empower the creative capacity of the 'originating' self in a modern liberal democracy (Rawls, 1980, pp 543–45). We, as a community, construct our own conception of reason by the very process of our dialogue or conversation. Rawls emphasised that the 'constructionist view accepts from the start that a moral conception can establish but a loose framework for deliberation which must rely very considerably on our powers of reflection and judgment'. Rather, these 'powers are not fixed once and for all, but are developed by a shared public culture and hence shaped by that culture'. Accordingly, 'a conception of justice is framed to meet the practical requirements of social life and to yield a public basis in the light of which citizens can justify to one another their common institutions' (Rawls, 1980, pp 560–61).

In subsequent essays, Rawls refined still further the idea of an 'overlapping consensus', as a 'consensus that includes all the opposing philosophical and religious doctrines likely to persist and to gain adherents in a more or less just constitutional democratic society'. Such a consensus is all inclusive and empowering. Democracy, he emphasises, is 'about' consensus, and the idea of such a consensus equips the 'citizens' of the political community to play an active role in creating a substantive politics 'in accordance with their own general and comprehensive views'. We all participate in the process of dialogue and the construction of our own community's conception of reason. It describes what Rawls refers to as a distinctive 'political liberalism', inherently democratic and necessarily pluralist and indeterminate in terms of political morality. An 'overlapping consensus' is necessary for liberal democracy, because it 'forces political philosophy to be, as far as possible, independent of and autonomous from other parts of philosophy', particularly 'from philosophy's long standing problems and controversies' in the areas of law and morality (Rawls, 1993, pp 133–72).

Once again, in the concentration on the processes of constructive rationality within a political community, there are clear echoes of the kind of communitarian theses which we will encounter in the next chapter. What remains distinctive about Rawls's theory of constructive rationality, however, is a determination to promote the potential for change against the stabilising tendencies of more conservative communitarian theories. This adherence is, thus, more immediately resonant of fellow Kantians such as Radbruch, rather than communitarians such as Sandel or MacIntyre. At the same time, whilst resisting the popular demand amongst so many communitarians for a return to the 'spirit' of 1776, Rawls fully acknowledged that his 'political liberalism' is itself merely the product of a particular historical tradition. Political liberalism should not be understood to be expressive of some innate principle of moral truth. It is merely a 'way of thinking', a willingness to be critical within a political community, whilst admitting the veracity of the criticism of others, and the 'overlapping consensus' is merely a mechanism for facilitating deliberation, an expression of the 'public political culture of a constitutional regime' (Rawls, 1985, pp 223–26, 229–33).

In its later invocations, Rawls's particular idea of political liberalism concentrated more and more on the relation between institutions and the facility of dialogue, 'the reciprocity between free and equal citizens in a well ordered society'. The facility for communication, he repeatedly suggested in *Political Liberalism*, 'deepens' the overlapping consensus, whilst the culture of democratic politics can 'broaden' it. It can therefore facilitate the articulation of a 'totality' of views, rather than just a 'compromise'. Democratic liberal politics is defined as a process of 'public discourse'. It is a strikingly functional definition, and in these terms Rawls's distinctively pragmatic liberalism is not a philosophy but a 'kind of view', a way of thinking that permits and cherishes the communicative participation of others (Rawls, 1993, pp 164–72, 213–15, 230–40). The 'overlapping consensus' that lies at the heart of Rawls's pragmatic political liberalism is one founded on an appreciation that political philosophy is, at root, a philosophy of language and communication. It is an insight that was noted by Cassirer half a century earlier, but it is also one that is common to the variety of critical theories of law which we address throughout this book.

In his final substantive work, *The Law of Peoples*, Rawls attempted to translate his constructive theory of 'domestic' justice into a jurisprudence which might accommodate the challenges of the 'new' world order. The model for *The Law of Peoples* was, as he explicitly acknowledged, Kant's famous essay on international and cosmopolitan justice, 'perpetual peace', and like Kant, Rawls embraced the inherently utopian nature of Kant's aspiration. And again like Kant, Rawls was convinced that such a world of 'Perpetual peace' is possible, simply because each group of societies, once they mature, must come to appreciate that their best interests lie in a state of stable and peaceful co-existence. Like many 'end of history' commentators, such as Francis Fukuyama, Rawls noted that genuine liberal democracies do not go to war with each other (Rawls, 2001, pp 10, 19–23). But whereas Kant's *Perpetual Peace* presumed the inevitability of States, simply because it was written in a era in which nation-states seemed to be inevitable, Rawls's *The Law of Peoples*, written in one in which the much-vaunted 'end' of the nation-states seems rather more likely, deals in terms of 'societies' or 'peoples'. It is, thus, a more 'general' jurisprudence (Rawls, 2001, pp 3, 23–30, 55). In simple terms, *The Law of Peoples* presents a strategy for converting all 'societies' to the virtues of liberal democracy; something which again aligns Rawls with the kind of 'end of history' triumphalism found in Fukuyama. Liberal democratic societies are distinguished from 'decent hierarchical societies', as well as a motley assortment of 'outlaw', 'burdened' and 'absolutist' societies. In order to nurture the conversion of this latter bunch, 'well-ordered' societies, primarily the liberal, but also the 'decent hierarchical', must be able to impress the virtues of common 'sympathies' and common 'moral character', meaning an acceptance of what is 'reasonable and rational' in a world of 'reasonably plural' societies. Above all, 'well-ordered' societies must sponsor a common sense of tolerance and dignity, whilst also advocating the particular virtues of human rights. The latter concept, he stressed, must assume a 'special role in a reasonable Law of Peoples' (Rawls, 2001, pp 11–18, 24–25, 59–62, 79).

THE EMPIRE OF INTEGRITY AND THE MORAL DOMINION

Rights in an interpretive community

Rawls's appreciation that a philosophy of law is about dialogue and reciprocity, as well as rationalism and rights, is also found in Ronald Dworkin's legal philosophy. Before addressing Dworkin's 'interpretive turn', it is important to appreciate the extent to which this jurisprudence is embedded in a distinctively Kantian understanding of natural rights. In his *Taking Rights Seriously*, published in 1977, primarily an attack against legal positivism, rather than seeking recourse to a traditional natural law theory, Dworkin shied away from any theological or metaphysical basis and turned to a conception of the morally determined individual. At the same time, he wanted to reinvest a theory of rights that lay somewhere beyond the purely political parameters of the modern State. The failure of legal positivism, according to Dworkin, is a failure to account for the fact of pluralism in modern society. It is pluralism which necessitates the Dworkinian distinction between 'rules' and 'principles'. A 'constellation of principles' does not 'decide' cases, but rather 'inclines' decisions (Dworkin, 1977, pp 42–44, 55–57). A theory of rights, because they vest in the individual, at least in the Kantian sense, are derived from principle and not from policy. Policy only ever reflects collective political goals. Arguments of fairness, Dworkin suggests, can only be supported by 'principles'. The crux of Dworkin's theory of judicial reasoning lies in his 'hard case' scenario. What does a judge do in a 'hard case', where there is no established 'rule' by which he can make an adjudication? The answer is that he seeks recourse to 'a scheme of abstract and concrete principles', derived from the 'community's moral tradition' and which can provide a 'coherent justification' for judgment (Dworkin, 1977, pp 81–83, 90–94, 116–26).

There is much here that bears comparison with Rawls's model of constructive reasoning. Indeed, Dworkin specifically approves the 'constructive model' because it does not make the mistake of assuming 'some fixed, objective existence', whilst at the same time not conceding to 'skepticism or relativism'. The 'constructive model', he continues, 'requires coherence ... for independent reasons of political morality' (Dworkin, 1977, pp 160–63). Dworkin extends the 'constructive model' by suggesting a 'deep' theory of it. Such a model, he suggests, can be either duty based, goal based or rights based. Dworkin, of course, prefers the latter option to either the positivist duty based or utilitarian goal based alternatives. Such a preference is not to succumb to metaphysics, but merely to accept the 'hypothesis that the best political program' is 'one that takes the protection of certain individual choices as fundamental, and not properly subordinated to any goal or duty or combination of these'. Such a theory of rights must 'presume rights that are not simply the product of deliberate legislation or explicit social custom, but are independent grounds for judging legislation and custom' (Dworkin, 1977, pp 176–77).

The interpretive turn in Dworkin's work was signalled in a 1982 essay in which he argued that 'legal practice is an exercise in interpretation not only when lawyers interpret particular documents or statutes but generally. Law so conceived is deeply and thoroughly political' (Dworkin, 1982, p 146). Legal interpretation is a process of constitutive or constructive interpretation because it is historically situated, and that situation describes a constellation of text, author and reader. Meaning is not 'fixed' in either author or text, or indeed reader, but varies with regard to the particular constellation or situation (Dworkin, 1985, pp 147–50). The publication of *Law's Empire* confirmed Dworkin's determination to reinvest a liberal theory of rights within the practical constraints of the political community. We can better understand Dworkin's theory of interpretation and 'integrity' by taking particular note of footnote number 2 in Chapter 2 of *Law's Empire*. In this considerable note, Dworkin pays tribute to the origins of modern hermeneutic theory and in particular to the work of Hans-Georg Gadamer. In 1975, Gadamer published *Truth and Method*, and in it emphasised the roles of author, text and reader as necessary constituents in a constructively rational political community. It is worth noting, of course, that Gadamer's theory of hermeneutics was founded explicitly on Kant's *The Critique of Judgment*.

More precisely, Gadamer suggested that the historicity of all texts meant that the reader, himself subject to socio-historical 'prejudices', would read a text that was also historical, and which had been created by a historically situated author. Hermeneutics is very much a theory of reading texts founded in their historical context. Moreover, according to Gadamer, the 'legal hermeneutic' enjoyed an 'exemplary significance'. Legal hermeneutics, he suggested, is a peculiarly 'purposive' hermeneutic, directed to 'practical measure[s] to help fill a kind of gap'. Furthermore, the practicalities of using legal texts demands the exercise of 'fidelity to the text'. In other words, the use and interpretation of a text demands that the reader uses the text honestly. The demands of use, in a legal scenario, means that the lawyer, in particular, should not release all to the free play of the text, but should instead seek to access the socio-historical constraints of the text and the author of the text. More than most readers who approach a text, the hermeneutic lawyer should be particularly inclined to read historically and to think 'productively'. Understanding, for the lawyer as historian, is 'a matter of placing a given text within the context of the history of language, literary form, style, etc, and thus ultimately within the totality of the living context of history' (Gadamer, 1975, pp 302–05).

The empire of integrity

It is Gadamer's theory of hermeneutics, and more particularly of 'fidelity' to the text, which Dworkin employs in *Law's Empire* as a complement to his theory of law as 'principle'. From the very beginning of *Law's Empire*, Dworkin is committed to the 'argumentative' character of legal reasoning (Dworkin, 1986, p 13). In such terms, the 'practice' of interpretation must always take account of the context of the argument. This is not a matter of searching for 'larger questions of history and society', but one of recognising immediate historical and social context. By adhering to this historicist thesis, Dworkin is keen to align himself with the 'constructivism' of Rawls, which he opposes to the kind of free standing 'conversationalism' of postmodernists. The key to a constructivist interpretation is a constructivist community; that is, a community with 'interpretive attitude'. There is, Dworkin suggests, a 'deep connection between all forms of interpretation', so the constructive form is represented as a directed form of conversational interpretation, but crucially it is directed from within the moral community, and not from some metaphysical 'without' (Dworkin, 1986, pp 50–55). The 'constructivist model' of interpretation provides the foundation for law's 'empire'. Each 'judge's interpretative theories are grounded in his own convictions' about the 'purpose or goal or principle' of his adjudicative role. This necessarily provides for a legal culture of difference and plurality, and thus, in turn, there is a need for a basic consensus for any interpretive theory. This can provide for a critical, 'non-metaphysical' theory of rights, founded on the Kantian model of the morally driven individual, and a constructive 'two way stage of reasoning' between this individual and the 'particularly deep personification of the community'. It is here, in this 'stage' or process, that the principle and the text, the philosophy and the language, come together (Dworkin, 1986, pp 151–52, 167–75).

Dworkin introduces his own constructive theory of law 'as integrity', both as a matter of interpretive and of political principle. As a matter of interpretive principle, 'integrity' is a specifically jurisprudential variant of Gadamer's idea of 'fidelity' to the text. There are two essentially interpretive principles of jurisprudential 'integrity' – legislative coherence and adjudicative integrity. Judges should adjudicate by seeing law as it is 'created' by the moral community, and they should also recognise that the law is 'created' as a hermeneutic process, as a process of historical evolution. The principle of 'law as integrity' demands that judges:

> ... assume, so far as is possible, that the law is structured by a coherent set of principles about justice and fairness and procedural due process, and it asks them to enforce these in the fresh cases that come before them, so that each person's situation is fair and just according to the same standards.

Such a 'style of adjudication respects that ambition integrity assumes, the ambition to be a community of principles' (Dworkin, 1986, p 243). In these terms, judges engage in an indisputably 'constructive' process of 'interpretation', and as an exercise in 'integrity', they must attempt to establish the 'best' possible adjudication. To do otherwise would be to act in 'bad faith', and to act irrationally, meaning against the constructed rationality of the community of which the judge is a member. In the hardest of 'hard cases', the judge will develop political morality, but will do so only in the 'direction' demanded by precisely that morality understood as something fashioned by the historical situation of the community. In other words, the judge will not invent law, but will develop it in a 'constrained' fashion. A judge can never simply make up the answer to a hard case. Rather, he articulates a decision prescribed by the morality of the community. It is not, then, simply a matter of understanding history, but of appreciating the role history plays in constituting the present, and present understandings of law and society (Dworkin, 1986, pp 348–49).

In like terms, the political community of 'integrity' is creative and evolutionary. It is always capable of changing, but does so as part of a historical process. Each new 'chapter' of legal theory is built on the foundations established in the previous chapter. It is, of course, an immediately historicist and interpretive theory of change. We fashion political changes by re-interpreting texts in the light of their previous interpretation. Integrity is thus a matter of political as well as interpretive principle. It provides for 'self-government' which lies at the heart of any liberal theory of law. Accordingly, 'integrity expands and deepens the role individual citizens can play in developing the public standards of their community'. At the same time, it 'insists that each citizen must accept demands on him, and may make demands on others, that share and extend the moral dimension of any explicit political decisions'. In such terms, 'integrity' thus:

> ... fuses citizens' moral and political lives: it asks the good citizen, deciding how to treat his neighbour when their interests conflict, to interpret the common scheme of

justice to which they are both committed just in virtue of their citizenship (Dworkin, 1986, pp 189–90).

Dworkin's 'empire' is, then, one developed from 'principle' rather than simple political compromise, constructed by an 'argumentative' community which argues on a foundation provided by the basic concepts of moral 'principle'. Dworkin describes this 'strong' community as one that 'insists that people are members of a genuine political community only when they accept that their fates are linked in the following way: they accept that they are governed by common principles, not just by rules hammered out in political compromise'. Such a political process is a 'theater of debate about which principles the community should adopt as a system, which view it should take of justice, fairness, and due process'. In short, Dworkin concludes, in such a community:

> ... each accepts political integrity as a distinct political ideal and treats the general acceptance of that ideal, even among people who otherwise disagree about political morality, as constitutive of political morality (Dworkin, 1986, p 211).

The ambition is clear. The process of interpretive 'integrity' provides for the constitutive role of the morally driven self. In other words, by taking note of the textuality of postmodern liberalism, as something which empowers individuals, Dworkin is able to reinvest the idea of 'principle' which is so central to modern liberal philosophy. In doing so, he is further able to infuse the philosophy of Kant with the textuality of the later Rawls. Law's 'empire' is determined, in the final analysis, by an 'attitude', an 'interpretive self-reflected attitude', and it is this 'attitude' which describes the active communicative participant and the political community within which he or she resides, and which he or she shapes. This community becomes a 'moral agent', representative of the Kantian moral self. In an eloquent concluding passage, Dworkin emphasises that:

> Law's attitude is constructive: it aims, in the interpretive spirit, to lay principle over practice to show the best route to a better future, keeping the right faith with the past. It is, finally, a fraternal attitude, an expression of how we are united in community though divided in project, interest and conviction. That is, anyway, what law is for us: for the people we want to be and the community we aim to have (Dworkin, 1986, p 413).

Moral readings

Having established his theory of interpretation, as a complement to the idea of legal 'principle', Dworkin has since returned to the matter of moral philosophy, and particularly its situation with regard to constitutional law and interpretation, and he has further refined the domain of law's 'empire'. In *Life's Dominion*, he applied the theory of 'integrity' to matters of moral philosophy, and most particularly two of the most enduring controversies in 'law and morality' debates – abortion and euthanasia – whilst in the more recent *Freedom's Law*, he applied the interpretive complement of the 'integrity' principle to readings of the US Constitution. The two studies represent, as it were, the two sides of the 'integrity' coin. The ambition of *Life's Dominion* is to transcend contemporary 'opinions' on ethical issues by means of establishing overriding principles. What Dworkin wants is a 'principled compromise', as opposed to a simple political compromise. The distinction is important because it demands more of a 'comprehensive' theory than is provided by Rawls's 'overlapping consensus'. With regard to the specific issue of a 'right to life', Dworkin advocates what he terms a 'detached objection', which means that the 'right to life' is an 'intrinsic' right derived from an absolute value to life. Any alternative, non-principled right, such as a right to control a woman's body or rights of a foetus at so many months, are 'derivative objections', rights premised on certain political or biological opinions. A modern liberal community must attempt to resolve such issues as a matter of principle, and this is always the case in any community which recognises its plural constitution (Dworkin, 1993, pp 32–34, 60–67).

The resolution of the liberal community must be a textual one. Problems with regard to legal and moral principle must be resolved by refining our way of reading our laws and constitutions. With regard to the use of a constitutional document as a mechanism for resolving such issues, Dworkin uses precisely the theory of interpretation which he advanced in *Law's Empire*. Constitutional interpretation must accede to two tests. First, it must fulfil the 'dimension of fit', which determines whether an interpretation is in accordance with legal practice or 'experience'. Secondly, it must be in accord with a principle of 'justice', which demands that such principles must reflect moral rights as reinterpreted by each generation. On both counts, the exercise is an eminently historical and hermeneutic one. The reading of the constitution is one which takes account of historical derivation, but which evolves from that derivation rather than remains entirely constrained by it. Accordingly, life's 'dominion', like law's 'empire', is one governed by argument, and this argument, founded on moral principle, is one conducted between the judiciary and the community. In this political and moral 'dominion', the principle of interpretive integrity 'insists that judicial decision be a matter of principle, not compromise or strategy or political accommodation' (Dworkin, 1993, pp 71–101, 146).

An alternative theory of interpretation, against which Dworkin is particularly keen to level his criticism, is termed 'original intent', and suggests that judges should interpret a constitutional document so as to give it a meaning as close as possible to that which was originally intended by those who wrote the text, back in 1776 in the case of the US Constitution, or perhaps 1215 or 1689 in the case of the British. Original intent theory is obviously historical; indeed it is entirely historical. But it is not historicist. In other words, it refuses to concede that contemporary society is anyway in part constituted by history, and that any reading of the constitution is anyway historical to some degree, and historicist too. At the same time, it also clings to the illusion that we can somehow return to the world of the constitution drafters, and appreciate precisely how they thought and what they intended when writing their texts. In these terms, 'original intent' theory is both impractical and unprincipled. Returning to the intensely moral issues surrounding the 'right to life', Dworkin suggests that any 'competent reading' of a constitution must appreciate the historicist evolution of the 'sanctity' of the moral person. The morality of today is not that of 1689 or 1776, even if it has evolved from it, whilst the Kantian moral right of individual autonomy anyway trumps any alternative legal rights. Dworkin suggests that the US Constitution, as interpreted by generations of judges, has refined precisely the 'detached objection', the 'intrinsic value' to life which attaches to the Kantian conception of the moral self. Interpretive integrity thus requires that judges must respect this moral principle, as indeed interpretive principle demands.

Freedom's Law develops this particular idea of constitutional interpretation. Dworkin refers to it as the 'moral reading' of the constitution, and aligns it with an impassioned defence of liberalism and liberal 'principles' against what he perceives to be the march of conservative communitarianism. All law, he advises, is 'anchored in history, practice and integrity' and, accordingly, 'constitutional interpretation is disciplined, under the moral reading, by the requirement of constitutional integrity'. 'Judges', Dworkin affirms, must 'not read their own convictions into' their constitution. At the same time, they must 'not read the abstract moral clauses' intrinsic to a constitution 'as expressing any particular moral judgment, no matter how much that judgment appeals to them, unless they find it consistent in principle with the structural design of the Constitution as a whole, and with the dominant lines of past constitutional interpretation by other judges'. Judges must see themselves as situated within an historical and narrative continuum. They 'must regard themselves as partners with other officials, past and future, who together elaborate a coherent constitutional morality, and they must take care to see that what they contribute fits with the rest' (Dworkin, 1996, p 10). The 'moral reading' is, in simple terms, a matter of reading 'in good faith'. As a matter of politics, particularly liberal politics, the 'moral reading' is a vital component of the political order which complements the presence of certain central liberal principles, most obviously autonomy. A political principle, such as autonomy, is of no use unless it is buttressed by the principle of interpretive integrity (Dworkin, 1996, pp 1–38).

In this way Dworkin grounds the constructively rational community in a conception of interpretive integrity which is itself founded on the critical idea of the moral self as deliberative judge. Liberalism has little meaning without the 'personal responsibility' of deliberative 'reflection' (Dworkin, 1996, pp 224–25, 239–40). Dworkin's 'moral readings' represent the realisation of a Kantian theory of law which seeks to describe all legal philosophies, regardless of the particular narrative history of their substantive legal and constitutional morality. In a strikingly Kantian conclusion, the echoes of which resonate sharply with Radbruch's conception of legal philosophy, Dworkin emphasises the need to move away from a simple dichotomy between the 'annihilating idea that critical interests are only subjective' and the 'equally unacceptable idea that everyone's critical interests are the same, over all history'. A critical legal theory must look for a space between the traditional alternatives presented by sceptics and positivists on the one hand, and natural lawyers on the other. It is 'important that we find life *good* and that we *find* life good'. The theory of integrity is, accordingly, a 'mark of conviction', not in some abstract metaphysical theory of natural order, but in 'the idea that the value of life lies in part *in* its integrity' (Dworkin, 1996, p 206). The idea of the moral self, as an end in its self, must emerge as the fundamental conception in a revised and critical philosophy of law.

And so must the principle of 'equality', the principle which, Dworkin has argued in his most recent substantive work, *Sovereign Virtue*, has become the 'endangered species' in contemporary political philosophy, and particularly American public philosophy. Once again, Dworkin suggests that certain perceived inadequacies in current constitutional and political practice are rooted in a failure to understand the basic premises of a liberal political philosophy. Equality is, quite simply, the 'sovereign virtue' in such a philosophy, and it is a virtue determined by the law. Any government that likes to call itself liberal must 'show equal concern for the fate of all those citizens over whom it claims dominion'. And this means more than simple formal equality, but also material substantive quality in terms of 'resources', as well as 'welfare'. It is, quite simply, a 'matter of justice that should be accepted by everyone because it is right' (Dworkin, 2000, pp 1–3, 23). The immersion in theories of equal resources and distributive justice resonates at least as much with Aristotle as it does with Kant. But it is the determination to effect the proper balance between equality and liberty that underlines the Kantian nature of Dworkin's thesis. Interestingly, in suggesting that such a 'conception of equality' should be understood in terms, not just of 'their welfare but in the resources at their command', there is also a striking similarity between Dworkin's idea of equality and the kind of 'capabilities' approach advocated by the likes of Amartya Sen and Martha Nussbaum. As we shall see in Chapter 6, for Nussbaum, as for Dworkin, the need to realign the principles of liberty and equality is the pressing issue in contemporary public philosophy. They are, as Dworkin alleges, 'mutually reflecting aspects of a single humanist ideal' (Dworkin, 2000, pp 87–89, 120–23, 134, 299–303).

Modern America, Dworkin argues, has forgotten this particular truth. More importantly, successive American Presidents and their administrations have failed to assume their primary responsibility, to 'make the lives of citizens better' and to 'act with equal concern for the life of each member'. Dworkin repeatedly uses the same word to describe the condition of public welfare and public philosophy in contemporary America, 'disgrace'. It is 'disgraceful that so prosperous a nation cannot guarantee even a decent minimum of medical care to all those over whom it exercises dominion', and it is a 'disgrace' that a purportedly open and liberal society should be so comprehensively corrupted by money. It is even more 'disgraceful' that its Supreme Court should collude in this corruption, by refusing to curtail it (Dworkin, 2000, pp 184, 318, 351–53, 384–85). The reason for Dworkin's visceral contempt for modern American public philosophy is not just an anger at the fate of those who are denied basic resources or the 'capability' to act effectively in the market. The failure to ensure equality also leads to the erosion of the sense of community necessary for any healthy liberal democracy to flourish. 'Citizens', Dworkin argues, 'identify with their political community when they recognise that the community has a communal life, and that the success or failure of their own lives is ethically dependent on the success or failure of that communal life'. And it is here, once again, that the importance of 'democratic discourse' comes into play. If citizens are to 'govern collectively' then 'they must also deliberate together as individuals'. A truly liberal and democratic community must never forget that it is indeed a community, not merely an aggregate of autonomous rights-bearing individuals. The true liberal, for this reason, is an 'integrated' liberal (Dworkin, 2000, pp 231–33, 364). It is to this thought that we shall now turn.

CHAPTER 3

THE POLITICS OF COMMUNITY

COMMUNITARIANISM

Aristotle and the idea of the political community

In the last chapter, we noted the extent to which a Kantian theory of law was determined by the need to account for the constructively rational political community. In this chapter we are going to consider further critical theories of law that are focused on the idea of community. Whilst the invocation of the necessary political community is made to counter more radical and sceptical alternatives, these communitarian and related theories are themselves irreducibly critical insofar as they concede that a metaphysics of natural order is not itself sufficient, either for describing or legitimating the exercise of law and government. Moreover, in order to trace the origins of communitarian politics, we must return to the first critic of Plato's idea of natural order, Aristotle, and his suggestion that man is an irreducibly political animal, parachuted into a pre-existing social world. We are never isolated from community, and accordingly, the idea of community is superior to any idea of the individual or individual right. It is for man to fit into his community, not for community to accommodate man.

This idea was present from the very earliest pages of *The Ethics*. The political community is the highest form of community, because it is devoted to perfecting government. In the opening sentences of *The Politics*, Aristotle affirms that:

> ... every State is an association, and that every association is formed with a view to some good purpose ... that association which is the most sovereign among them all and embraces all others will aim highest ... This is the association which we call the State, the association which is political.

The purpose of the State is to promote the 'perfect and self-sufficient life' of all its citizens (Aristotle, 1981, pp 54, 198). In *The Ethics*, government had been described as an intellectual virtue. In turn, the purpose of government is to promote good and virtue. A political community is a virtuous community, and a necessarily just one. Such a community is constituted, not so much by individuals, but by numerous micro-communities, of which families, villages, tribes or religious associations are examples. Each of these communities is natural, and so the macro-community, the State, is also natural. In these terms, Aristotle can affirm that, 'It is clear then that the State is both natural and prior to the individual' (Aristotle, 1981, pp 59–61).

What distinguishes man from a 'dumb animal' is that man will wish to 'participate' in government, and thereby to contribute to its constitution. Discussing the concept of citizenship, Aristotle affirmed that 'what effectively distinguishes the citizen proper from all others is his participation in giving judgment and in holding office'. A citizen is one who has a 'share in honours', and a virtuous citizen is one who realises that the common good lies in a preparedness to contribute to the government and 'constitution' of the State. It is this sense of citizen participation which not merely permits political change, but actually applauds it. The very term 'constitution' implies the active constitution of the citizenry. As Aristotle suggests, 'Now in every case the citizen body of a State is sovereign; the citizen body is the constitution' (Aristotle, 1981, pp 169–87). Political virtues and ideals will remain constant in form, but their substance may, indeed will, change. It is this which explains why different polities may have different laws, even different forms of government, but may still be just and virtuous.

On each occasion, the ideal community is a mean community; a community of moderate size, not too big and not too small, enjoying a moderate climate, moderate population, moderate vegetation and so on. A good climate promotes 'friendly disposition'. Commoners become fractious, and democracy prospers, where climates are unpredictable and hot summers too long (Aristotle, 1981, pp 401–18). *The Politics* is devoted to describing the various means by which the community interest can be promoted. Like Plato, Aristotle approves of communal feasts, though without the inebriation, and provides a comprehensive guide to productive sexual activity (Aristotle, 1981, pp 419, 441–42). At the same time, as we noted in Chapter 1, Aristotle further stresses that 'friendship' and 'affection' are essential in any political community, and it is significant that he closes *The Politics* by affirming that the most important factor in promoting a sense of communal 'affection' is education. As in *The Ethics*, he emphasises that education is the responsibility of the State, and must be directed towards those likely to be more receptive to knowledge, the aristocracy. Clearly borrowing from Plato's extensive proscriptions for good education, he suggests that students must be taught four disciplines: reading and writing, gymnastics, music and drawing, together with the importance of hard dieting. Most importantly, they must not be allowed to learn to play the pipes, an evil instrument which merely encourages orgies and civil dissension (Aristotle, 1981, pp 198, 452–69).

In the context of promoting the good of the community, slavery is a good thing. It might not be much fun for slaves, but cheap labour is vital for maximising the wellbeing of the community and maintaining social order (Aristotle, 1981, pp 64–69, 95). At the same time, excessive wealth is a bad thing because it destabilises a community by promoting aggressive competition between citizens and a complementary ethic of self-interest. In like terms, trade is itself inherently destabilising, whilst pure monetary exchange or money lending is an evil because it produces gain which is not the product of honest labour. In fact, there are only three truly honest ways of making a living from labour: from rearing stock, from tilling land and, from bee keeping (Aristotle, 1981, pp 83–89). Of course, this does not apply to slavery, for gaining profit from slaves is quite natural. Relatedly, the possession of property in any form is always potentially destabilising. It is not the concept of private property itself which is a problem: it is human nature. Men tend to be greedy, whilst women, as the history of Sparta apparently revealed, are greedier still. The Spartan constitution was fatally weakened by the failure to control the amount of property women could possess. At the other extreme, excessive communal property holding, as idealised by Plato, was also detrimental. In Crete, it had led to homosexuality and a dangerous reduction in procreation. As always, moderation was the key, and property holding was only virtuous in moderation (Aristotle, 1981, pp 142–52).

Classicism revisited

The particular idiosyncrasies which pervade Aristotle's ideal community, the products of his particular historical context, should not detract from the enduring influence of the basic idea of a politics defined in terms of communities. During the 16th and 17th centuries, much of Europe was swept by a complementary political and intellectual renaissance, part of which sought a return to Aristotelian principles of law and government. In many ways it reflected a sense of acute disorder, generated to a considerable extent by the challenge of the protestant reformation, and which concentrated on establishing some lost ideal which could be revisited in order to restabilise early modern politics.

Perhaps the most influential exponent of this political renaissance was Niccolo Machiavelli. Although, as we shall see in Chapter 4, Machiavelli enjoys a reputation as one of the most sceptical and pragmatic of political commentators, he was also one of the most creative and idealistic. His work *The Discourses* graphically portrayed the merits and demerits of classical government. Rome, and its greatness, were founded on a conception of citizen virtue, as exemplified by 'good education' and 'good laws'. The role of law in securing the republic, and indeed the importance of princes governing through a rule of law, was essential to classical virtue, and was something which Machiavelli was keen to impress. Indeed, as he confirmed in his more notorious *The Prince*, the ideal prince may be acutely pragmatic, even hypocritical, but he is not a tyrant. Tyranny, like democracy, breeds chaos. The only security in a polity is that preserved by law, along, of course, with arms. The communitarian form of Machiavelli's republic is undeniable. Nothing binds together a community as effectively as a feeling of 'fellowship', and a constitutive sense of active citizenship, and there is no good community without 'citizens of good repute'. Of course, the 'repute' is more important than the 'good'. For Machiavelli, government was always a form of 'theatre' (Machiavelli, 1983, pp 113–14, 459–71, 481).

Another to embrace the liberating potential of a revitalised classical humanism was Francis Bacon, whose *New Atlantis* betrayed a similar desire to remodel society in line with an image of classical virtue and goodness (Bacon, 1974, pp 215–47). At the root of Bacon's appreciation of humanity lay a belief in classical ideas of virtue and goodness, recast in terms of natural science, and, crucially, our observation of it. 'There is no hope', he asserted, 'except in a new birth of science; that is, in raising it regularly up from experience and building it afresh; which no one (I think) will say has yet been done or thought of' (Bacon, 1974, p vii). It was for this reason that Bacon rejected theatrical medieval displays of honour and nobility, preferring an immanent Aristotelian virtue defined in terms of education and knowledge. Classical humanism was founded on this concern for improvement of the mind, for the stability of a society depends ultimately on 'education, which is, in effect, an early custom' (Bacon, 1985, p 180). As the opening sections of Bacon's *The Advancement of Learning and New Atlantis* stressed, the search for order in renaissance Europe was to be found though a judicious mixture of classical wisdom and 'new' science. Philosophy might inspire 'contemplation', but 'knowledge' must not be 'as a courtesan, for pleasure and vanity only', but 'as a spouse, for generation, fruit, and comfort'. It was this reliance on empiricism, and this desire for its practical application in civil life, which made an active education all the more critical. The renaissance man learned, not just to satisfy himself, or indeed just for the sake of it, but in order to benefit the wider community, and the 'good ends' that were 'set before' such a man, the ends which prescribed his political 'virtue', were always ends directed towards the application of knowledge within a community (Bacon, 1974, pp 34–36, 167).

Renaissance humanism was defined by its desire to revise traditional ideas of virtue, and benevolence, whilst also emphasising the overriding importance of education. The Aristotelian 'virtues' of order were learned in both church and 'pettie' school, the two institutions which characterised the early modern determination to transfer education from the 'private' sphere of the family to the 'public' sphere of the community. Erasmus's *Manners for Children* announced the arrival of a particular interest in the educational process as a means of providing for better citizens. The education of magistrates was, for obvious reasons, a particular concern. Sir Philip Sidney, in many ways an archetypal Renaissance humanist, required magistrates to be both rational and virtuous, in the ultimate cause of preserving the good of the English commonwealth. Virtue was an essential attribute of good and godly government. English humanism was, then, not just intellectual, but carried a distinctive and urgent political ambition. In his influential *Book of the Governor*, Sir Thomas Elyot advised that the product of reason and virtue was good counsel; that 'which is rightwise is brought in by reason. For nothing is right that is not ordered by reason'. Moreover, 'Goodness cometh by virtue. Of virtue and reason proceedeth honesty'; so he could thus conclude, 'Wherefore counsel being compact of these three, may be named a perfect captain, a trusty companion, a plain and unfeigned friend' (Burgess, 1996, p 55).

A good magistrate was an Aristotelian one, imbued with all the virtues of citizenship. Classicism and godliness were elided, and, at the more puritan Calvinist extremes, government became the duty of every Christian citizen, and the determination to govern the ambition of the protestant crusade. The veneration of classical government was translated into justification for a reforming godly communitarianism. An intellectual model for this elision was provided by Erasmus's *The Education of a Christian Prince*. A godly prince is one 'complete with all the virtues', and in the ideal Christian commonwealth, the role of the virtuous and well educated citizenry is critical. The citizenry, if they are to enjoy a share of political power, must be educated with regard to what is 'conducive to common good' and be 'familiar with' a 'sense of honour and disgrace' (Erasmus, 1997, pp 36, 79–81). The various utopias recommended during the 16th and 17th centuries all effected this particular marriage of classicism and godliness. Bacon's *New Atlantis* was overtly Christian. Thomas More's *Utopia* prescribed a 'single community' directed towards a 'single way of life', governed by a philosopher-king. *Utopia* was perfected when the hitherto pagan communitarians, anyway 'unconsciously inclined' towards godliness, were 'easily' converted to Christianity (More, 1965, pp 57, 79, 118).

As we have already noted in Chapter 1, the Aristotelian idea of commonwealth took a particular hold of 16th and 17th century English jurists. It founded Richard Hooker's *Of the Laws of Ecclesiastical Polity*, as well as Richard Baxter's *A Holy Commonwealth*. It also took centre-stage in James Harrington's *The Commonwealth of Oceana*, written during the interregnum. Harrington's *Commmonwealth* made much of a presumed affinity between the English common law tradition and classical ideas of commonwealth and 'common good'; for only such a commonwealth, one of 'laws and not men', can be a commonwealth of 'virtue' (Harrington, 1992, pp 19, 35, 39–40, 221). The same tone could be found in Algernon Sidney's *Discourses Concerning Government*, written a decade later. The *Discourses*, as its author conceded, was a paean to classical conceptions of law, government and justice. The particular concern for the educated and virtuous magistrate was, once again, central. A good magistrate is defined, quite simply, by his understanding of justice and his capacity to preserve the 'public good'. It is for this reason, following the likes of Milton, that Sidney could elevate the removal of tyrants from a mere right to a duty of the good citizen (Sidney, 1996, pp 44–49, 70–74, 80–82). Alongside this particular interest in the virtuous magistrate was a determination to effect government at the lowest practicable level, and in doing so, Sidney argued, nourish within citizens a particular concern for the good of their immediate political community. True democracy, he suggested, 'can suit only with the convenience of a small town'. Participation in government 'makes men generous and industrious; and fills their hearts with love to their country' (Sidney, 1996, p 199).

As the 17th century passed into the 18th, the godly tones were increasingly replaced by the kind of secular, and explicitly classical, arguments found in Sidney's *Discourses*. The model civic republic became a centrepiece of Scottish Enlightenment political philosophy, articulated by the likes of David Hume and Adam Ferguson. The latter's *An Essay on the History of Civil Society* was founded on the basic Aristotelian premise that 'Mankind are to be taken in groups, as they have always subsisted' (Ferguson, 1995, p 10). Betraying the growing influence of utilitarian arguments that the purpose of life is largely defined by the capacity to promote happiness and minimise pain, Ferguson emphasised that the great practical value of community lay in its capacity to promote, not merely virtue, but the 'greatest happiness'. Echoing Sidney's similar injunction, Ferguson affirmed that:

> That is the most happy state, which is most beloved by its subjects; and they are the most happy men, whose hearts are engaged to a community, in which they find every object of generosity and zeal, and a scope to the exercise of every talent, and of every virtuous disposition (Ferguson, 1995, p 59).

Reinvesting community

A decade after the publication of Ferguson's *Essay*, assorted delegates found themselves gathered in Philadelphia charged with the responsibility of devising a constitution, and public philosophy, for an America that was determined to assert its independence. It would be here, across the Atlantic, that Aristotelian ideas of community would really take root. One of its most strident, and influential advocates, was in fact an itinerant English polemicist and republican, Thomas Paine. The publication of Paine's *Rights of Man* in 1791 served to refocus everyone's mind, not just the American, on ideas of civic republicanism and democracy. At the centre of Paine's thesis, inspired by the American and French revolutions, was the determination to empower individuals so that they could cultivate their own personal morality as well as define their role as citizens within a democratic community. The idea that democracy could be a political tool with which the congruent interests of individual and community could be nurtured was, of course, resonant of classical political philosophy. However, for Paine there was no question of natural order somehow ensuring the intellectual superiority of the democratic polity. Paine's concerns were acutely political. Democracy could not be left to its own devices, and neither could the community. Democracy must be argued for. As he had earlier suggested in 'Common sense', democracy and the idea of the State were antithetical, and radical democracy must serve an idea of civil society, primarily in the form of local self-government. The

American revolution of the same year seemed to offer the ideal opportunity for genuine radicalism. Paine argued vehemently for a constitution that extended certain rights to all, and a federal polity within which everyone could participate in government.

Rights of Man concentrated its fire at the forms of despotism which were pervasive in a conservative society such as England, from tyrant monarchs to unrepresentative parliaments to patriarchal families. The role of the democratic constitution was central to Paine's political model. Certainly, it must be above mere government, and the role of the judiciary in preserving the 'rights' of the constitution is paramount. The idea of 'natural rights' which cannot be legislated away by any government was resonant, both of the natural law theory which underpinned the distinctively English notion of the ancient constitution, and of the naturalism of Rousseau, which was so influential in the intellectual utopianism of the French Revolution. They were not, therefore, theological, but rather political, secular natural rights, and the political nature of these rights was most apparent in the series of social rights which Paine included in order to fashion a sense of solidarity within the civil society. Only a deep 'natural yearning' for social solidarity can really seal a civil society, and it was this 'yearning' which a radical democratic constitution must preserve (Paine, 1985, pp 159–209).

Aristotelian ideas of civic governance found an indigenous expression in the writings of 'founders' of the American constitution such as Thomas Jefferson and John Adams. According to Adams, Sidney's *Discourses* in particular excited 'fresh admiration' each time he perused them. But it was Jefferson who perhaps took their defence of localised communitarian governance most to heart, most obviously in his strident defence of the 'ward republic'. Such a republic was composed of myriad constituent commonwealths, all of which enjoyed extensive autonomy to run their own affairs, subject only to a minimal range of reserved matters of federal competence. According to Jefferson, such 'wards' would be 'pure and elementary republics, the sum of all of which, taken together, composes the State, and will make of the whole a true democracy'. They are the 'vital principle' of genuinely democratic government, and 'by making every citizen an acting member of government, and in the offices nearest and most interesting to him, will attach him by his strongest feelings to the independence of his country, and his republican constitution' (Hart, 2002, pp 8–9, 66, 77, 92–97).

The extent to which communitarian ideas of democracy were taken to the heart of an emergent American political philosophy during the first decades of the 19th century was evidenced in the observations of a French visitor, Alexis de Tocqueville. Tocqueville's *Democracy in America* identified a distinct 'spirit of association' in 19th century America, which was attributed to the sense of active participation in government at a radically decentralised level. Such democratic empowerment served to realise the ideals of popular 'sovereignty' enshrined in the American constitution, whilst the experience of participation encouraged a sense of responsibility and affinity, realising in the American citizenry a genuine sense of Aristotelian virtue. The American 'learns to know the laws by participating in the act of legislation' and the 'political education' of a citizenry is completed by the 'gentle motion' of participatory democracy. Moreover, if men are to promote civilisation, then 'the art of associating together must grow and improve' (Tocqueville, 1980, pp 54–59, 95–98, 114–15). Perhaps most perceptively, Tocqueville noted that the sense of affinity within a political community is dependent upon an image of ideal government which the citizenry feels that it shapes through its participation (Tocqueville, 1980, pp 70–71, 130–33, 150). This sense of 'narrative' community has proved to be influential in more recent communitarian theses.

In many ways, Tocqueville's account of his experiences in America reads as utopian as those projected by the likes of Bacon, More or Harrington. But the image which he bequeathed has proved to be enormously influential. The 20th century witnessed yet another renaissance in the idea of the political community, the immediate impetus for which was generated by a perceived sense of crisis with regard to the ideas of both community and democracy, together with a wistful invocation of a lost 'spirit' of communal solidarity. The specific invocation of Jeffersonian ideas of democracy has been most recently expressed in Gary Hart's *Restoration of the Republic*. According to Hart:

> In the current age, Jefferson's democratic republican ideal might yield a new political culture or a polity founded upon humanity's essentially social nature; a new destiny founded on participation in community life; the restoration of a public ethic that supercedes the private, commercial self; and the elevation of the common good and of commonwealth institutions, such as public schools as instruments of civic education, community welfare as a political and moral function of the ward, and local security provided by the citizen-soldier (Hart, 2002, p 23).

Such a communitarianism, Hart impresses, would encourage, even demand, 'qualitative' personal engagement in promoting the 'common good' (Hart, 2002, p 61).

The wistful tone finds a still clearer expression in Alisdair MacIntyre's suggestion that there is a 'grave disorder' in western moral and political philosophy. The late 20th century is characterised by the 'dissolution of historically founded certitudes', and it is the individualism championed by a utilitarian liberalism which communitarianism attacks. MacIntyre admits that there are no moral absolutes, but invokes Aristotle's idea of community to suggest that a community can establish a political, as opposed to universal or natural, ethics. Communitarianism must be refounded securely on such a conception, and present a bulwark against the kind of moral nihilism represented by more radical critical legal scholars (MacIntyre, 1985, pp 2–7, 62–74, 113–17; 1988, p 362). The essential concept in a renewed communitarian politics is justice, because it is justice which underpins the idea of 'virtue'. The two are co-determinative, for to be virtuous is to be just in all dealings with fellow citizens. The nature of the ethical community is determined by justice, not by the mechanics of law, and the communitarian, accordingly, is concerned less with laws, and more with the political philosophy of justice. Contemporary communitarianism, MacIntyre suggests, must be invested with precisely the same pervasive 'virtue' of justice. Whereas liberalism is founded on the legal 'rights' of individuals, communitarianism must follow Aristotle in founding itself on the ethic of 'justice' in the community (MacIntyre, 1985, pp 146–60).

Thus MacIntyre employs Aristotle to provide a theoretical foundation for a renewed 'politics of community' (MacIntyre, 1985, pp 141–42). In contrast to much received Aristotelian scholarship, which used Socratic philosophy as authority for establishing universal metaphysical principles, MacIntyre uses Aristotle as evidence that even the most revered of ancient philosophers admitted a degree of relativism. Political ethics are relative to each community, because it is that community which forms and re-forms its own 'virtues' (MacIntyre, 1985, pp 52–61, 146–60, 256–58). Political philosophy, then, is about judgment and choice in particular political situations. But whereas Plato resolved these particular choices by means of universal metaphysical ideas, Aristotle, according to MacIntyre, grounded them in community ethics, or 'virtues'. In other words, political problems were grounded in political ethics, not meta-ethics. Accordingly, philosophies of politics, and of law, are always contextual. In other words, they are historically situated, relative to a particular historical situation. At the same time, each philosophy of law is itself constituted by history, by previous philosophies of law. There is no such thing as a purely original idea (MacIntyre, 1985, pp 190, 213–20; 1967, pp 92–93). Moreover, being ethical, rather than meta-ethical, such philosophies are contingent, forever changing in line with changing contexts.

A populist variant of the same essential thesis can be found in Amitai Etzioni's *The Spirit of Community*. Like MacIntyre, Etzioni perceives a modern political world defined by 'increasing moral confusion and social anarchy' (Etzioni, 1995, p 12). Etzioni's appeal is different from MacIntyre's in that he also advocates the return of community 'morality', and in this sense derives much of his intellectual inspiration from Judeao-Christian theology. He advocates a politics in which 'communities are social webs of people who know one another as persons and have a moral voice' (Etzioni, 1995, pp ix–xi). At the heart of Etzioni's Aristotelianism is the belief that this 'moral voice' can only be heard if the political institutions remain open to the citizenry. Accordingly, much of his thesis is devoted to advising forms of decentralised and participatory government. Strong central government is the antithesis of community, and it was for this reason that Aristotle had warned against permitting the accretion of power in any particular institution of government. The radical dispersion of power amongst an active political citizenry is the only sure mechanism for protecting against what Aristotle rightly identified as potential majoritarian dictatorship (Etzioni, 1995, pp 44–50). The ideological enemy is very definitely liberalism and its idea of a realm of privacy which cannot be infringed by any demands of the wider community. As Etzioni concludes, it 'has been argued by libertarians that responsibilities are a personal matter, that individuals are to judge which responsibilities they accept as theirs'. In contrast, the communitarian perceives 'responsibilities' as being 'anchored in community'. As Aristotle emphasised, politics cannot be understood outside the idea of community (Etzioni, 1995, pp 266–67).

THE POLITICS OF SOLIDARITY

Unger's society

One of the most strident modern defences of a distinctive politics of communal solidarity has been presented by the critical legal scholar Roberto Unger. As we shall see in Chapter 6, the 'critical legal studies' movement, of which Unger was one of the early leading lights, has tended to align a critique of liberal legalism with a programme for social and political reform. The latter aspiration lies at the heart of Unger's particular variant of critical legal thought. In his *Knowledge and Politics*, he advocated the 'practice of total criticism' as something that requires both deconstruction and reconstruction. Rather than merely destroying liberalism, Unger wishes to uncover the 'deep structure' of liberal politics, so as to fashion a reconstructive 'superliberalism'. Such a liberalism, he announces, must address both individual and society, and serve more effectively to marry the two together. This ambition, to address the 'private' and the 'public' so as to overcome any barriers between the two, and to refashion 'communities of shared purpose' founded on a 'moral sentiment' of reciprocal respect, remains consistent throughout Unger's work (Unger, 1975, pp 3–25).

This concept of 'respect' is central, and a new theory of radical politics is premised on a philosophy of the self with is determined in terms of the 'reflective judgment' which individuals employ in relations with one another. Interestingly Unger recasts this as a 'morality of sympathy'. The new Ungerian 'self' must accept right and duty as a control and a determination of community, must accept the contingency of ends, and finally, must accept the indeterminacy of individualism. A 'superliberalism' is distinguished by its appreciation of 'difference', as opposed to the traditional liberal assumption that all individuals can be generalised in terms of liberty and political equality (Unger, 1975, pp 38–58). The mechanism for translating this fuller understanding of individual relations in a community into a radical democracy is through institutions which facilitate greater dialogic participation. If we come to appreciate that our relations with others are governed by our ability to converse on terms of equal respect, then our politics can be redefined accordingly. It will be a community which can thus fashion a 'conception of shared values', and it is this co-determinative relation of self and community which lies at the heart of Unger's vision of radical democracy (Unger, 1975, pp 82–102).

At the same time, Unger is careful to emphasise that these 'shared values' do not enjoy any particular or fixed moral authority. There is no metaphysical or philosophical foundation to his morality. It is purely shaped by the individuals within a particular society at a particular time, and it is for this reason that he rejects any socialist notion of a bureaucratic welfare state. People must not be assumed to be alike and to have certain shared ambitions, but rather, precisely because they are shared, these ambitions or 'values' cannot be assumed to be anything, but are constantly changing in accord with circumstances. Echoing Karl Popper's idea of an 'open society', Unger refers to a radical politics facilitating an 'open community' and founded ultimately on only one fixed political principle, liberty. Liberty presumes the capacity for change (Unger, 1975, pp 174–90). The congruence of individual and social interest, and their capacity to reshape one another, was captured in one particularly resonant passage:

> Community is held together by an allegiance to common purposes. The more these shared ends express the nature of humanity, rather than simply the preferences of particular individuals and groups, the more would one's acceptance of them become an affirmation of one's own nature; the less would it have to represent the abandonment of individuality in favour of assent and recognition. Thus, it would be possible to view others as complementary rather than opposing wills; furtherance of their ends would mean the advancement of one's own. The conflict between the demands of individuality and of sociability would disappear. Each person, secure in his individuality, would be able to recognise his own humanity in other persons (Unger, 1975, pp 220–21).

The reconstruction of the idea of community on this conception of 'sympathy' will transcend the traditional notion of government by institution. Government will be from within each individual, because the form of politics will be an expression of each person as articulated through the 'shared values'. It will, Unger concludes, be a 'democracy of ends' (Unger, 1975, p 267).

The ideas in *Knowledge and Politics* must be placed in the context of Unger's wider theory of the development of modern society. In *Law in Modern Society*, Unger concluded that a radical liberal democracy must be based on consensus politics. He traced the evolution of modern government as a form of institutionalised bureaucracy in which the individual is crushed, alienated and disempowered, and similarly seized on the experience of totalitarianism as an acute form of administrative government. Liberal legalism must be overcome by reinvesting a critical sense of human difference and individualism. Law, Unger suggests, has become the keystone of traditional liberal ideology, whilst the 'myth' of individual rights, because it denies individuality and difference, disguises widespread social, political and economic exploitation and disadvantage. The politics of modernism is premised upon denying the relevance of community and encouraging an ethic of competition between atomised individuals who refuse to acknowledge the 'respect' which others deserve. Unger refers to the need to reinvest a sense of liberty within a community context, and terms this 'solidarity', the 'kernel' of which is 'our feeling of responsibility for those whose lives touch in some way upon our own and our greater or lesser willingness to share their fate'. Solidarity, he concludes, is the 'social face of love' (Unger, 1976, p 206).

In more immediately jurisprudential terms, 'solidarity implies that one is never permitted to take advantage of his legal rights so as to pursue his own ends without regard to the effects he may have on others'. The holder of rights must always exercise them in the wider 'interest in maintaining a system of social relations'. Rights are not purely legal instruments, but also social instruments, the primary purpose of which is to encourage 'compassion for each other'. Against traditional liberal legalism, this superliberal jurisprudence will describe the 'latent and living law' of 'human interaction'. Once again, Unger seeks recourse to a communicative method of democratic participation. Liberalism must promote participation by facilitating opportunities for discussion, whilst jurisprudence must develop in terms of understanding law as something discussed and thus interpreted. Once understood in these terms, as a conversation piece, then the fluidity of law will be better appreciated, as will be our greater sense of empowerment. No law is set in stone, and any law can be changed if a society persuades itself that it should be (Unger, 1976, pp 209, 249–58).

Politics and passion

The publication of Unger's *The Critical Legal Studies Movement* in 1986 was significant for two reasons. First, it represented, or at least hoped to represent, a definitive statement of the reconstructive critical legal project. Secondly, after a gap of several years, it represented Unger's turn to a more intensive analysis of the politics of law. The basic ambition, to facilitate the realisation of a more 'reflective' politics, remained, but Unger's critique was now directed more immediately against the formalist pretensions of positivist theories of law. The ability to engineer change, in both society and its laws, is the essential quality of a radical liberal community. Unger termed this facility for change 'enlarged doctrine', and it inhered three qualities. First, it transcends any pretended distinction between what is and what ought to be. Secondly, it cherishes the 'transformative' potential of conflict and argument. Thirdly, it emphasises the empirical in order to reveal the politics of law (Unger, 1986, pp 16–19). The political import of this 'transformative practice' is to advocate effective decentralisation of power.

At the same time, it does not necessitate the abandonment of rights. Indeed, rights are essential in the superliberal polity. But they are political, not metaphysical, rights, and cannot be allowed to 'stabilise' the law. Rights must, of necessity, serve to emancipate the individual. Unger suggests four 'kinds of rights': 'immunity' rights, which are absolute against all others; 'destabilising' rights, which destabilise institutions; 'market' rights, which preserve a right to compete in the market; and 'solidarity' rights, which offer a legal entitlement to communal rights. Such rights are intended to revise the existing liberal conception of rights, which he characterises as essentially negative implements used against others. In contrast, Unger's rights are intended to facilitate participation in society and, moreover, require the acknowledgement of that responsibility. Once again, rights must be exercised, not purely in the interest of the individual, but in recognition of wider social responsibilities, and by advising the importance of participation in the legal process such a critical legal attitude is representative of the spirit of 'transformative action' which underpins contemporary radical politics (Unger, 1986, pp 22–36, 41, 93–103).

Unger's project pivots upon the basic Platonic desire to redefine the relation between the individual and society. The duality of the project is essential, and is reflected in his subsequent and complementary set of works, *Passion* and *Politics*. *Passion* addresses the situation of the self in modern society, whilst *Politics* suggests a complementary rewriting of political institutions in order to reflect and enhance this refined idea of self. *Passion* is dedicated to refining an idea of 'sympathy', which is founded on the 'opportunity for discovery and self-expression'. The critical sense of social 'solidarity' comes from the empowerment that is experienced by self-assertion and expression. People feel a greater affinity with others within a community if they feel that the community is, at least in part, their creation. This is why the idea of 'sympathy' must be understood as constitutive of, and constituted by, radical democracy (Unger, 1984, pp 8–15). The idea of 'passion' itself must be seen as complementary to reason. Unger does not deny the idea of reason, but he does deny that reason is the only dynamic behind the actions of individuals. The rational actor is another of the myths that must be 'debunked'. When individuals make choices, or participate in democracy, the workplace or wherever, they may act rationally, but at the same time they will also act with regard to their emotions.

It is passion which expresses individuality against the depersonalising potential of universal reason. Our lives are filled with passion, every bit as much as they are determined by reason. Once again, it thereby follows that our politics and laws are themselves also expressions, not just of reason, but of passion. Passion, as the determination of individuality, is the dynamic of change, just as reason is the justification for stabilisation, and so a radical politics, and a critical legal politics, must be founded on this passion. Passion, also, is the emotion that is capable of understanding community – the relation between self and others. A 'personality' that lives out 'passion' is one that appreciates the 'utter contingency of his own being and of the world' and, moreover, cherishes such contingency as a virtue, rather than as a threat to order. Such a person is 'self-reflective', one who understands his own situation as being solely determined in relation to others (Unger, 1984, pp 126–35, 146–57). No one lives in isolation, any more than anyone lives by reason alone. Passion, ultimately, describes the 'brio and panache, the sheer vibrant life, of a personality'. It heightens our 'sense of experiences of human power', whilst reconciling us to our contingent political lives. Finally, we find ourselves 'set down in particular social and mental worlds', where the 'modes of discourse and explanation available' to us 'never exhaust the possibilities of understanding and communication' (Unger, 1984, pp 260–61).

The complementary *Politics* is characterised by the pervasive demand for mechanisms of participatory government. Community, echoing Aristotle's original injunction, is an 'artefact', something created by us. Such an insight alone is intended to be uplifting and empowering. A society is ours and so we can change it, and the same applies to its laws. The critical legal project, by reinvesting the importance of the creative self in the political process, has revealed the possibilities of a new normative vision of society. The newly appreciated 'antinaturalistic conception of self and society can inform the life projects of the individual'. At its centre is the essential injunction to deny any pretended metaphysical foundations. Such an injunction must facilitate our 'freedom from false necessity', the belief that certain 'truths' are natural and simply have to be. There are no social or legal 'truths' (Unger, 1987, vol 1, pp 18–35, 135–37). With this knowledge, there is nothing which can stop the liberated individual from participating in the endless shaping and reshaping of society and its laws. There is no 'reason' not to change the law. It is the fundamental appreciation, across all human and social sciences, 'that all things or some things might be otherwise than they are'. Our situation in society is always changing, and so are our ideas, and so the only 'truth' is that every 'truth' is contingent. Unger finds 'encouragement not only in the constructive work that modern social thought has silently begun to accomplish but also in the emergence in many areas of thought of an image of man that emphasises both his context bound predicament and his context smashing capabilities' (Unger, 1987, vol 1, pp 173, 192–204).

Unger thus returns to ideas of participatory democracy in order to furnish a radical political model, and law is at the centre of such a model, because law is the part of politics which people most immediately experience. It is law which effects political ideology. As ever, the key is to convince people that, because law is indeed merely an expression of political ideology it is malleable and can be reshaped by precisely those people who feel oppressed by it. But such a potential for change can only be realised if the institutions of democracy are truly radical. In the second volume of *Politics*, therefore, Unger presents a series of models for radical democracy, all of which emphasise the necessity of 'democratic pluralism' and 'economic destabilisation', and all of which employ a radical model of rights. All citizens must have rights to participate in democratic institutions and in the market, as well as to be protected from the infringement of those rights by others. There must be a rewriting of the constitution in order to effect these rights. Here, of course, there is an essential problem, for if these particular rights are indeed entrenched, then all the rights in the political regime are not malleable. Some are more important rights than others, and, it seems, themselves contradict the fundamental quality of transformation. Unger's solution is to acknowledge that such rights are not entrenched because they are somehow 'natural' or 'neutral', but because they are recognised, in purely political terms, as being necessary in a participatory democracy. Their entrenchment is therefore itself tenuous. Such rights, and, indeed, such a democracy, must be understood in terms of expressing an 'attitude' rather than defining 'structures'. We, who define the attitude, rule in a participatory democracy, not the structures (Unger, 1987, vol 2).

Telling stories

It is notable that Unger's later, more refined and reconstructive work, has increasingly turned towards a distinctively narrative and imaginative conception of community. In modern society, he argues in *Politics*, law is 'the place at which an idea of civilisation takes detailed institutional form', and the hope of political reform, the 'marriage between social realism and social prophecy', thus depends on an intellectual capacity for 'institutional imagination'. We must be able to imagine alternative ways of governing and living within communities, and so Unger refers to a 'democratic experimentalism' as a counter to the 'institutional fetishism' which pervades so much classical liberal ideology. The role of dialogue between citizens is central to the possibilities of institutional reform and the experimental dynamic. Rather than any metaphysical notions of reason, all we have, and all we need, are 'historically located arrangements and historically located conversations' (Unger, 1996, pp 1–23).

An appreciation that political institutions are only legitimate in so far as they promote the conditions for conversation between citizens is an explicit recognition that we now live in a radically plural world devoid of metaphysical foundations. Radical democracy, in turn, must be about respecting difference and accommodating it within political institutions. The jurisprudential import of Unger's thesis lies in the pivotal role which he assigns to lawyers and judges, whose primary responsibilities lie in preserving the capacity for self-expression, choice and individuality. Above all, they lie in an appreciation that the law belongs to everyone, not merely to lawyers, and that lawyers provide a service, not just to clients, but to society itself (Unger, 1996, pp 36, 76–77, 106–18). Ultimately, social progress and institutional reform depend on co-operation, both between lawyers and non-lawyers, and between citizen and citizen. Whilst securing the liberal principle of freedom, a radical liberalism must recognise the reality of community and, accordingly, concentrate on the pressing need to facilitate narrative 'arrangements' for genuine participatory democracy. As Unger concludes, radical democracy must 'connect conditions for the development of freedom' with the 'demands of practical progress through practical experimentalism' (Unger, 1996, pp 184–90).

This narrative injunction is shared by a number of communitarian critics. Charles Taylor, for example, asserts that a community is an historical and narrative artefact, constituted by generations of dialogic participants. Democracy is not a matter of voting in elections, but participation in an 'ongoing conversation' with our 'immediate historic community' (Taylor, 1989, pp 25–52). The same narrativity lies at the heart of Michael Sandel's *Democracy's Discontent*. As the very title of his work implies, Sandel argues that the demise of modern democracy cannot be distinguished from the collapse in community 'spirit' in contemporary America. Alluding to a more global crisis, Sandel alleges that our modern world is 'rife' with a 'discontent' that is founded on a shared perception that 'we are caught in the grip of impersonal structures of power that defy our understanding and control' (Sandel, 1996, pp 3, 201–02). According to Sandel, liberal political theory has driven a wedge between the private and public spheres of life. Modern humanity has been forced into a private world, largely alienated from a sense of empowerment in, and thus affinity with, the political community. Invoking Tocqueville's ideal, he advises that a return to genuine democracy 'requires political communities that control our destinies, and citizens who identify sufficiently with those communities to think and act with a view to the common good'. Moreover, such a sense of political identity will only be nurtured in communities founded on a shared 'narrative understanding' of communal goods, worked out by the resolution of 'competing interpretations' of what a particular political community cherishes (Sandel, 1996, pp 274, 350–51).

Perhaps the most strident advocate of a restored narrativity in modern theories of law and society is Martha Nussbaum. In *Cultivating Humanity*, Nussbaum suggests that the idea of a liberal education, including a legal one, is premised on a 'particular norm of citizenship', and the ability to relate 'stories of people's real diversity and complexity' is essential to such an ambition. What must be reinvigorated in the citizen, and the lawyer, is the 'compassionate' and 'narrative imagination', the 'ability to think what it might be like to be in the shoes of a person different from oneself'. Literature, accordingly, plays a 'vital' role in 'cultivating the powers of imagination that are essential to citizenship' (Nussbaum, 1997, pp ix, 8–11, 85–86). It is this appreciation, of the immanent relation between literature and the political community, and the 'passionate engagement' with political life which it describes, which has been lost in the modern world. The 'future of democracy' depends upon a return to the classical understanding of politics as a narrative engagement, between 'author and readers' (Nussbaum, 1997, pp 15–41; 1990, pp 3–7, 55–101, 142–43, 148–76). What Aristotle understood, and what we appear to have forgotten, is the simple fact that democracy is only democracy if everyone feels they belong, and no one feels oppressed, excluded or disempowered.

This idea of a narrative sense of justice and community bears an obvious resonance with the kind of 'compassionate' jurisprudence we encountered in Chapter 1. A politics of compassion is necessarily relational. It is founded on a principle of reciprocal engagement, and such engagement must be narrative. It is, in simple terms, a matter of telling what Richard Rorty terms 'sad and sentimental stories' (Rorty, 1989, p 186). As we noted before, the context within which Tutu has advocated such a jurisprudence is determined by the immediate experience of the South African Truth and Reconciliation Commission. The Commission did not replace the function of ordinary courts. But it did provide an alternative institutional mechanism by which individuals might retrieve a sense of dignity and justice simply by taking the opportunity to relate their personal histories, and by listening to the shared experiences of others. As Tutu announced at the very opening of the first session of the Commission, the 'healing of a traumatised and wounded people' would be better achieved simply by listening to 'stories' (Tutu, 1999, pp 86–87). In this capacity, the Commission represented a particularly striking example of narrative justice in action.

Of course, the experience attracted both applause and scepticism (Dyzenhaus, 1998, pp 136–83). But there can be little doubting its impact. As Antjie Krog commented, in her personal account of the Commission hearings, 'Week after week; voice after voice; account after account. It is like travelling on a rainy night behind a huge truck – images of devastation breaking in sheets on the windscreen'. Deploying a resonant, if slightly mixed, metaphor, Krog suggested that a restorative principle of justice was 'quilted together from hundreds of stories' (Krog, 1999, pp 259, 278–79). And for some deponents, the process of story-telling was enormously restorative. According to one, it 'allows me to remember but also to believe that we as human beings are all interdependent, that we can only exist through our community humanity'. For 'everyone has a story to tell', and 'people need to be given the opportunity to tell these stories, since there are different perceptions of the truth'

(Henry, 2000, pp 170–73). According to another oral deposition, of a young man blinded by South African police, what had 'brought my sight back, my eyesight back, is to come here and tell the story. I feel what has been making me sick all the time is the fact that I couldn't tell my story'. But now, he concluded, 'it feels like I've got my sight back by coming here and telling you the story' (Krog, 1999, pp 45–46; Tutu, 1999, pp 127–29).

RETHINKING DEMOCRACY

Towards an inclusive society

Injustice is the product of exclusion: the deeming of certain individuals to be outside society, and its presumed norms. Conversely, the idea of a political community is premised upon some notion of inclusivity. This irreducible tension was brilliantly analysed by one of the leading Aristotelian political philosophers of the last century, Hannah Arendt. What is most striking about Arendt's agenda, and indeed her own personal history, is the absence of geopolitical roots. It is for this reason that her analysis remains so pertinent today, as we all try to make some sense of the 'new' world order in which we live. As someone who throughout her life identified with the outsider, the alien, Arendt was in a particularly informed position to argue for the importance of an idea of democracy that was both inclusive and cosmopolitan, and one that respected the idea of a discrete community in which everyone plays a constitutive part. From a very early age, Arendt felt that her Jewishness set her apart from fellow children. Born in 1906 in Koenigsberg in eastern Prussia, she spent most of her youth moving around avoiding the Russian army. Later expelled from junior school for organising a boycott of one particularly incompetent teacher, alienated by authority, by race and by invading armies, it is small wonder that she should so readily empathise with those excluded by society.

Arendt just escaped from Nazi Germany in 1933 as Hitler came to power, and between then and receiving US citizenship in 1951 was effectively 'stateless'. In political terms, she did not exist. The peculiarity of a human being having no political existence made a profound and lasting impression, and for a number of years she worked with various Jewish movements striving to secure a homeland in Palestine. It was the first of many occasions when Arendt actively supported revolutionary movements, even force when necessary, in order to realise what she perceived to be a necessary human right. The experience of the Holocaust finally convinced her that Europe could never provide a secure home for the Jewish people. A Jewish State was a human right on a vast political scale, and a commitment to human rights emerged as the centrepiece of Arendt's work. The problem of democracy and belonging was intrinsically a matter of human rights as political and social rights. In 1949, commenting on the idea of a 'rights of man', she observed that, post-1945, no one seemed sure what human rights really were. It was, she suggested, the most pressing matter in legal and political thought, and until the question was resolved there could be no new world order, whilst the condition of alienation would be one experienced by everyone (Young-Breuhl, 1982, pp 113–88, 256–57, 309–10). Later, she was to champion the rights of black and other ethnic minorities in the US, campaigning in particular against the forced segregation of black schoolchildren. Similarly, some of

Arendt's most immediately political work with regard to 'otherness' concentrated on the situation of women in the modern world. Her first major publication was a semi-biographical study of an early proto-feminist Rahel Varnhagen. In studying Varnhagen's life and career, and then considering her own, Arendt experienced a very real sense that the most common form of political exclusion in a modern society was gender based (Young-Breuhl, 1982, pp 95–97).

For the rest of her life, Arendt struggled with the idea of identity and belonging. The only solution, she time and again resolved, lay in a notion of political community to which all human beings were entitled to belong as of right. In terms of intellectual influence, it is not surprising that Arendt's almost utopian view of universal political and intensely 'human' rights should owe much to the combined influences of Aristotle and Kant. Arendt detected in Kant's later work on judgment and community the germ of a possible political philosophy of modern human rights. In her final uncompleted work, *The Life of the Mind*, she concentrated on the demise of freedom, and the extent to which real individual and political freedom had been suppressed by modernity. The three essential constituents of being human, the ability to 'think', to 'will' and to 'judge', have been systematically suppressed as the modern world has sought to regiment the individual. Ultimately, what was suppressed was intellectual, political and jurisprudential freedom (Canovan, 1992, pp 110–26; Hansen, 1993, pp 195–200). It was not, of course, a pure libertarian freedom, but rather a more sophisticated freedom to which was attached a responsibility for others in the political community.

Kant's legal theory, she suggested, was founded on the idea of subjective individual 'judgment'. This 'judgment' is the peculiar faculty of political jurisprudence, and it is a faculty which we all employ throughout our lives. We are all, therefore, politicians and judges, and we all carry the wider responsibility for community that judging others demands. Rather than representing the epitome of a libertarian philosophy of individual right, Arendt argued that Kant's later works described a community-based political jurisprudence, one which demanded the active participation of all community members in the cause of realising effective political justice (Arendt, 1982, pp 17–27). It was in the later Kant, then – the Kant of community and respect for others – that Arendt found a distinctive tradition of civic and political humanism. Human rights must be removed from metaphysics and notions of universalism, and relocated in communities and politically empowered individuals. A human right, like any form of legal right, is at root a political right which can only exist in democratic politics. Moreover, it is particular, just as justice itself is particular to real political situations. Above all, human rights exist only in the minds of men and women, and so must be understood in terms of human relationships (Arendt, 1982, pp 10–12).

In 1951 Arendt published *The Origins of Totalitarianism* as a 'frontal assault' on European modernism itself, and the philosophical and political baggage which came with it. The Enlightenment fantasies of universalism had proved illusory, destroyed by the perverse inclination of modern political communities to reward those who triumph self-interest over the wider interest of the community itself. The essential political choice established in modernity is that which lies between totalitarianism and democratic pluralism. The historical triumph of totalitarianism was premised on the resignation of democracy in favour of administrative bureaucracy, and to emphasise the intimately jurisprudential nature of this triumph, Arendt opened the first part of

Origins with an account of the notorious *Dreyfus* case, in which a Jewish army officer in the French Third Republic was wrongfully convicted of treason, scapegoated and convicted (Arendt, 1951, vol 1, pp 91–120). Dreyfus was condemned because of a lack of justice and a lack of democracy. The two are integral. Dreyfus's fate was both prophetic and symbolic. The subsequent triumph of totalitarianism in the 20th century world would be premised on a critical failure of justice. The implication was clear. It is not just in regimes such as Hitler's Germany or Stalin's Russia that totalitarianism is to be found. Rather, totalitarianism is present in any polity, even superficially democratic ones like the French Third Republic, where there is no genuine participatory democracy in which justice can flourish. If justice does not belong to everyone in a political community, if it is not preserved by the institution of participatory democracy itself, then law will simply belong to particular sectional interests which enjoy political power.

Totalitarianism is the antithesis of individualism. It suggests that the interests of all are alike, and therefore denies the need for individual political participation. This ambition, 'to organise the infinite plurality and differentiation of human beings as if all of humanity were just one individual', lies at the heart of the modernism which pronounces universalism and ultimate truths, whether they are located in God, in reason, in science or whatever (Arendt, 1951, vol 2, pp 21–28, 136). The first step in any totalitarianism, any establishment of an ultimate truth, is to 'kill the juridical in man', to deny the need for the individual to undertake the responsibility of judgment. The murder of the juridical man is a murder of humanity itself. Humanity is defined by the idea of justice, by enacting a fundamental fairness in the relation between individuals within a political community. Thus, after 'murder of the moral person and annihilation of the juridical person, the destruction of the individuality is almost always successful' (Arendt, 1951, vol 2, pp 91–92, 145, 153).

The denial of justice is the denial of the intrinsic value of humanity, the denial that man is necessary or can in any way contribute to the wellbeing of the community. It is this denial of political and jurisprudential purpose which finally describes the situation of the alien or outsider, and it is this situation that modern man finds himself in. The 'totalitarian attempt to make men superfluous reflects the experience of modern masses of their superfluity on an overcrowded earth'. The modern world is a:

> ... world of the dying, in which men are taught they are superfluous through a way of life in which punishment is meted out without connection with crime, in which exploitation is practised without profit, and where work is performed without product (Arendt, 1951, vol 2, p 155).

It is only in a world of alienation, a world without justice or democracy, a world which denies the intrinsic value of humanity, that the acute evil of totalitarianism can flourish.

Arendt's interest in the politics of evil did not end with *Origins*. She returned to it in her hugely controversial account of the trial in Israel of the captured Nazi war criminal, Adolf Eichmann. According to Arendt, Eichmann's torture, and experimentation on concentration camp inmates, was not the product of some especial evil. Rather, it was 'banal', devoid of substance. What really mattered was its situation within modernity. Eichmann, she suggested, was the product of modernism, and its denial of humanity. Eichmann was the classic modern man, alienated, incapable of communication during his trial as he had been in life, quite unable to comprehend any notion of humanity and quite incapable of exercising judgment. The responsibility for Eichmann was not Germany's, or even simply Eichmann's. The responsibility for Eichmann was everybody's. We, the human race, let Eichmann happen. The trial of Eichmann in Jerusalem was, then, a shirking of responsibility, a refusal to acknowledge that the concentration camps were an intrinsic part of a modernity which had lost its sense of humanity. Her critique of the modernist presumption that justice can always be resolved in formal trials can, of course, be set against the very different conception of justice that underpinned the Truth and Reconciliation Commission in post-apartheid South Africa. According to Arendt, it was not Hitler alone who had suddenly denied his fellow man: it was centuries of egoism and self-interest, of a sense of liberty without responsibility. Moreover, the trial was itself a piece of judicial violence little better than that inflicted by Eichmann on his victims. Unsurprisingly, Arendt's analysis caused a storm of protest. The post-war world was desperate to purge itself of any sense of guilt for the millions of lives lost between 1939 and 1945. It wanted scapegoats. It did not want intellectual arguments which suggested that only a wholesale rethinking of what modernity and its collateral notions of justice meant could really furnish a 'new' world order.

Politics as artefact

Arendt was convinced that radical thinking was itself a virtue. Individuality within any community is best expressed by thinking radically and by challenging established political and social norms. 'Social nonconformism', she emphasised, 'is the *sine qua non* of intellectual achievement'. Implicit in this statement is the essential idea that politics is not natural. In *The Human Condition*, she firmly aligned herself with Aristotle's assertion that politics is a human artefact, something created and fashioned by men. It is, therefore, a matter of human responsibility, not metaphysics or theology or such like. Politics demands active engagement, and the principle of democracy requires that it should be the engagement of everyone (Arendt, 1958, pp 29–77, 175–238). It was this idea of politics as artefact and as a matter of human responsibility which lay behind her critique of the Eichmann trial. Eichmann was our responsibility. It was in the final epilogue to *Eichmann* that Arendt presented an alternative politics based around the establishment of 'public spaces' which would facilitate the participation of all whilst nurturing the sense of jurisprudential responsibility which a new world order needed (Arendt, 1963, pp 290–98; Dossa, 1984).

It was precisely this approach to politics which also framed Arendt's reinterpretation of Kant's legal theory so as to emphasise the communitarianism of *The Critique of Judgment*. It was Kant's idea of a *sensus communis* which reinvested the lost Aristotelian idea of participatory democracy in the political community. Justice is only possible in a polity in which each member is empowered to contribute to the political process of judging others. Freedom, she stressed in *The Life of the Mind*, exists only in real political circumstances protected by real legal provisions which are the creation of active participating citizens 'engaged in changing our common world'. Such freedom is 'possessed by the citizen rather than by the man in general, it can manifest itself only in communities, where the many who live together have their intercourse both in the word and in deed regulated by the great number of rapports – laws, customs, habits and the like'. Such communities, Arendt added, facilitate real political freedom because they institutionalise the conditions for radical democracy in a 'sphere of human plurality' (Arendt, 1978, p 200).

The politics of freedom and justice demands a radical democratic constitution, with power relocated in micro-communities, geographically localised, in workplaces, in families and so on. It was, of course, a classically communitarian vision. But what really distinguished Arendt's particular communitarianism was the extent to which it was founded on the fundamental philosophical ideas of freedom and justice. Aside from the Aristotelian, Arendt suggested two further models for political community. The first was the Jewish model of community, the kibbutzim. The kibbutzim, she suggested, is a genuinely democratic 'society based on justice, formed in complete equality, and indifferent to all profit motives' (Young-Breuhl, 1982, p 164). The second model of communitarianism was to be found in the American republican tradition and Tocqueville's idea of 'associational politics'. The political rights cast into legal form in the US Constitution were merely paper rights, valueless unless cherished by citizens prepared to undertake the responsibility for effecting them in their civil society. Rights, like democracy itself, are not something handed down from above. They are purely political entities which must be fought for and defended. In both *Origins* and again in *The Human Condition*, she emphasised that the ideas of right, democracy and community were integral and their fate intimately related, for as the power of the modern State rose, it was these virtues which had been lost. Though an admirer of the American republican dream, Arendt became increasingly critical of the reality of US politics. It had represented an idea of rights and democracy, and its loss had been all the more symbolic. More particularly, being a constitutional failure, the loss of the idea of human and civil rights in America was a fundamental jurisprudential failure.

It was, then, not so much a failure of universal ethics as of immediate political judgment. The fault, she suggested, lay not so much in the constitution as in the willingness of the judicial system to support it. In 1970, Arendt controversially advised a programme of civil disobedience as the only remedy for the apparent inability of the legal system, and in particular the Supreme Court, to respect the human rights of disadvantaged Americans. The 'law' she said, was 'dead', and civil disobedience, as a popular expression of group action, was the necessary means of reinvesting a sense of justice in political life. It was a taking of political responsibility by a community of disadvantaged, whether they be black, women, poor, student or whatever, for to take such responsibility, to act in civil disobedience, was to act as a citizen. As Paine had advised, civil disobedience was a civic duty, not a crime. Her pronounced support for the civil rights movement placed Arendt at the very edge of radical democratic politics. It also earned a fierce response from the more conservative elements of American political life. Once again, Arendt was marginalised and cast out of the political community.

In *On Revolution*, she again tried to reinvoke the spirit of the 'founding fathers' of America, of Paine, Tocqueville and the other proponents of radical and participatory democracy, emphasising the 'intimate connection between the spirit of revolution and the principle of federation'. The comparable, if temporary, success of the Hungarian revolution and its institution of a 'council system' of radically decentralised power enthused Arendt enormously. The Hungarians, she maintained, had reawakened the spirit of Aristotle and of 1776. The council system expressed 'nothing more or less than this hope' for 'a new form of government that would permit every member of the modern egalitarian society to become a participator in public affairs' (Arendt, 1990, pp 264–65). In *On Revolution*, she closed with an impassioned appeal for a 'completely different principle of organisation, which begins from below, continues upward, and finally leads to a parliament'. Such a system of localised and decentralised government would be one facilitated by 'a number of public spaces', in which everyone can 'participate', 'debate' and effect 'justice' (Arendt, 1972, pp 231–33). As ever, the causes of democracy and justice were inseparable, and continued to define the fundamental questions of modern law and politics.

Democracy in a post-metaphysical world

Arendt's reception in modern legal and political thought has been mixed. So radical is her brand of political activism, civil disobedience, even judicious use of violence, that she is often accused of being an apologist for anarchy (Isaac, 1992, pp 246–47). Yet, the heroes of democracy, as Arendt was only too well aware, are the revolutionaries, the Thomas Paines of the world. Arendt certainly wanted to be a revolutionary, to challenge the cosy complacency of modern liberalism, and at the heart of her critique is the assertion that the idea of law as some sort of independent arbiter governed by universal metaphysical rules that can secure individual justice is a nonsense. Arendt traced the mythology of liberal legalism to its constitutional heart. In its place she suggested a fundamental rethinking of constitutionalism in terms of realising a genuine radical democratic legitimacy. Whilst the aspiration might be quintessentially communitarian, it is certainly not exclusively so. And, as we shall shortly see, it has gained an increasing currency as legal and political theorists try to make sense of the impact of globalisation and the much-vaunted 'new' world order in which we live. For at the heart of this experience, the relation of included and excluded, self and 'other', is writ large.

One of the most interesting chroniclers of the fate of community and democratic solidarity in the modern world is the German social theorist Juergen Habermas. In *Between Facts and Norms*, Habermas emphasised the extent to which legal and political thought must concentrate on the failures of democracy and the need to reinvest an idea of justice through reinvigorated democratic institutions. This will require the recasting of a public philosophy for the 'post-metaphysical world'. It will also require the complementary reinvestment of a 'kind of communitarianism', a reinvestment of Aristotelian 'public spaces'. At the same time, Habermas shares the opinion common to so many communitarian critics, that the demise of democracy is a direct result of the triumph of liberal legalism and its underlying need to support the emerging dynamic of the modern political economy. The dominant discourse in contemporary legal thought has become that of 'private' right, essentially a right to property and commerce, rather than 'public' democracy. Accordingly, law has been recast in specifically economic, rather than political or moral terms (Habermas, 1996, pp xlii, 44–52; 2001, p 126).

Like Arendt, Habermas again isolates the rise of the administrative, bureaucratic State as the key to the suppression of democracy in the modern polity. In contrast to the 'administrative State', the 'principles of the constitutional State' will depend on the establishment of 'new forms of participation and arenas for deliberation into the decision making process of the administration itself'. The reinvestment of the constitutional State will depend on the restoration of democracy (Habermas, 1996, pp 191, 430–52). At the same time, democracy is not merely restored through political institutions, though it is a necessary step. It is also restored by reinvesting a sense of community and 'social solidarity', and this investment is made, in large part, through law. Thus Habermas places a stress on the role of courts and lawyers in acknowledging their responsibilities as political actors fashioning a community and securing a principle of democracy. If anyone is going to restore democracy and ensure a sense of justice it is lawyers and legal theorists, for it is the legal theorist who can prescribe the constitution of democracy and the lawyers and judges who can protect it. The responsibility of the law is not merely to effect justice between individuals, but to act whenever necessary to protect the 'public spaces' of democracy against any legislative which seeks to constrain them. Like Arendt, Habermas suggests that the responsibility for the failure of democracy in the modern western world lies with lawyers and an ethic of liberal legalism which has hidden behind a mythology that law is somehow a discipline distinct from politics and power (Habermas, 1996, pp 196–286).

Though committed to the idea of a political community, Habermas is enormously suspicious of the kind of moral or theological totalitarianism which underpins so much contemporary communitarianism. We only exist in real 'social situations', and 'social solidarity' reflects the need to refine the politics of community without infringing the liberty of the individual. Law, he repeatedly asserts, is a matter of politics and power in a social context. Law and politics are mutually 'constitutive', and in a world that no longer believes in universal values, the only means by which the exercise of power in the form of laws can be legitimated is through properly democratic institutions. Central to Habermas's democratic vision is the theory of 'communicative discourse' which is firmly 'embedded' in real 'lifeworld contexts'. The issue of legitimacy is central to Habermas's thesis, such that 'one cannot adequately describe the operation of a constitutionally organised political system, even at an empirical level, without referring to the validity dimension of law and the legitimating force of the democratic genesis of law' (Habermas, 1996, pp 21–27, 285–88, 457).

Law is only legitimate if it is constructed as a result of a broad 'background consensus' fashioned by the discussion of all participants in a community. In this there is, of course, a sharp similarity to Rawlsian ideas of an 'overlapping consensus'. Law will thus be rational, but it will be a rationality constructed by the participants through the very process of participating itself. The importance of 'public spaces' lies in their ability to provide the political structures for these discussions. The elusive notion of 'social solidarity' will ultimately be realised only by effecting a sense of 'reciprocal recognition' amongst citizens for the mutuality of the rights and responsibilities which they have themselves prescribed (Habermas, 1996, pp 3–4, 28–33, 80–81, 110–23, 171–73). But the possibility for such a solidarity always depends upon adequate democratic institutions. The 'success of deliberative politics depends', he confirms:

> ... on institutionalisation of corresponding procedures and conditions of communication, as well as the interplay of institutionalised deliberative processes with informally developed public opinions (Habermas, 1996, p 298).

In such a context, law becomes the:

> ... medium through which the structures of mutual recognition already familiar from simple interactions and quasi-natural solidarities can be transmitted, in an abstract but binding form, to the complex and increasingly anonymous spheres of a functionally differentiated society (Habermas, 1996, p 318).

Law, as enacted in a constitutional order, is the key mechanism through which a radical democracy can be preserved, and the more 'complex' and 'differentiated' the society, the greater the need for a strong constitution which can preserve the principle of democracy (Habermas, 1996, p 373).

In a striking echo of Arendt's writings on the situation of women in the modern world, Habermas uses the issue of gender disadvantage as an example of the need to effect genuine participation in modern democratic polities. Whimsical notions of sex equality written into constitutional texts are of no practical use unless enforced in the real political world. To write a constitutional clause on equal gender rights, without providing adequate democratic institutions within which to realise them, is a classic example of the structural inadequacies of liberal legalism. Liberal rights can only 'empower women to shape their own lives autonomously' if democratic structures 'also facilitate equal participation in the practice of civic self-determination, because only women themselves can clarify the relevant aspects that define equality and inequality for a given matter' (Habermas, 1996, pp 417–20). The situation of women, like all those marginalised and excluded from power in the contemporary world, graphically describes the failure of liberal law and constitutionalism to prevent the 'disintegrating' sense of 'social solidarity' which has come to characterise modernity. The solution, in the final analysis, is to resolve the tension between individual and community, liberalism and communitarianism, by relocating this sense of solidarity as a mean between the alternatives. Rights must be supplemented by responsibility, and the law by institutions of participatory democracy. Accordingly, law:

> ... can be preserved as legitimate only if enfranchised citizens switch from the role of private legal subjects and take the perspective of participants who are engaged in the process of reaching understanding about the rules for their life in common (Habermas, 1996, p 461).

In his more recent work, Habermas has translated his broader critique of modern democracy to the more particular question of the 'new' world order, and especially the European bit of it. The future challenge for Europe in the coming century, he argues, will be the challenge of democracy. As the scale of political communities grows, to over 400 million citizens in an enlarged European Union, the idea of centralised democracy becomes ever less credible. And so, correspondingly, the need for alternative forms of localised, participatory and deliberate democracy becomes all the more pressing. There must, Habermas argues, be a revitalized conception of 'cosmopolitan solidarity' (Habermas, 2001, pp 53–57). In *The Postnational Constellation*, he has again asserted that the politics of the 21st century will be defined by the search for 'appropriate forms' of democracy and citizenship 'beyond the nation-state' (Habermas, 2001, pp 60–61, 70, 76–77). In the specific European context, Habermas argues that:

> If Europe is to be able to act on the basis of an integrated, multilevel policy, then European citizens, who are initially characterized as such only by their common passports, will have to learn to mutually recognize one another as members of a common political existence beyond national borders (Habermas, 2001, p 99).

In this context, Habermas has flirted with an idea of 'global governance'; an idea that has been vigorously presented by commentators such as David Held. According to Held it is possible to conceive a grand global community founded on principles of democracy and self-government, an 'international cosmopolitan' model of governance wherein internal democracy 'within' communities can be reinforced by 'regional and international agencies' that are located 'outside' (Held, 1995, pp 22–23, 236, 267–78). Thomas Franck has similarly appealed to a transnational system of government, one that 'portends to a new global political culture supported by common rules and communitarian implementing institutions' (Franck, 1992, pp 46–47, 79–80, 90). Some kind of 'global civil society' has also been recommended by advocates of a 'third way' political philosophy, such as Antony Giddens and Will Hutton (Giddens and Hutton, 2000, pp 23, 38–39). Habermas is not, however, convinced, preferring instead the idea of a global 'community' described in more 'diffuse' terms, a 'dynamic picture of interfaces and interactions between political processes that persist at national, international, and global levels' (Habermas, 2001, p 110). Time will tell which prophecy is the more acute.

CHAPTER 4

THE POLITICS OF POSITIVISM

THE ORIGINS OF LEGAL POSITIVISM

An age of (un)certainty

Forever cautious for his own health and safety, the 17th century political philosopher Thomas Hobbes became one of the first fitness enthusiasts of the modern age, playing tennis well into his seventies, turning vegetarian, and singing frequently in order to keep his lungs strong. Throughout his life, he remained convinced that men died of too much moisture, eventually drowning internally, and so in order to counter this threat, he spent hours each day deliberately making himself sweat. It is easy today to scoff, but it seemed to work, for he lived until he was 91 (Rogow, 1986, pp 10–12). Hobbes was right to be wary, for the age in which he lived was one of acute and persistent political unrest, caused in large part by the break up of Hooker's tenuous constitutional settlement. By the time he attended university, James I had come to the throne, and by the time Hobbes started to pen his most influential texts, his son, Charles I, had succeeded and was threatening, not just to return the Church of England to a form of high church catholicism, but also to return the practice of government to a more continental form of absolutism. In the years leading up to the outbreak of civil war in 1642, the kingdom slid ever further into a mood of dissension and dispute. England was troubled politically, theologically, economically and socially. But for Hobbes, the essential problem lay in the absence of authority, and this was primarily a matter of government and church.

The constitutional context of these 17th century struggles is central to any understanding of Hobbes and his major political treatise, *Leviathan*. The English constitution was founded on the mythology of the Ancient Constitution, which, in turn, was founded on the common law. It did not enjoy its authority in any founding document or written constitution, but rather in the mists of time, with various ancient Anglo-Saxon princes and long lost tracts. It had been encapsulated in the Magna Carta of 1215 and had found rhetorical support in the tracts and treatises of revered juristic authorities such as Bracton and Fortescue. In the common law tradition, the monarch was ascribed a role within a 'balanced' or 'mixed' constitution, along with the Houses of Lords and Commons. The monarch did not lie above the constitution, and enjoyed no authority outside it. Although he was not subject to the rule of law, he was subject to the constitution. It was this 'balance' which Charles disputed, and which Parliament went to war to enforce. Later, in both *Behemoth* and a treatise entitled *A Dialogue between a Philosopher and a Student of the Common Laws of England*, Hobbes firmly aligned himself with this particular view of the Ancient Constitution. The sovereign was indeed part of the constitutional order, but could not be limited by it. A properly rational theory of the constitution could not support the idea of a 'sovereign' subject to law. Charles lost the intellectual argument, and the war, and was executed in 1649. The country, by all accounts, was stunned, as indeed was Hobbes, who had spent all of the war in exile in France, for a period as mathematics tutor to the future Charles II. He returned in late 1650, apparently invited by Oliver Cromwell to serve as his private secretary, and to design a constitution for the new English Republic. Although there was to be no constitution, Hobbes did publish *Leviathan* as an attempt to provide some sort of constitutional legitimation for the Republic.

Before we turn to *Leviathan*, there is an immediate intellectual context to be noted. Hobbes lived in the age, not just of revolution, but of scepticism, and Hobbes was a confirmed sceptic. In *De Cive*, published privately in 1640, he proclaimed that 'we cannot ... conclude, that any thing is to be called just or unjust, true or false, or any proposition universal whatsoever'. The rejection of universal propositions lies at the heart of philosophical scepticism. Niccolo Machiavelli suggested that law was an instrument of value only in exercising power, and that this is a good thing. In *The Prince* and *The Discourses*, Machiavelli acknowledged that 'knowledge of honest and good things' comes from one source and one source only – the sovereign. He decides what is good and what is not, not God, and certainly not commoners. The overwhelming majority of men and women are 'ungrateful, shifty, simulators and dissimulators', and the one sure truth of politics is that the world is 'inhabited by rational brutes hellbent on ruin'. Subjects need to be ruled because they are quite incapable of ruling themselves. Moreover, the only thing that can guarantee good order is fear. Again, precisely like Hobbes, Machiavelli was convinced that man's natural state of fear could be exploited in order to preserve social stability (Machiavelli, 1961, pp 17–20; 1983, pp 226–33, 252–61; de Grazia, 1992, pp 34, 73–82).

The intellectual ferment which founded this scepticism threw up two alternative, though not incompatible, disciplinary approaches to scholarship. It was Hobbes's achievement to take these alternatives, history and science, and from their conjunction produce a political science of government. His early interest in history was enhanced by a study and translation of the Greek historian Thucydides. Thucydides came to believe that the whole purpose of politics was to prevent warfare, and Hobbes followed suit. It is perhaps appropriate that his very last works, including most obviously his history of the civil wars, *Behemoth*, testified to a continuing interest in the illuminating value of history. Hobbes opened *Behemoth* with the observation that 'There can be nothing more instructive towards loyalty and justice than will be the memory, while it lasts, of that war'. If history in general, and the civil wars in particular, taught anything, it was the ever present danger of civil collapse and the concomitant need for strong government. According to Hobbes, the experience of the civil wars revealed the dangers of rival sources of power within a commonwealth, whether they be clerics, lawyers or those that 'babble' about the philosophy of Aristotle (Hobbes, 1990).

Just as history could be used as an instrument to reveal the fallacies of universal theological and metaphysical truths, so could science. Whilst visiting Geneva in 1629, Hobbes apparently came upon Euclid's *Elements*, and fell 'in love' with geometry. Suddenly, he was convinced that scientific method, which seemed so capable of discovering truths in the natural and physical worlds, could also be applied to discover historical and political truths. And seven years later, he had met the great Italian mathematician Galileo, who had suggested that the earth circulated the sun, an observation which led to his persecution by the Vatican authorities. The threat of science against metaphysics was appreciated on all sides of the debate, and no one was likely to be more sensitive to possible persecution than Hobbes. In early works such as the *Elements* and *De Cive*, he applied scientific principles in order to present an analysis of government stripped of any metaphysical guise. By analysing each constituent part of the legal order, the *Elements* presented the 'true and only foundation of such science ... of justice and polity'. Such a science identified a supreme source of authority from which various arms of government descended. The most striking facet of the code of laws in *De Cive* was its hierarchical nature, as well as its inclusiveness. Every law was authorised by some superior law. Legal positivism has descended from Hobbes's *De Cive* (Johnston, 1986, pp 26–65).

Leviathan and the constitution of humanity

The theory of man's constitution which underpinned Hobbes's theory of the political constitution was founded in his understanding of physical and natural science. As a matter of science, many of Hobbes's ideas were decidedly bizarre, and recognised as such by his contemporaries. He spent all his life producing a series of geometrical 'proofs' for squaring the circle. At the same time, however, he also anticipated a number of future scientific discoveries of considerable import, such as Newton's third law. Against theological wisdom, which suggested that the natural state of everything was static, Hobbes, like Newton, was convinced that the natural state was one of movement, and developed this thesis so that every action taken by an individual is a reaction to some sort of motion against the body. The suggestion that individuals react against immediate physical sensation, and nothing else, was a major to the assumptions of metaphysics and theology. According to Hobbes, the individual has no natural physical propensity to anything, and just reacts to sensations, most particularly those of pain and pleasure. As we shall see shortly, a distinctive utilitarian theory of ethics developed from this basic premise.

Leviathan was published in 1651. The four parts of the book address, in turn, the constitution of humanity, of government, of theology, and of 'darkness'. At its very core is the thesis that government is simply a matter of effective power, and law is merely an instrument of this power – good if effective, bad if ineffective. Law is a matter of politics, not philosophy, and the individual is a political, not a philosophical, animal. Of course, Aristotle had noted that 'man' was a political animal. But whereas Aristotle also thought that he or she had a propensity to the good, and to be contemplative, Hobbes thought that the individual had a propensity to nothing. Left on his own, Hobbesian 'man', in his natural state, was more likely to beat up his neighbour than sit in the sun and contemplate metaphysics. The first part of *Leviathan* is devoted to exploring the character of 'man'. Chapters 1–5 explore the senses, imagination, speech and powers of reason, whilst Chapters 6–11 then examine how men react to one another. Man has two general 'inclinations'. The first of these is self-preservation. The central characteristic is not savagery *per se*, but a violence founded on fear and the desire to preserve the self. Because Hobbes lived his fears and anxieties, he assumed, quite naturally and probably correctly, that so does everyone else. It is fear which destabilises society. Prior to civil constitution, the individual exists in a 'state of nature', and a state, unlike the natural state of Adam which is one of perfection and bliss, of chaos and perpetual strife, 'of warre ... of every man, against every man'. In a famous passage, Hobbes described such a 'state' as one in which:

> ... there is no place for Industry; because the fruit thereof is uncertain ... no Arts; no Letters; no Society; and which is worst of all, continuall feare, and danger of violent death; And the life of man, solitary, poore, nasty, brutish, and short (Hobbes, 1985, p 186).

The second of man's natural 'inclinations' is to exercise power, a 'general inclination of all mankind, a perpetuall and restlesse desire of Power after power, that ceaseth only in Death'. In part, power is exercised in a pre-emptive sense, as a defence against personal danger, 'because he cannot assure the power and means to live well, which he hath present, without the acquisition of more' (Hobbes, 1985, p 161). At the same time, in a related sense, it is also exercised in order 'to obtain some future apparent Good'. Ultimately, in political terms, an individual's value is measured in relation to the degree of power he or she enjoys (Hobbes, 1985, pp 150–51). These two 'inclinations' relate to Hobbes's idea of sensations, and were the most immediate and primitive 'political' reactions; the desire to resist danger, and to do so by controlling others. Hobbes refers to 'appetites' and 'aversions'; the desire for certain things, such as power, and the dislike of others, such as pain and death. Moreover, because 'man' lives in a world of constant motion, he is continually subject to these 'appetites' and 'aversions' (Hobbes, 1985, pp 118–30). His reactions are, at all times, appropriate to this particular calculus of pleasure and pain. This empiricism, which underpins Hobbes's idea of 'appetites' and 'aversions', and which evolves into a distinctive philosophy of utilitarianism, seeks to justify political and legal measures only if they benefit the condition of the majority, as calculated in terms of gross happiness against gross misery. Utilitarianism, and legal positivism, as a response to the theory of happiness as an ultimate measure of effectiveness, run hand in hand, and are both found in their original form in Hobbes's theory of individual personality and the 'constitution' of humanity (Tuck, 1992, pp 168–69).

The final two parts of *Leviathan*, on the role of theology and the 'kingdom of darkness', are intimately related to the theories of both government and humanity, and serve to reinforce the intensely naturalistic, and indeed secular, theory of human nature already asserted. It is here that Hobbes emphasises that his political philosophy is founded, not on theology, but on the individual's natural and civil state. It is the nature of humanity which determines politics, not the nature of some metaphysical illusion. Because 'man' is essentially natural, and not theological, Hobbes suggested that there was no particular need for an institutional religion, certainly no particular religion or theology. In terms of contemporary politics, it aligned with a dissenting 'Independency', the assertion that the State should not prescribe any particular theology, but should, as a secular force, merely preserve religious toleration of all sects. This was seen by many as heresy, and by just about everyone as an apologia for atheism. Thus, although various chapters on witchcraft, demons, and the king of the Fairies, who Hobbes suggested was probably the Pope in disguise, might seem rather obscure and irrelevant today, in mid 17th century England their tone was devastating, suggesting, above all, that theology should no longer be regarded as a credible discipline around which to fashion a public philosophy. In *Behemoth*, as we have already noted, Hobbes attributed much of the responsibility for the civil wars to theological dogma.

Contract and covenant

Leviathan is, then, primarily a text on effective secular and civil government. Effective government depends upon an effective sovereign power. Laws 'without the Sword', as Hobbes declared at the beginning of the second part of *Leviathan*, 'are but Words, and of no strength to secure a man at all' (Hobbes, 1985, p 223). For Hobbes, effective government meant effective monarchy, though it could just as easily be vested in an effective republican leader, such as Cromwell. The actual title, *Leviathan*, relates to the biblical story of the chastened Job, witnessing the power of the Old Testament God in invoking all powerful monsters, including Leviathan and Behemoth, in order to instill fear into man. Law and order would be restored to England, Hobbes clearly implied, if a new Leviathan could be visited upon the land. Cromwell was precisely such a Leviathan. Most importantly, though, the mark of the effective monarch, and indeed the source of his effectiveness, was an understanding that strong leadership comes not from communion with God, but from an appreciation of human character. A strong leader is a bully who knows that bullying succeeds where persuasion rarely can (Hobbes, 1985, pp 81–83). Law, Hobbes affirmed, 'is not counsel, but command; nor a command of any man to any man; but only of him, whose command is addressed to one formerly obliged to obey him' (Hobbes, 1985, p 312). The importance of effective power cannot be overemphasised, and Hobbes's reliance upon it foreshadowed the evolution of legal positivism, and the place of what became known as command theory. It should also be noted that it is precisely this rationale which lies behind Hobbes's strong rejection of democracy as a form of government. Democracy and effective government do not go hand in hand, for history has shown that democracy always tends to 'anarchy', and so the English commonwealth of the future would be best served by making only the merest and most superficial gesture towards the idea of democracy.

In order to move out of the 'state of nature', individuals must establish a 'common Power to keep them all in awe'. Such a power is established by 'contract' and 'covenant'. The idea of a 'social contract' was not original to Hobbes. Continental philosophers such as Grotius had used the idea, and it was common in Protestant, particularly Calvinist, theology to refer to solemn 'covenants' binding consciences to God, and by implication short circuiting obligations to a civil sovereign. But what was most striking about Hobbes was his use of the 'social contract', not to empower the individual, but rather to underline his or her powerlessness subject to sovereign authority (Lessnoff, 1986, pp 1–69). Hobbes's description of the 'social contract' along these lines can be ascribed to the particular historical circumstance within which he found himself. In 1651, with a country in very real danger of falling apart, Hobbes was far more interested in strong government than he was in the niceties of Calvinist theology and any embryonic notions of individual right and conscience. The contract tames humanity's natural inclinations. The passage from the 'state of nature' to a social contract is described as the movement from a 'right of nature', of absolute autonomy, to a 'law of nature', which is a 'generall Rule, found out by Reason, by which a man is forbidden to do that which is destructive of life'. A 'law of nature' can then prescribe a civil law which furthers the possibility of self-preservation. Whereas 'Right consisteth in liberty to do, or to forbeare', the 'Law determineth, and bindeth to one of them' (Hobbes, 1985, p 189). From the first natural law, that humanity 'ought to endeavour Peace', Hobbes can then deduce a second:

> That a man be willing, when others are so too, as farre-forth, as for Peace, and defence of himselfe he shall think necessary, to lay down this right to all things; and be contented with so much liberty against other men, as he would allow other men against himselfe (Hobbes, 1985, p 190).

The heart of *Leviathan* lies in Hobbes's theory of contract, the 'Artificiall Chain' that can hold a society together. In turn, this theory is itself derived from Hobbes's empirical theory of humanity's constitution. Because man lives in fear for his life, it is entirely rational that he should make the necessary sacrifices of his liberty in order to preserve his own safety. The contract is recognition of humanity's need to make such sacrifices in the social situation. Because everyone with whom he lives is a potential killer, 'man' must make some necessary social and political provision. This core idea had been evident in earlier works such as *De Cive*, and in *Leviathan* it is absolutely central. Natural 'right' is 'layd aside, either by simple Renouncing it; or by Transferring it'. The transferral is effected by the contract: 'The mutuall transferring of Right, is that which men call Contract.' All individuals, thus, contract together to transfer their natural rights, and they then covenant these collected natural rights to a designated sovereign (Lessnoff, 1986, pp 49–50; Gauthier, 1988, pp 136–38). Crucially, at no time is the sovereign contractually bound. Rights are covenanted away unilaterally. According to Hobbes, any contractual or conditional restraint on the sovereign would render that sovereign power less than absolute (Hobbes, 1985, p 313).

The process of contract then covenant is of considerable importance. The existence of the contract preserves the individual's civil condition, and prosperity. Hobbes clearly implies that if there had been a strong 'power' in England in 1642, there would have been no need for war. The precise nature of the contract was caught up in the wider constitutional disputes which we have already noted. According to common law, a contract was valid if formally prescribed; in other words there was offer and acceptance and clear evidence of consideration passed. According to the courts of prerogative, most importantly the Court of Chancery, contracts must be equitable, and that degree of equity was a matter for the king's courts to decide. If a contract was inequitable, whether or not it was formally valid, the courts of equity could strike it down (Atiyah, 1979, pp 141–43). In these terms, the contract was itself a symbol of the wider constitutional dispute, and it was, of course, within the context of this dispute that Hobbes wrote *Leviathan*.

The distinction between covenant and contract here becomes vital. A covenant was an agreement to convey an interest in return for some future performance. The promise created an obligation to perform, and equity looked upon this obligation as consideration. So did the common law, but unlike the common law, which would merely award damages for failure to perform, by the 17th century the Courts of Chancery were increasingly prepared to demand performance. When Hobbes described the process of contract then covenant, he chose with deliberation. The covenant conveyed rights subject to effective performance. It was the only condition in the conveyance, but it was a condition, a limitation on the power of the sovereign. In such terms, a failure to perform could void the entire covenant. It is here that the particular context of 1651 is so important. In January 1650, the government of the new English republic decided that every man over the age of 18 should take an Oath of Engagement, which declared that: 'I do declare and promise, that I will be true and faithful to the Commonwealth of England, as it is now established, without a King or House of Lords.' For many royalists, who had taken a similar oath of allegiance to Charles I, the republican demand caused an acute crisis of conscience. Hobbes's definition of the process of contract and covenant was designed to guide them through this crisis, at the same time as stabilising any tendency to disobey the new republican rulers. The failure to perform the covenant rendered it void. Thus, although there is no philosophical or theological constraint on a sovereign, there is a practical one: it had to work. There was no question of any open ended covenant of the theological kind (Hobbes, 1985, p 197). Individuals were perfectly capable of reasoning their own contracts, and the conditions for them, and whilst there was no general right of disobedience, they retained the residual right to a reciprocal breach of covenant if non-performance was such that their very lives were threatened (Hobbes, 1985, pp 196–97).

By the same token, if government was effective, anyone who sought to disobey was acting unlawfully, by definition acting in breach of contract and obligation (Hobbes, 1985, p 191). Accordingly, Hobbes could then proceed to present a very simple definition of justice based on performance of obligations under the covenant: 'And the definition of Injustice, is no other than the not Performance of Contract. And whatsoever is not Unjust, is Just' (Hobbes, 1985, p 202). In this sense, then, obedience was never absolute, but was always subject to the dictates of reason. But there was no question of legitimating disobedience as a general principle. Government, as ever, is a matter of practical reason and politics, not philosophical nicety. Charles I was now dead, and his son could not claim any practical political authority. In such terms, the prior oath of allegiance to Charles was no longer in force, for it had been abrogated by Charles himself, and therefore royalists could subscribe to the 1650 Engagement without any sense of breaching their own earlier covenant unilaterally. That covenant was no longer lawful, and the only lawful covenant was the one taken with the Rump Parliament (Ward, 1993). It was in such a very precise historical context that Hobbes refined his theory of the social contract, and with it laid the foundations for the future development, not just of social contract theory, but also the authoritarian constitutional theory of sovereignty which underpinned legal positivism through the 18th and 19th centuries. As we shall see, it has served to convince generations of jurists that a credible constitution must be possessed of some identifiable, unitary and effective sovereign body or institution.

LIBERTY, ANARCHY AND THE SCEPTICAL MIND

Locke and the Glorious Revolution

A generation after Hobbes, another social contractarian, John Locke, confirmed the particular relation between the jurisprudence of legal positivism and the Whig interpretation of the British constitution as it was apparently confirmed by the 'Great and Glorious' Revolution of 1689. Locke shared Hobbes's underlying scepticism, and, like his illustrious predecessor, was convinced that a modern political theory must break from medieval notions that metaphysics could provide some sort of order and meaning to life. Metaphysics, he remarked to a friend, was simply so much 'fiddling'. There are, he observed in his *Essay on Human Understanding*, 'no innate ideas', and the truth is merely what seems right in the particular circumstances in which we live. The king of Siam, he noted, refused to believe traders' stories of ice, simply because such a thing could not be found in Siam. Truth depends upon the experience of the community which constitutes it. In terms of methodology, again like Bacon and Hobbes, Locke turned to science, forging close friendships with the likes of Robert Boyle and Isaac Newton. Instead of metaphysics, there is science, and our political ideas are always shaped by our individual engagement with political science. As well as a particular intellectual context, Locke also wrote within an immediate political context, dedicated to reassuring middle England that revolution against a particular monarch did not need to threaten its economic or social security. Indeed, he advised, the deposition of James II in the Glorious Revolution of 1688 was designed to enhance its economic and social authority. Not only had James threatened religious freedom and constitutional absolutism, by extension of the royal prerogative, but he had also threatened the economic interest of the landowning middle classes. The immediate threat of oppressive taxation was the ultimate justification for a theory of individual political resistance (Marshall, 1994, pp 270–83). Locke's primary audience, then, consisted of approximately 10–15,000 gentlemen, around 2% of the population; the 2% that just happened to control around 65% of English land and wealth. The Glorious Revolution was their revolution, and the settlement Locke prescribed was designed to confirm their ability and right to govern England for the next three centuries.

Locke liked the middling classes, and liked to think himself one of them. Proud to pronounce his affiliation, he was an appalling snob and social climber, ever eager to impress that he was not just the Earl of Shaftesbury's employee, but also his friend. Not surprisingly, he maintained a particular distaste for the common horde, 'always craving, never satisfied', and as a lecturer in moral philosophy at Oxford during the early 1660s, he warned his students, mostly putative Church of England priests, against the disgusting condition of the average common man (Marshall, 1994, pp 18–32). Not that Locke was particularly inclined to alleviate their economic deprivation, remaining a consistently brutal and exacting absentee landlord of his own Somerset estates. The greatest minds are not necessarily the most enlightened. When he later advocated the importance of education, it was to benefit the middle classes, and not the ordinary man who was predestined, in economic terms, to ignorance and squalor. In 1697, he recommended to the Board of Trade a system of workhouses for poor orphans, within which they could be trained to labour for 14 hours a day in return for 'watery gruel', and to come to realise that such a condition was both natural and necessary (Marshall, 1994, p 324).

Locke's political affinities had already been established at least two decades prior to the revolution of 1688. In his *An Essay Concerning Toleration*, published in 1667, he had firmly aligned himself with minimal government, confirming that the private sphere was always prior to the public, and that government was only justified in so far as it facilitated individual autonomy. More particularly, Locke emphasised that government should play no role in asserting any particular moral philosophy or theology. Religious affinity is purely a matter of individual conscience. This was not to admit atheism. In his *Constitution for the Government of Carolina*, Locke advised toleration for all those except atheists, who should be subjected to the most rigorous oppression. Certainly Locke was right to see that religious turmoil was a prime threat to social order. Yet, consistently fearful for the fragile condition of human and political life, he nevertheless espoused the most radical political and theological ideas, and devoted his life to justifying revolution. The extent to which he was forced into this contradictory stance because of his desire to provide intellectual nourishment for his employer and 'friend', the leading Whig politician, the Earl of Shaftesbury, must remain a matter of speculation. As is ever the case with any political theorist, it is impossible to say with any real certainty how much is the product of deeply held belief, and how much is the result of particular personal circumstance. Though Locke, of course, would have held firmly to the latter supposition. Towards the end of his life, Locke moved ever closer to the radical nonconformist theology of Socinianism, and certainly such an affinity fits the evolution of Locke's own theological writings. It just so happens that it also fitted the theological affinity of Damaris Cudworth, the woman with whom he had gone to live in his declining years and upon whom he was dependent for financial support. Much earlier in his life, Locke had railed against adulterous woman, primarily as an attack against Charles II and his many mistresses, but by the 1690s, he was quite happy to live in an openly adulterous liaison under the same roof as his mistress and her husband.

Throughout his early writings on toleration and freedom, there is one particular consistency, and that is a belief in the dynamics of happiness. An original statement of utilitarianism can be found in Locke's *An Essay Concerning Human Understanding*, in which he aligns it with the sceptical dismissal of 'innate' ideas. In such an intensely empirical political condition, man is driven by reactions to 'two roots out of which passions spring', being pain and pleasure. The efficacy of anything, including government, can be gauged by its relation to these two 'roots'. The whole purpose of government, and the individual's very existence, 'could not but follow happiness', and any pseudo metaphysical notion of 'good' could be stripped down to simply what tended 'to the advancement of happiness'. Ultimately, 'justice is established as a duty and will be the first and general duty of happiness'. Toleration of religious conscience promoted individual happiness, as did limited government, and, most importantly, money. Not only did Shaftesbury impress upon Locke the importance of toleration and limited government, but he also convinced him that the future prosperity of England depended upon its ability to trade, and to trade from secure economic conditions. All political, religious and economic stability depended upon commercial success, and commercial success, in turn, depended on political, religious and economic stability. Locke devoted his life and career to presenting a political theory which could legitimate the Whig politics of his employer, whilst convincing his wider audience that revolution would in fact stabilise their natural right and duty to govern (Dunn, 1969, pp 46–47; Marshall, 1994, pp 65–70, 177–93).

The idea of a liberal constitution

Locke published his *Two Treatises of Government* in 1690, the year following his return to England from exile in France. The first *Treatise* was devoted to a critique of Sir Robert Filmer's *Patriarcha*, which, as we have seen, had provided intellectual depth to the classic Stuart idea of the 'divine right' of kings by justifying the hereditary principle of monarchical government in terms of biblical authority. The absolute right of Filmer's monarch, Charles I, was founded on direct descent from the biblical Adam. Locke, having developed a particular contempt for absolutist monarchy whilst in France during the late 1670s, was determined to refute any pretended justification for absolutism. The idea of Adamic descent, he suggested, was patently absurd. Virtually every monarch was a usurper or descended from a usurper. Indeed, Charles's father, James I, was only the most recent example of a monarch with a decidedly dubious right to the throne. By the time Locke published his *Treatise*, there had been at least two further revolutions and accompanying depositions – of Charles I and James II. Monarchs, he concluded, 'are but men'.

Having dismissed Filmer's argument, the second *Treatise* then presented an alternative 'true origins' of government, at the core of which lies a social contract. However, Locke's contract is very different from Hobbes's. For a start, it vests power in the community, not in any sovereign body, and so the power of Parliament, entrusted by the community, remains held on 'trust' alone and is limited accordingly. Government must always 'move' with the dictates of the majority. Such is the essence of democracy, and such is demanded by the very notion of a social contract (Locke, 1989, pp 165–79). If it does not move of volition, it must be moved by force. If Parliament fails in its responsibilities, it and any monarch who is a constituent part of Parliament can be replaced. A Parliament can always be dissolved, and a monarch removed, without threatening the existence of society. Accordingly, the dissolution of James II's Parliament, indeed the dissolution of his monarchy, was entirely defensible, even laudatory, as was the Convention settlement of 1688–89. This theory of individual resistance is perhaps Locke's most famous bequest to English political thought. It is not a 'licence' for individuals to take up arms and create civil confusion, but it is 'liberty' to appeal to the community for a change of government. The actual revolution will then depend upon the political will of the majority.

Having determined the 'true origins', Locke then addressed an appropriate alternative model of government. The second *Treatise* opened by affirming that the role of government is to facilitate happiness and stability. It should do nothing more, for legitimate government is 'directed to no other end but the peace, safety, and public good of the people' (Locke, 1989, pp 117–18, 182). In terms of political institutions, such a government can be described by certain limits and balances. Most importantly, there must be a separation of powers between the legislative, executive and judicial arms of the constitution. These arms will serve to check one another and to effect the long desired ideal of 'mixed' or balanced government. Not only is Locke writing to legitimate the settlement of 1688, so too is he writing to prevent, or at least advise against, any temptation to vest greater powers in central government in the future. The history of tyranny and despotism must be used to educate against the danger of future tyranny and despotism, and only firmly delimited constitutional powers can preserve Englishmen and their property against any future tyrants. 'Wherever law ends', Locke soberly concludes, 'tyranny begins' (Locke, 1989, pp 190–219).

Providing it does not lose this balance or seek to exceed its limits, there will be a perfect harmony between the institutions of government, as well as between the interests of government and citizenry. In terms of constitutional jurisprudence, there will be a harmony between the private and the public interest. In this, Locke consciously echoes Plato, but whereas Plato tended to align government with natural order, Locke time and again stressed that government is not itself natural. Following Aristotle, Locke emphasised that government is an artefact, something created by humanity and fashioned by humanity, and accordingly, exists subsequent to existing natural rights. Certainly, Locke shared Hobbes's belief that without government, humanity would remain in a state of nature, but unlike Hobbes, Locke did not see government as some sort of necessary evil. Rather, properly limited government represented an epitome of humanity's political abilities, by serving to confirm an appreciation that individual 'liberty' did not mean individual 'licence'. It also meant that individuals appreciated that government was created by them for their benefit, and was not something to which they should ever be 'enslaved' (Locke, 1989, pp 119–28, 179–80).

Paradoxically, at the same time as establishing the constitutional frame for the liberal polity, so too Locke sowed the seeds of a liberal communitarianism, and it is for this reason that Locke is often presented as the intellectual father of the American

Revolution. His is a 'commonwealth' of 'common wealth', wherein everyone's interest lies in the reciprocal respect for political and economic rights. Political liberty brings its responsibilities, and these responsibilities must be educated into the putative citizen. Law is a product of this reciprocal relation between liberty and responsibility, being:

> ... in its true notion ... not so much the limitation as the direction of a free and intelligent agent to his proper interest, and prescribes no further than is for the general good of those under law (Locke, 1989, pp 143, 183).

God requires the individual to take up his political responsibilities. He has driven humanity 'into society', establishing basic family units around the core political responsibility of child and parent, and complementing it with various forms of political community. The parent's responsibility for educating his child (and it was the father's responsibility to provide political education) was a responsibility owed not just to the child, but to the community. It was, indeed, part of the gentleman's wider duty to 'serve' his commonwealth. The tension which is always exhibited in the relation between liberalism and visions of community is present in Locke's discussion of individual infringements against the community interest. The mark of a 'civil society' lies in the ability of a community to legitimate the punishment of offenders, whilst acknowledging the fundamental autonomy of all. Moreover, setting the foundation for the utilitarianism to follow with the likes of Hume, Bentham and Mill, this means that only those infringements which are directed against the persons and property of fellow citizens can be punished. Echoing his earlier essays on religious and political toleration, Locke affirmed that there was never any justification for punishing citizens simply for what they believed (Locke, 1989, pp 154–60).

The paradox of Locke's constitutional and communitarian liberalism is striking, and is one which has served to haunt a series of subsequent liberal thinkers, including, as we shall see shortly, the utilitarians Jeremy Bentham and John Stuart Mill. At the same time, as we saw in Chapter 2, it has continued to force sometimes uncomfortable compromises from Kantian liberals such as John Rawls and Ronald Dworkin. It could be concluded that Locke's theory is a form of communitarian utilitarianism; the maximum freedom of the individual, limited only in so far as necessary for the wider utility of the Christian commonwealth. According to Bertrand Russell, Locke can be presented as the intellectual founder of most modern political theories, from communitarianism to capitalism to utilitarianism to legal positivism (Russell, 1961, pp 605–11). The liberal constitutional State has consistently sought to justify itself in terms of preserving both the politics of a distinct national community and the principle of liberty, and so writing at precisely the time that the English variant of such a confused aspiration came into being, Locke found himself to be necessarily obliged to defend the respective causes of liberty, utility, capitalism and community.

A sceptical justice

The 18th century Scottish philosopher David Hume is one of many who accepted the tenor of Locke's intellectual scepticism, the basic denial of innate ideas. In his *Treatise*, he affirmed that 'mankind' is 'nothing but a bundle or collection of different perceptions, which succeed each other with inconceivable rapidity, and are in perpetual flux and movement'. Both the 'idea' of the self and that of knowledge is entirely contingent (Hume, 1978, pp 1–25, 69–123). Unlike Locke, who remained constantly tempted by religion, Hume accepted the logic of Hobbes's implied atheism. Belief, as a form of knowledge, was itself entirely contingent and unfounded, part of social custom and habit. The counter to theology was enlightenment, and the power of education. The sceptical 'man of sense' must learn to 'judge of things by their moral, unprejudicial reason, without the delusive glosses of superstition and false religion'. The liberating potential of education, advanced by renaissance humanism, was taken on by a number of subsequent utilitarian reformers, including Bentham and Mill. It was education, Hume suggested, that could reorient human love, from its devotion either to God or to self, to the interest of the community. At the root of Hume's political philosophy was a deep belief that humanity must be educated away from a Hobbesian inclination to self-interest. It is a 'just political maxim that every man must be supposed a knave', and politics, ultimately, is about facilitating a compromise between the interests of self and community founded on a common practical 'utility' (Hume, 1966, pp 48–49, 108; 1978, pp 494–95; 1994, pp 11–12, 24).

Not surprisingly, Hume presented a theory of justice which owed far more to a sense of community and fellowship than it did to any notion of intrinsic goodness. In his *Enquiry Concerning the Principles of Morals*, he suggested that any morality, including an idea of justice, is derived 'from taste and sentiment' (Hume, 1966, p 2). As we saw in Chapter 2, it was from this Humean premise that Kant developed his theory of constructive political judgment, and an idea of community was central to Hume, who shared Locke's concern with the 'selfish hypothesis' of acute individualism. Everyone has within 'some spark of friendship for human kind', and as a matter of both sentiment and political expediency, the relative 'happiness and misery of others' cannot be a 'spectacle' of indifference to the political community. Community, though itself an 'artifice', is unavoidable, even desirable, and the interest of the individual lies in the interest of their 'fellows' (Hume, 1966, pp 79, 109–19). Revealing a sharp appreciation of the narrative constitution of a political community, Hume asserted that the strength of such a community lay in its hold over the political imagination. The stability of a society depends upon maintaining certain mythical affinities and identities, none of which accord with any naturalistic idea of reason, but which can be justified in terms of constructive political rationality. The quality of a civilised society lies in its ability to use the 'subtlety of imagination' in order to define politics in terms of community rather than self-interest. In this sense, politics is an expression of 'poetical fiction' (Hume, 1966, pp 21, 49–55, 140; Postema, 1986, pp 126–37).

A second 'artifice', and one which engendered a certain ambivalence in Hume, was 'commerce' and its tendency to 'predominate in society'. Financiers in particular are a 'race of men rather odious' to any community. Being an artifice, commerce is only legitimate if it serves the utility of the wider political community. Accordingly, the fluidity of possession, promoted by the idea of a free trading market, appealed to Hume in that it made individuals further dependent upon each other, and could thus promote a sense of community and fellowship, as well as the spread of knowledge. Yet, the accretion of possessions, and the encouragement of an ethic of self-interest, could be equally destructive of this sense. It was a crucial ambiguity which haunted later political economists such as John Stuart Mill, and, as we shall see, the emergence of utilitarianism complemented, yet also reacted against, the excesses of the liberal idea of the free market. According to Hume, the role of law is to balance these countervailing dynamics and thereby seek to resolve them. All the 'tools' of trade, including the legal mechanics of promise, contract and exchange, are themselves artifices, and enjoy no deeper natural foundation than their utility in regulating the market for the benefit of the political community. According to Hume, the legal contract for future performance is akin to the theological rite of 'transubstantiation', and should be treated with the same critical utilitarian faculty, judged legitimate only if it serves a purpose (Hume, 1978, pp 520–25; 1994, pp 57, 63–64, 93–104, 127–30).

Justice, like community and commerce, is also an 'artifice', legitimated solely in terms of being 'useful to society', and laws should be calculated in terms of their 'public utility'. The 'virtue' of justice lies in its 'necessity' for the 'support of society'. It is its 'sole foundation', and there is no deeper 'morality' of law. Moreover, its validity is dependent purely upon effecting popular acceptance, which can only be achieved if civil laws are seen to tend towards the 'good of mankind'. Here, therefore, Hume refines a utilitarian jurisprudence with an ethical component defined solely in terms of a popular perception of the good of the community. According to Hume, Locke's 'great political defect' was his determination to found society on a right to property. The notion of 'natural rights' is a 'very gross fallacy'. Rights are purely legal, and what is natural is simply that which is useful to the community. Thus, whilst acknowledging that a conception of property founds the idea of political justice, any legal right to property is only valuable if it stabilises relations between individuals. Indeed, civil laws 'extend, restrain, modify, and alter the rules of natural justice, according to the particular conscience of each community'. Thus, the ill distribution of wealth and goods can cause covetousness and be contrary to the interest of particular communities. Indeed, one of the redeeming benefits of a free market is its ability to furnish a redistribution of resources, and moreover, it is the only redeeming benefit of centralised taxation (Hume, 1966, pp 15–45, 116–19, 147–54; 1978, pp 477–91, 505–13; 1994, pp 124–30, 162–63).

Unsurprisingly, Hume was equally sceptical of any notion of law or government being formal or apolitical. Being founded on the 'artifice' of property, law could not itself be justified in terms of natural order. Like Locke, Hume shared a political affinity with the Whig party, and sought to use his particular understanding of constitutional government in order to legitimate the events of 1688. For Hume, being historically contingent, laws were irreducibly political expressions, human constructs described by a constantly changing pattern of social and political interaction. It is, he affirmed, 'on opinion only that government is founded'. If the experience of tyranny was to be banished once and for all, then there must be a popular understanding that liberal democratic politics is about opinion, persuasion and contingency (Hume, 1994, pp 16–27). Although he remained opposed to its foundational tendencies, his account of the historical and political origins of a body of common law played a considerable part in forging an affinity between it, the emergent doctrine of constitutional sovereignty and a complementary jurisprudence of legal positivism (Postema, 1986, pp 81–143). Certainly in terms of methodology, committed to a rational scepticism of natural order, Hume asserted that only science could furnish a proper understanding of political matters, and thus the study of law is a matter of scientific observation and analysis, not moral or theological reflection. The common law is not innate and so cannot be understood in terms of innate moral principles, but is an historical construct which must be scientifically analysed (Hume, 1994, pp 33–34).

In turn, the institutions of government and justice are themselves legitimated only in terms of their utility in facilitating the 'public interest'. The origin of law and government, as Hobbes had instructed, lies in mutual security. However, unlike Hobbes or Locke, Hume rejects any notion of social contract or government by consent. Obligation 'takes root of itself', and is implied by existence within a political community. Indeed, revealing a strongly positivist sense of legal validity, Hume emphasises that law and government are 'entirely useless' unless power is absolutely effective and capable of enforcing an 'exact obedience'. Such an 'obedience' is necessary if government is to fulfil its own utilitarian obligations. At the same time, this does not deny the right to take up arms against tyranny. The 'preservation of public liberty' is the most 'essential to public interest', and Hume could thus articulate the classic Whig justification for the deposition of James II. Politics is a 'perpetual intestine struggle' between 'authority and liberty', and a utilitarian theory of political morality is, by definition, about practical contingent compromise. It was this understanding of politics, as defined in terms of difference and accommodation, which ameliorated Hume's weary acceptance of incessant party factionalism in early 18th century British politics. The British constitution and the 'protestant succession', he concludes, is defined and validated precisely in terms of its facility for political accommodation. Such accommodation defines liberty, and the facility for it defines a liberal constitution (Hume, 1978, pp 534–67; 1994, pp 20–23, 34–45, 186–94, 204–20).

Against the law

There is an implicitly anarchistic streak to the sceptical tradition; something which inheres a very obvious paradox. The same basic political philosophy, of radical utility and liberty, it seems, can promote both the most rigorous jurisprudence, that of legal positivism, and also the most virulent critique of the very idea of law, philosophical anarchism. The nature of the paradox became ever more obvious as the 18th century progressed, and reached something of an apogee in the extreme libertarianism of the self-styled 'friends of liberty' during the 1790s. Fired, in large part, by the example of the French Revolution, the 'friends' loudly proclaimed the case for a similarly radical revolution in England, one that would sweep away all the presumptions of the Whig constitution, its laws and its constitutions. Tom Paine recommended that the English should follow the French and bring their constitutional mythologies 'to the altar' and make 'of them a burnt offering to reason' (Paine, 1985, pp 51–66, 81, 142–43). Even William Wordsworth, in later years a paragon of conservative respectability, urged his compatriots to enjoin the 'dances of liberty'. 'Bliss was it that dawn to be alive' he famously declared in his epic autobiographical poem, *The Prelude*.

The most strident, and momentarily most influential, of the 'friends of liberty' in the early 1790s was William Godwin. To a certain extent, Godwin's family circle is dramatically more famous than Godwin himself. His wife was the great feminist Mary Wollstonecraft. Their daughter was Mary Shelley, the author of *Frankenstein*. His son-in-law was to be the romantic poet Percy Bysshe Shelley. And his social circle was equally impressive. Friends and acquaintances, all admiring, included fellow radicals Tom Paine and John Thelwall, as well as literary figures such as Charles and Mary Lamb, Coleridge and Byron. Anarchy, today, has a bad name. It is deemed to be almost beyond the pale of civilised political debate. But the cause of radical liberty, which Godwin cast as a 'species of anarchy', was a cause that many enjoined in the England of the 1790s. In his *Rights of Man*, Paine had likewise noted that the mark of a 'perfect civilization' would be the absence of law (Paine, 1985, p 165). And it is one that can be placed indelibly at the heart of a distinctively sceptical tradition in English legal and political thought.

Godwin's most influential work was undoubtedly his vast three volume *An Enquiry Concerning Political Justice*. According to Charles James Fox, the parliamentary leader of the radical Whigs, given its density and sheer length, Godwin's *Enquiry* was a book about which everyone knew, and upon which everyone was inclined to pontificate, but which no one had actually managed to read through. It is certainly true that Godwin's *Enquiry* was weighed down by its expectations. As he later admitted, he had ventured upon his great work in the 'vain imagination of hewing a stone from a rock, which by its weight, should overbear and annihilate all opposition, and place the politics on an unmoveable basis'. The observation is telling, not least because it betrayed the sheer utopian confidence that Godwin and his fellow 'friends' shared. For them, the age of revolution was a universal experience, a world without law an inevitable state of human 'perfectibility'. Godwin's own commitment to this latter concept, tied as it was to the broader Enlightenment belief in progress, was unswerving. Progress and perfectibility were guaranteed, if nothing else by the faculty of reason, what Paine famously termed in his essay of that name, 'common sense'. 'Reason', Godwin affirmed in his *Enquiry*, 'is the only legislator, and her decrees are irrevocable and uniform' (Godwin, 1993, pp 395–96).

And if we are all indeed rational, then we must all, Godwin assumed, crave the maximum liberty with which to live our lives. It was for this reason that his dismissal of law and government was so uncompromising. The fifth book of the *Enquiry* opened with the following notorious injunction:

> Above all we should not forget, that government is an evil, an usurpation upon the private judgment and individual conscience of mankind; and that, however we may be obliged to admit it as a necessary evil for the present, it behoves us, as the friends of reason and the human species, to admit as little of it as possible, and carefully to observe whether, in consequence of the gradual illumination of the human mind, that little may not hereafter be diminished (Godwin, 1993, p 206).

And if government is an evil, then so is the law. In time, the 'simple' exercise of 'omnipotent' reason will replace the tyranny of 'positive' laws. In the meantime it is well to remember that 'Law tends no less than creeds, catechisms and texts, to fix the human mind in a stagnant condition, and to substitute a principle of permanence, in the room of that unceasing perfectibility which is the only salubrious element of mind'. For this reason, Godwin continued, 'Every lover of justice will uniformly in this way contribute to the repeal of all laws, that wantonly usurp upon the independence of mankind' (Godwin, 1993, pp 379, 407, 413).

Of course, the dismissal of law cast no aspersions on the idea of justice. On the contrary, Godwin was convinced that the cause of justice lay precisely in this dismissal of law. The Aristotelian tone of his passages on the relation between justice and the idea of the 'good' was undoubted:

> We ought to love nothing but good, a pure and immutable faculty, the good of the majority, the good of the general. If there be any thing more substantial than all the rest, it is justice, a principle that rests upon this single postulatum, that man and man are beings of the same nature, and susceptible, under limitation, of the same advantages (Godwin, 1993, p 441).

Justice is a particular virtue. As Godwin affirmed, there is 'no ingredient that so essentially contributes to a virtuous character as a sense of justice'. But it is also something, as Aristotle advised, which exists only in a relational sense. As Godwin put it, justice is a 'rule of conduct originating in the connection of one percipient being with another' (Godwin, 1993, pp 49, 146). And it is for this reason that Godwin felt comfortable in aligning the Aristotelian premise with the principle of utility advanced by the likes of Hume and Jeremy Bentham, whose ideas we shall encounter shortly. The idea of good or justice that matters is not an abstract idea, but an idea that must work. Whilst the utopian in Godwin urged the goodness of all, the utilitarian recognised that reality suggested that the maximum goodness, and happiness, of the maximum number was a more realisable aspiration.

But what really troubled so many of Godwin's more conservative contemporaries was not just the belief in perfectibility, and the concomitant assertion that a truly perfect world would be one in which justice meant everything, and law nothing. Only the most ardent 'friends of liberty' really articulated such a utopian vision. It was Godwin's defence of democracy that attracted such visceral criticism. Godwin was convinced that rational beings are quite capable of governing their own lives. In a justly famous passage of the *Enquiry*, one which still carries a certain inspirational charge, Godwin held:

> Democracy restores to man a consciousness of his value, teaches him by the removal of authority and oppression to listen only to the dictates of reason, gives him confidence to treat all other men as his fellow beings, and induces him to regard them no longer as enemies against whom to be upon his guard, but as brethren whom it becomes him to assist. The citizen of a democratical state, when he looks upon the misery and injustice that prevail in the countries around him, cannot but entertain an inexpressible esteem for the advantages he enjoys, and the most unalterable determination at all hazards to preserve them (Godwin, 1993, pp 268–69).

The causes of justice and democracy, liberty and anarchy. For Godwin they were, at their conceptual root, indistinguishable.

UTILITY AND THE EVOLUTION OF LEGAL POSITIVISM

Bentham, utility and reform

As both Hume and Godwin in their different ways implied, utilitarianism is defined by its deeply pragmatic concern that a political philosophy must actually work. The politics of utility, accordingly, is founded on the belief that political actions can only be justified if they are indeed of use. During the late 18th and 19th centuries, utilitarianism became increasingly aligned with an identifiable reform movement, and perhaps the most important force in forging this affinity was Jeremy Bentham, a jurist whose positivist affinities were securely founded on a passion for jogging and racquet sports, together with an equally healthy disrespect for the pomposity of the legal profession. It was altogether right, he commented, that lawyers should be 'treated throughout as the scum of the earth and the arch enemies of mankind'. Indeed, the only persons he disliked more than lawyers were priests. Theology, which provided the intellectual fuel for natural rights theories, was, he famously opined, 'nonsense on stilts'. Ideas of law and sanction should not be left to a residual 'fear' of a 'splenetic and revengeful Deity'. Neither should they be constrained by ancient ideas of virtue or honour. In a famously satirical passage in his *An Introduction to the Principles of Morals and Legislation*, more resonant of Nietzsche's visceral distaste than Kant's critical reason, Bentham launched into a critique of all the philosophies of men who imagine themselves on a 'road to holiness' and who want to be 'miserable' (Bentham, 1982, pp 17–33).

However, unlike Nietzsche who, as we shall see, prophesied the collapse of western civilisation, Bentham shared the more optimistic Enlightenment belief in the inexorable improvement of humanity's social condition. Moreover, such an improvement will be effected by marrying the principle of utility with the instrument of law. First, however, the modern world must recognise that natural law is an historical anachronism, an intellectual and rhetorical feint designed to stabilise society against the desirable progress of social, political and legal reform. The cause of legal reform must harness the powers of reason and science. It is significant that Bentham would far rather have trained as an architect than a lawyer, and his infamous model of a reform prison, the Panopticon, was the result of these frustrated architectural ambitions. The design of institutions, within which criminals might be reformed and re-educated, represented an epitome of modern technology. The ideal society, with its ideal architecture, could manufacture ideal citizens, just as his fellow intellectual traveller Adam Smith thought that ideal factory institutions could realise ideally efficient workers. When Bentham was not designing model prisons, he was designing model legal and penal codes, in turn for Greece, the Argentine, Columbia, Grenada and Guatemala. Each politely declined the offer of assistance, though ironically, when Geneva did actually ask for his help in designing a code, Bentham declined, thinking the jurisdiction to be too small to be worth the effort. The desire to employ legal and institutional order to reform both individual and society remained the central concern of Bentham's career. It was for this reason that he recommended that drunkards who commit criminal damage should be made to garden. Gardening, he opined, inclucates an appreciation of order as well as a sense of responsibility. The recalcitrant must be taught the virtue of industry. It was for this reason, likewise, that he advised a fourteen hour day of forced labour.

Like so many reformists, Bentham's politics were in fact innately conservative. He was every bit as troubled by the events of 1789 as Godwin was enthused. If the masses were to be prevented from revolting, something had to be done to relieve their situation. The self-interest which Adam Smith suggested underpinned all human motives and actions had to be realised, and the mechanism for realising it was the law. The value of all laws must be tested against a 'calculus of felicity'. In other words, laws are justified if they add to the sum of human happiness, which can be calculated in terms of the greatest happiness of the greatest number. The very first sentence Bentham ever published stated that 'it is the greatest happiness of the greatest number that is the measure of right and wrong'. In his *An Introduction to the Principles of Morals and Legislation*, the principle was stated in the Humean terms of 'two sovereign masters, pain and pleasure'. It is 'for them alone to point out what we ought to do, as well as determine what we shall do', and it is for 'reason' and 'law' to establish this 'fabric of felicity' (Bentham, 1982, pp 11–13). Even if its motivation was essentially conservative, Bentham's idea of law was progressive and instrumental. Law was cut loose from any innate natural or constitutional moorings, and cast in the service of political reform, not merely a mechanism for stabilising society but a proactive mechanism for reforming society.

If the dynamic of political life is utility, and utility is about making as many people as possible happy, and people are made happy by being satisfied, by becoming affluent and by having money, then the role of law is determined by this political imperative. The 'principle of utility' was dedicated solely to enhancing the happiness and 'interest' of the individual subject, for a political community, Bentham affirmed, was an essentially 'fictitious body' which enjoyed no meaning outside that of its constituent members. All of Bentham's legal and political writings were underpinned by this particular rationale. Though 'fictitious', Bentham's idea of community was pivotal. The principle of utility served to link the interests of individual and community, in the same way as Plato had used the principle of natural order, and Aristotle, virtue. A 'man may be said to be a partisan of the principle of liberty', Bentham affirmed, if his actions are rationalised in terms of the 'happiness of the community' (Bentham, 1982, pp 12–13). It is this residual commitment to an idea of community, even if essentially imagined, which shaped Bentham's critique of the common law. Whilst recognising that any law was, in terms of substance, the enactment of a community political morality, Bentham remained convinced that the form of the law must be rationalised through codification. Rather than providing consistency through precedent, the common law merely served to retard reform by distancing a backward looking law from contemporary society. The common law was 'dog law' and acted as a check against statutory reforms. The recourse to precedent, he suggested, represented a refusal to employ the powers of human reason, and social justice could not be reduced to learning 'maxims by rote' (Postema, 1986, pp 154–55).

Unable to convince the authorities to either codify the law or construct Panopticons, Bentham's most important legacy was to reform the study of law, to rid it of the common lawyer's reverence of 'rights' and to assert in its place the rigours of analysis. According to Macaulay, Bentham was 'the man who found jurisprudence a gibberish, and left it a science'. Law should be understood purely in terms of its utility, and the study of law should have no greater pretensions. The law should enhance the happiness and wealth of people. Thus, penal law must educate the criminal into appreciating the virtues of industry, whilst private law must only enhance the potential for production and the capacity of each economic actor to compete to his or her advantage, and that of the community. As a matter of constitutional jurisprudence, the role of the sovereign authority is not to provide a link with God, but to present a recognisable authority which can found the laws necessary to a reformed and reforming free market society. In *Of Laws in General*, Bentham affirmed that the sovereign in the modern political State must, by definition, have the powers of command and sanction, so that the rational economic actor can be forced, not only to be rational and economic, but also to be free (Postema, 1986, pp 218–62). It is no surprise that the most rigorous of 20th century free market liberals, such as Friedrich Hayek, champion Bentham as the founder of a jurisprudence which dedicated law to the service of the political economy. In this sense, Bentham played a critical role in the evolution of modern jurisprudence, for whilst he may have stripped it of its intellectual pretensions, the turn to analysis in fact represented an acknowledgment that legal theory was fundamentally a critical and interdisciplinary exercise. Law, Bentham affirmed, only existed as a function of something, of liberty, of the market, of social and political reform.

Mill and the politics of liberty

The march of Victorian industrialisation and the increased difficulties experienced in governing it became the pervasive concern of 19th century government, and it was John Stuart Mill who tried hardest, perhaps, to accommodate the countervailing dynamics of the free market, the movement for social reform and the mythologies of liberal legalism. To a considerable extent, Mill's intellectual endeavours were a response to those of his father, James Mill, who was also a committed reformist and close friend of Bentham. James consciously educated his son so as to equip him to continue the reform project. As his *Autobiography* reveals, the young John Stuart was reading Greek at the age of three and writing histories of Rome aged six. Between the ages of four and seven, he recalled walking around Hornsey with his father debating the relative merits of Hume, Gibbon and Roman agrarian laws (Mill, 1989, pp 28–41). His education was indeed prodigious, and Mill remained convinced that the key to unlocking social reform lay with better and universal education throughout Britain. A far better grip of Roman history and agrarian laws, it seemed, would finally realise the emancipation of the British working classes. However, at the age of 23, Mill went through what he termed his 'crisis', precipitated by two 'torturous' problems, the exhaustibility of the possible constitutions of the octave and the 'destiny of mankind'. In essence, he was tormented by the thought that the best possible education, like his own, did not actually ensure any particular improvement either in his condition or in that of society itself.

Mill's enduring influence was secured by the publication of *On Liberty* in 1859 and *Utilitarianism* in 1861. In his *Autobiography*, Mill recalled his early commitment to the need to address the 'defects of the law', along with his determination to follow Bentham in dedicating his life to being a 'reformer of the world', and towards the end of his life, Mill sat as an MP for Westminster, and fought a number of political causes, including female suffrage and the promotion of further parliamentary reform (Mill, 1989, pp 83, 111). What distinguishes Mill's utilitarianism is a determination to emphasise its ethical component. Utilitarianism, he argued, should not be seen as analytical or purely expedient, but as a rich philosophy of life with a politics which was itself 'moral and educational' (Mill, 1989, pp 96–98, 136). Mill suggested that his own 'crisis' owed much to the absence of 'emotion' in Bentham's coldly analytical assumption that humanity could only be estimated in terms of how useful it can be. Bentham, he suggested, was emotionally 'inadequate'. There is more to life than utility alone.

In his 'Essay on Coleridge', Mill suggested that the poet, though an 'arrant driveller' in his political commentaries, better appreciated that happiness cannot be merely analysed with regard to individual estimation. Happiness is not a purely personal experience, but something which only exists in a social context. In other words, our general happiness always depends on others. If only Bentham had liked poetry, Mill concluded, then the utilitarian project would already have effected social revolution (Mill and Bentham, 1987, pp 132–227). *Utilitarianism* set out to address the deficiencies in Bentham's analysis, and to suggest that there could be a moral philosophy even without a natural or theological base. Certainly the core of utilitarianism, the calculus of pain and pleasure, is correct. Any non-metaphysical moral philosophy must be based on a theory of sensory experience. Happiness is clearly subjective, particular to certain conditions relevant to the individual and the community, and there is no natural condition which can ensure it. Any amount of wealth cannot ensure happiness if the individual is about to be hanged, and the most impoverished of citizens could find happiness in personal relations. At the same time, however, society can be fashioned so as to increase the prospects of wealth, decrease the need to commit crimes which might lead to hanging, and increase the conditions for productive personal relations.

The most important mechanisms for improving the conditions of life are law and education, or 'mental cultivation'. People must be helped to be free and to compete, and the first step towards fashioning social conditions in which they can then compete, and by definition participate in society, is the relief of poverty. Poverty must be 'extinguished' by the legislative 'wisdom of society'. At the same time, both law and education must encourage individuals to appreciate that their own best interest lies in enhancing the 'collective happiness' of the wider community. The 'multiplication of happiness' throughout the community is the 'object of virtue' in a utilitarian moral philosophy (Mill and Bentham, 1987, pp 286–91). The great error amongst critics of utilitarianism is to see it as defending the idea of 'self-interest'. Utility, as a moral philosophy, is dedicated to refining the idea of the modern political economy so as to emphasise that any economy is a collective enterprise. The 'social State' is a 'natural condition', without which modern humanity cannot function or realise happiness, and it is only the 'social State' which can ensure the conditions of 'justice' and write the laws which can help individuals to realise this happiness (Mill and Bentham, 1987, pp 304–05). As a matter of jurisprudence, justice is something which exists and is itself determined by immediate social conditions, and so a utilitarian conception of justice is entirely relative. Moreover, justice is also something which exists only in the real practical situation. Ultimately, Mill concluded, justice lies at the heart of the very idea of utilitarianism. The:

> ... principle ... of giving to each what they deserve, that is, good for good as well as evil for evil, is not only included within the idea of Justice as we have defined it, but is a proper object of that intensity of sentiment, which places the Just, in human estimation, above the simply Expedient (Mill and Bentham, 1987, p 334).

On Liberty, which was dedicated to resolving the emergent problem of how to reform society without impinging upon the sanctity of individual freedom, was dedicated to the 'simple principle' of liberty; the necessary requirement for any inquiry, pursuit of truth or political reform. Liberty is not merely a political end, but a prerequisite for the entire utilitarian and reformist project, and Mill opened his essay by stressing that a liberal political theory was necessarily dedicated to defining the nature of the constitution of an entire community. The essay is a study into the 'nature of the power which can be legitimately exercised by society over the individual' (Mill, 1985, p 59). At the root of any political theory there must be a principle of liberty, for unless grounded in liberal principle, law is likely to become the caprice of majoritarian preference, the 'mere likings and dislikings' current in society at the time. Individual liberty can only be legitimately constrained in order to 'prevent harm to others'. The role of law is thus reduced to this and nothing more. If this 'simple principle' is not observed, then history shows us that power can be seized by despots and tyrants. Moreover, the worst and most dangerous form of despotism was not political, but moral; the desire to impose 'opinions and inclinations' on others as ethical 'rules of conduct' (Mill, 1985, pp 69–74).

Liberty was threatened in the modern world, as it always has been, by intolerance. But the danger is all the greater, because the individual is 'lost in the crowd' in a modern world in which 'public opinion now rules' (Mill, 1985, pp 130–31). In such a world there is an ethical void. No one believes in God, yet no one seems to have located an alternative. At the same time, the vast majority do not express any strong aspiration for improvement. Sadly, the majority of people are stupid and lacking in ambition, and it is this twin failing which has led to the moral decline of Britain. In its place, people just want to engage in 'business', and seem only too willing to sacrifice individual liberties in the hope that collectivism will realise greater economic rewards. The political economy has become all consuming, threatening the very fabric of society, and it is in response to this threat that utilitarian liberalism must address its call for educational and legal reforms (Mill, 1985, pp 134–38). The political economy represents both a potential solution to the miserable condition of mankind as well as the greatest threat to individual liberty. But, if the ethical dimension of the political economy is better appreciated, then it can be harnessed as the strongest weapon with which to defend the liberal society. The fluidity of exchange upon which the free market of the political economy depends necessarily frees up social order, promoting movement between classes and interests.

The role of the State must be to preserve this fluidity and to maintain the political conditions for economic and social liberty, and laws must be limited to preventing any economic exchange which might unduly injure another party. But there must be no further interference with the processes of production, exchange or distribution. Accordingly, it is important to refer all such laws to a private sphere, quite apart from the temptations always present in public law to impose constraints justified by spurious moral imperatives. With public law always comes the danger of a 'moral police' (Mill, 1985, pp 139–41, 149–57, 164–65). Aside from the obvious arguments of liberal principle in support of limited government, there is also the matter of efficiency. History has revealed that a society where central power is severely limited is a more productive society, not least because it is a happier society and a happy individual is a more productive individual. Most importantly, such an individual is educated by experience into appreciating that his or her own worth is determined by the worth and condition of the society in which he or she lives. It is certainly no coincidence that Mill consistently referred to the authority of Plato (Mill, 1985, pp 185–87).

Positivism revised

For both Bentham and Mill, the jurisprudence of legal positivism was always secondary to the primary interest in accommodating social reform in the emerging political economy, and utilitarianism provided a philosophical rationale that was dedicated to facilitating this particular and deeply pragmatic ambition. The reduction of legal theory to a purely analytical role, to assess the utility of law as a political instrument, was thus innately critical, though certainly not in the constructive sense suggested by the Kantians. Unsurprisingly, given the political geography of utilitarianism, legal positivism emerged as the dominant influence in English jurisprudence during the 19th century, and indeed retained a certain authority in the 20th. Legal theory is still regarded by some jurists as being an empirical science, the legitimacy of which remains subject to the wider demands of practical utility. In Chapter 6, we will encounter a series of pragmatic and critical theories of law which are founded on this same commitment to empiricism, but which tend to impress the politics of law whilst denying the value of scientific analysis.

An essential conduit in the process of designing a universal positive jurisprudence was Bentham's pupil, John Austin. It was Austin who refined Bentham's positivism and took to heart the need to systematise legal theory. As we noted above, in his *Of Laws in General*, following the authority of Hobbes and Hume, Bentham had clearly demarcated law 'as it is', from law 'as it ought to be'. He had also, again following Hobbes and Hume, redefined the constitution in terms of recognisable sovereign authority, legitimated in terms of commands and sanctions, themselves defined in terms of the 'sovereign masters' of pain and pleasure. In his influential *The Province of Jurisprudence Determined*, published in 1832, Austin adopted this basic schema and sought to refine the particular idea of sovereign authority. It is the 'rapid advancement of science', Austin asserted, that can rid humanity of its nostalgic and irrational 'love of things ancient'. Like Bentham, Austin denounced the idea of natural right as 'stark nonsense'. It was not that Austin denied the possibility of divine law. Indeed, the first sections of the *Province* were devoted to extricating a definition of the 'law of God'. But such laws were not of concern to civil jurisprudence, and any attempt to legitimate civil laws in terms of any deeper metaphysics could only result in the kind of 'muddy speculation' into which predecessors such as Hooker and Blackstone had slipped. Accordingly, like Bentham, Austin rejected the 'senseless fictions' of ideas such as the 'rights of man' or 'unalienable liberties' or 'social contracts' (Austin, 1995, pp 19–20, 38–57, 73, 154).

Law, Austin appreciated, must be understood in terms of pragmatism and power, and so it was utilitarianism which again provided the intellectual authority for any theory of law. Once again, Austin did not deny the deeper ethical components of utility, or its relation to the wider ambitions of political reform. He was as committed to the overriding imperative of the market as Hume, Bentham and Mill, and shared their belief that the law should be used as a political instrument dedicated to maximising the efficiency of the political economy. At the same time, he affirmed that utility was a 'guide to moral sentiment', a mechanism for enhancing the 'good of the individual' and, as a related albeit 'secondary' condition, that of the community. But the components of utility are not the same as those of law. Law is merely an instrument, utility an end. Laws should instrumentally approximate the dictates of utility and moral sentiment, but they need not, and the definition of law must be understood in terms of its formal, rather than substantive, legitimacy (Austin, 1995, pp 51–52, 64–66, 80–99).

Sovereignty is the key concept in Austin's jurisprudence, and its redetermination was premised on these pragmatic and utilitarian foundations. All laws, Austin affirmed, are species of command, which impose 'relative duties' on subjects, and the very first sentence of the *Province* premised that laws 'properly so called, are commands'. Moreover, a command is 'distinguished' by the 'power and purpose of the party commanding to inflict an evil or pain in case the desire be disregarded' (Austin, 1995, pp 10, 21). In order for such commands to be valid, they must be issued by a recognisable authority, the locus of sovereignty, and positive law can be distinguished from 'positive morality' precisely in terms of it being articulated and enforced by this authoritative body. The 'command is a rule of positive morality set by a determinate author' (Austin, 1995, pp 116–24). The role of sanction is pivotal, because it is positive sanction, as opposed to morality or conscience, which enforces real political duties (Austin, 1995, pp 154–57). In the modern political State, then, there is law and legal order if the 'bulk of the given society are in the habit of obedience or submission'. The political State is a 'State of subjection', and the whimsical notion of political freedom, residing either in an individual or a popular body politic, has no practical meaning. Austin advised that any notion of 'limited' monarchy must not be translated into a form of 'political mongrel' which implied that sovereign authority is somehow shared between sovereign and subjects. Sovereignty must be unified in one recognisable body, to which all subjects acknowledge their subjection. Interestingly, Austin justified this uncompromising position in terms of the overriding interest of the 'common weal' against that of the individual subject. If liberalism and the idea of the free market provided the impetus for utilitarian philosophy, then the practicalities of the liberal community define political and legal sovereignty. The individual interest, and the happiness of each subject, can only be effected through the recognition of the political community, for political sovereignty and political community are 'bottomed in the principle of utility' (Austin, 1995, pp 166–72, 183–200, 223–26, 244–47).

Austinian jurisprudence retained a dominant position in English legal thought throughout the 19th century. It found a famous expression in Albert Venn Dicey's *An Introduction to the Study of the Law of the Constitution*, with its strident assertion that the Briitsh constitution could be understood solely in terms of a system of rules deriving their authority from one supreme constitutional principle, parliamentary sovereignty (Dicey, 1959). A generation later, the banner of positivism would be taken up by Herbert Hart, whose critique of resurgent natural law was discussed in Chapter 1. In his *The Concept of Law*, Hart attempted to marry the shared analytical ambitions of Austinian and linguistic positivism. In the final chapter, we will take a look at various theories which suggest that law, like any other idea or concept, must be understood as a form of language. Linguistic positivism, as articulated by the early Wittgenstein, sought to found the meaning of ideas in linguistic use, and Hart remained convinced that law could, moreover, be stripped down to basic linguistic and conceptual meaning, and that such an exercise was the proper discipline of legal theory. Accordingly, what is perhaps most interesting about Hart's *The Concept of Law* is what is absent. Although much of it is directed towards refining Austin's idea of command, and adopts Austin's particular determination to impress the critical limitations of legal theory, there is no trace of any deeper political or utilitarian justification. Hart's notorious admission of certain 'truisms' of 'human nature' – such as vulnerability, approximate equality, limited altruism and resources and limited understanding – was a descriptive rather than conceptual gesture (Hart, 1961, pp 189–95). There is no prescription in *The Concept of Law*. The theoretical study of law is simply a matter of analysis and identification, and though the methodology may be critical, it does not actually serve any deeper purpose.

The revision of Austin's command theory concentrated on the need to distinguish specifical legal commands from wider general commands. Law could not, Hart asserted, be reduced to mere command, but has to be legitimated in terms of a sovereign authority. Though Austin had acknowledged the importance of sovereignty, he had not sufficiently determined the alternative forms of command. There is, therefore, a fundamental difference between being under a legal 'obligation' to perform a duty and being 'obliged' by some illegitimate force to perform an act (Hart, 1961, pp 18–48, 80–81, 86–88). Like Austin's sovereign, Hart's was identified by the absence of any 'legal limits on his law creating power' (Hart, 1961, pp 64–65). The ability to identify the sovereign authority is pivotal, and expresses Hart's particular ambition to provide a foundation for the law, albeit a necessarily political and pragmatic one. There is, thus, a 'rule of recognition', an 'ultimate' rule, which can be used to identify the locus of supreme sovereign authority, and the validity of all laws can only be 'assessed' in relation to it. This rule and process of recognition, Hart suggests, describes the 'foundation' of law, and there is nothing deeper for which a jurist should search (Hart, 1961, pp 92–93, 97–114).

It is Hart's sovereign, accordingly, which founds the meaning of a legal order, just as Wittgenstein had hoped that the individual word could found the meaning of a particular communication. Of course, the problem lay in identifying the sovereign power, and it was this which generated Hart's desire to refine the idea of command. Indeed, Hart was himself critically aware that the indeterminacy or 'open texture' of language militates against precise meaning in a legal order. A rule, he perceptively acknowledged, is more than the simple sum of its words, but operates within a contextual 'penumbra' of meaning. Accordingly, the duty of the jurist is to explore this penumbra and to seek clarity of meaning, aware that it, too, is a matter of process rather than resolution (Hart, 1961, pp 121–50). Thus, if there is, ultimately, a deeper purpose in jurisprudence, it lies in effecting the exercise of political power by clarifying the relation between subjects and sovereign. The concession to effective identifiable power, and the denial of the need or desirability of legal theory to search for deeper intellectual legitimacy, is what ultimately defines legal positivism. It is not a concession explicitly made by utilitarians such as Bentham, Mill or even Austin, but it is a logic admitted by Hart. If critical legal theory is characterised by a desire to dismiss the possibilities of metaphysical foundation, then legal positivism, in its determination to restrict legal theory to the matter of description rather than prescription, is perhaps the most critical theory of all. The formalism sought by Hart is one determined purely by contingent political relations, and is devoid of any deeper rationalisation. This is not to condemn Hart's analysis, but it does serve to emphasise the nature of its self-imposed limitations. It is also to suggest that there is an inexorable logic that stretches from the political scepticism of Hobbes and Machiavelli, through that of Locke, Hume and Godwin, and through the attempts of Bentham and Mill to establish an intellectual legitimacy in utilitarian ethics, and which arrives finally in a jurisprudence which abandons any notion of legitimacy which rests deeper than the effective exercise of authority.

The search for a general jurisprudence

Whilst the age of analytical positivism might have finally passed, the universal assumptions that underpin Benthamite and utilitarian legal thought have recently been revisited by jurists in search of some kind of 'general' jurisprudence. It is suggested that such a jurisprudence might be able to furnish a coherent account of law in our 'new', and possibly postmodern, world. The leading advocate of such an approach is William Twining. In his *Globalisation and Legal Theory*, Twining admits that whilst the arrival of this 'new' world order might appear to demolish all universalist pretences common to the various modernist theories of law, classical, Kantian or utilitarian, in fact our 'increasingly cosmopolitan' world makes the 'revival of a more general jurisprudence' all the more timely. More than ever, Twining ventures, 'We need jurisprudence that can transcend jurisdictions and cultures, so far as that is feasible and appropriate, and which can address issues about law from a global and transnational perspective' (Twining, 2000, pp 3, 49). Making sense of what law appears to be, and how it works, is not the same as positing some grand unifying theory that seeks to suggest that law is everywhere the same, or that it should be. There is, very clearly, an empirical pull in Twining's search. Its methodology is obviously comparative, focussing upon identifying certain common principles, and perhaps more importantly common practices, across apparently disparate legal regimes. As he confirms elsewhere, 'we are in an important sense all comparatists now' (Twining, 2002, pp 99–100). The comparative approach, of course, is premised on the assumption that there is something common to be found. As we shall see in Chapter 6, there is a very clear resonance with the attempts of American realists during the first part of the last century to investigate legal institutions and practices elsewhere in order to better inform debates surrounding legal reform at home. This time, however, it is not a matter of effecting reform at home, so much as trying to make sense of the world out there.

It is an aspiration which, Twining alleges, lay at the heart of Bentham's jurisprudence. Bentham's search for a 'general' jurisprudence explicitly 'recognised the existence of law at multiple levels from the very local to the world as a whole', including, Twining adds, 'something that looks remarkably like non-state law'. As such, Benthamite jurisprudence immediately lends itself to our supposedly postmodern age. Indeed, the 'modern Benthamite' is, Twining affirms, a true 'citizen of the world' (Twining, 2000, pp 65–66, 102). The reason, in simple terms, is that whilst the assertion of a 'general' jurisprudence might seem to be rather bold, in truth Bentham did not aspire to do too much. Declining to look for universal theories of justice, he settled instead for commonalties of practice, commonalties that could be experienced and seen. A 'general' theory of legal practice or social utility can, in short, be evidenced, perhaps even proved. According to Twining, it can be 'mapped' (Twining, 2000, pp 137–40). A theory of natural justice, in contrast, can only be surmised. This is very probably so. But as with the fate of analytical jurisprudence, it leads to a simple but not very satisfying conclusion. Whilst various peoples might appear to resolve or adjudge legal disputes, what realists term the 'law job', in a broadly similar way, such observations do not equip us to make any kind of normative judgment about how we might best live our lives, or how the ideas of law or justice might help us to do so. The same self-imposed limitations apply to Twining and Bentham, as they did to Hart and Austin.

More recently, the search for a revitalised 'general' jurisprudence has been enjoined by Brian Tamanaha. The aspiration of his *A General Jurisprudence of Law and Society* is to identify and analyse all the 'elements and concepts common to all systems' of law. It is, once again, a necessarily comparative exercise. It is also rigorously positivist in that Tamanaha explicitly denies any kind of 'mirror' theory, by which law might be thought to reflect, or even be the product of, social dynamics or conditions, as well as any suggestion that the concept of law must have some kind of normative, even moral, component (Tamanaha, 2001, pp xiii, 154–55, 209–11). And equally inevitably, it leads to what can only be termed a very 'thin' conception of law. By the time all the complexities have been simplified, all the subtleties removed, all the social dynamics cast aside, there is not, for obvious reasons, much left (Twining, 2003, pp 238–41; Guardiola-Rivera, 2003, pp 794–97). There is, of course, a system of rules. And for the avowed Austinian this is pretty much all there needs to be, provided the system is broadly coherent and the rules can be effectively commanded and enforced. But if we want to conceive of a legal order as something more than a mere system of rules, then Tamanaha's account will disappoint. Once again, we find ourselves at the same position: recognising the validity of the positivist account of systems of legal rules, but wondering what the point is. We might be able to devise a 'general' jurisprudence that is sufficiently thin to account for the challenges of the 'new world order', or indeed any other order. But it will not help to understand all the intellectual complexities that define the idea of a critical theory of law.

It is for this reason that Twining has more recently urged that a 'general' jurisprudence, to have any real critical value, must embrace an element of normativity, a way of making a qualitative distinction between different kinds of legal systems, the 'enormous range of networks, coalitions, alliances, diasporas, and groupings that are an increasingly prominent feature of the contemporary world'. It is for this reason that a more Benthamite, as opposed to Austinian, jurisprudence is appropriate. Bentham's jurisprudence, designed for the 'citizen of the world' can take account of 'differentiated' legal orders, whereas Austin's more rigorous variant, like Dicey's too, presumed that there could be no coherent legal order outwith the modern nation-state. A 'general' jurisprudence, if it is to be useful and appropriate, must be conceived in terms of cosmopolitan, rather than statist, legal orders (Twining, 2002; 2003, pp 243–46). This is undoubtedly true. But the thicker that a 'general' jurisprudence aspires to be the more it risks being corrupted by the pluralism that characterises alternative Kantian and post-modern attempts to 'map' law at the beginning of the 21st century.

CHAPTER 5

LAW AND THE POLITICAL ECONOMY

THE CHALLENGE OF POLITICAL ECONOMICS

Locke, property and the free Englishman

According to the eminent economist Alfred Marshall, economics is 'a study of mankind in the ordinary business of life'. We are all economists to some degree, for we all shop, bank, get into debt. We all manage our own personal finances, even if we do not participate in politics or muse for too long upon the mysteries of life or metaphysics. Just as law plays a pivotal role in shaping our politics, so does it both fashion and then serve our dominant ideas of economics. Aristotle, as we have already noted, reduced economics to the service of ethics. Property, he suggested, is justified in so far as it better facilitates the pursuit of a good life. It was for this reason that he was so critical of usury, which he saw as contrary to the virtues of charity or industry. It was a philosophy which endured during the middle ages, and it was only towards the end of the period that a distinctive economic science began to emerge. Nicole Oresme wrote the first tract suggesting that control of money was a responsibility of government. The suggestion that some sort of free market might operate against the established tenets of classical moral philosophy or indeed the benefit of the wider community took increasing hold on the late medieval and then early modern imagination, and the result was the idea of a political economy.

Before taking a look at the more mature theories and critiques of political economics, we should return again to the Lockean settlement of the late 17th century, for it was this settlement which sought to align the idea of property with political liberty. For Locke, property is a matter of natural right, and in such terms precedes any subsequent political institutions or laws. Property is superior to law, and law, in turn, is only justified in so far as it protects and does not threaten these natural rights. The facility of happiness and stability was necessarily coincident with the protection of property and possession. In the second *Treatise*, Locke affirmed that the entire rationale which lay behind the 'original compact' is the need to unite in order to preserve 'lives, liberties and estates'. The preservation of estates is the 'great and chief end' of government (Locke, 1989, p 180). Property rights underpin political rights, and political rights serve to illustrate and preserve property rights. Although it was not a matter of metaphysics or any kind of innate intuition, in his *Essay Concerning Human Understanding*, Locke had already asserted that the right of property was of a form of 'morality' that was 'capable of demonstration'. In other words, we can experience that possession is a good and a matter of justice and right.

The natural right to property founds the political right to liberty, for if we own things, we experience liberty. The political philosophy of the *Treatises* is founded upon precisely this theory of property, and Locke emphasises the natural, indeed theological, authority for property ownership. God, he suggested, gave 'the world to men in common'. But he only did so on condition that they used it, and it is the 'use' of land which legitimates its apportionment to particular individuals. Appropriation of land is justified by the very fact that we need to eat to survive. Writing in the particular context of radical Whig opposition to slavery, Locke emphasises that, most obviously, we all have property in the possession of our own bodies. Of course, non-institutionalised slavery was fine, and Locke was happy to exploit the labourers on his own estates, just so long as they maintained the nominal right to walk away from his employment and starve themselves to death instead. Just as the constitutional settlement of the *Treatises* was aimed at the middling interest, so too was Locke's theory of property. It was never intended that the common horde should hold land, at least not as anything more than insecure tenants. Their existence was necessarily one 'but from hand to mouth', their needs limited to 'victuals', clothes and the 'tools' necessary to 'use' the land.

Concentration on the 'use' of land introduces a particular context which lay at the heart of modern theories of political economy, the 'labour mixing' theory. Our right to possess something comes about from our work upon it, for 'it is labour indeed that puts the difference of value on everything' (Locke, 1989, p 136). We mix our labour with the thing itself, most obviously by working on land. The theory enjoyed a very obvious and immediate affinity with the protestant culture of the work ethic. Humanity was called by God to work for the benefit of itself and the commonwealth. Towards the end of his life, Locke became convinced that he had not worked sufficiently hard, either for himself or for his fellow citizens, and so put in a minimum of three hours' hard labour a day, together with frequent jogging and games of tennis. We liberate ourselves through ownership of goods and property, and in such terms only do so through industry and endeavour. Indeed, it is the hallmark of the free Englishman that he devotes himself to creative industrious pursuits. The free Englishman is defined by his ownership of land and goods, and in such terms Locke can affirm that:

> God gave the world to men in common, but since He gave it them for their benefit and the greatest conveniences of life they were capable of drawing from it, it cannot be supposed He meant it should always remain common and uncultivated.

Rather, he 'gave it to the use of the industrious and rational (and labour was to be his title to it); not to the fancy or covetousness of the quarrelsome and contentious' (Locke, 1989, pp 132–37). God intended the harder worker to be the richer. But what God does not appear to have contemplated is the prospect of scarcity, that there might not be enough to go around. If someone starves to death, it is not because there is simply no food. It is because they are indolent. Lack of food, like lack of property, is not misfortune, but negligence. At the same time, God does not appear to have thought quite enough about greed. Reason dictates that individuals will only want to possess what they need, a 'very moderate proportion'. Locke, however, did think about scarcity and greed, and the reason for it, he concludes, is money (Locke, 1989, pp 134–35).

It is here, of course, that Locke can be distinguished from political economists to follow, such as John Stuart Mill and Friedrich Hayek. Whereas Mill and Hayek will see the political economy as a means of preserving a particular theory of politics and government, Locke sees it as a primary threat against social and political order. For Locke, fixed property rights found the constitutional order, and they alone. It was for this reason that he consistently advised against the alienation of property. Of course, law must not prevent a free Englishman from selling his own property, but its greater and primary responsibility was to protect property by fashioning social and economic conditions where such alienations were not necessary. It was inconceivable to Locke that anyone should want to alienate property, unless forced to do so by adverse economic conditions. The political economy is something that must be constrained, by law, rather than merely let loose to fashion a polity for itself. In an essay on the *Value of Money*, Locke affirmed that, whilst trade was a conditional good, the interest of the landholder 'is chiefly to be taken care of, it being a settled and immovable concernment in the common wealth' (Marshall, 1994, pp 165–73). In the second *Treatise*, he asserted that the 'great foundation of property' lies within the individual. It does not lie in the gift of law or government. In turn, all laws are valid in so far as they serve this 'foundation' and do not threaten it. The preservation of property rights against government is the first of two justifications for law. When discussing the 'extent of legislative power', Locke affirms that, as preservation of property is the true 'end of government' it would be absurd if government was to threaten it. Accordingly, government has no right to arbitrary seizure of property or taxation. Such abuses of private property are characteristic of absolutist governments and tyrannies (Locke, 1989, pp 188–89).

If the first justification for law is to preserve property against an avaricious government, the second is to preserve it against avaricious fellow citizens. The civilised 'community' has a primary duty to protect property against the ravages of the political economy. The necessary laws which serve to 'regulate the properties of private men' only do so in order to preserve the principle of property against those who suffer from a 'scarcity' of money, and are only valid as products of free 'compact and agreement'. In terms of jurisprudence, the same model of contract governs both the public and the private spheres. The emergence of monied economies validates the need to fashion laws of property, and does so in order to serve the deeper principle of property upon which the entire constitutional order is founded. So, by consenting to the idea of a political economy man has consented to 'unequal possession', but has done so only in so far as it does not threaten the sanctity of property itself as a symbol of fundamental individual liberty (Locke, 1989, pp 138–41, 188–89). It is in this way that Locke hopes to preserve the principle of property at the centre of political and constitutional theory, whilst accommodating the countervailing idea of the political economy. Accordingly, it is also in this way that he hopes to ease the worries of the landed gentry of middle England with regard to the security of their estates, whilst legitimating their endeavours to make even greater wealth from the emerging and clearly irresistible strength of the international political economy.

The idea of political economy

It can be argued that the mercantilist era, with its control of trade in order to stabilise and secure property holding interests, finally gave way to the economics of the free market in 1776. It was in 1776 that the American colonies revolted against their political masters in Britain, championing the cause of individual liberty against the interest of the British mercantile and governing classes, and it was also in 1776 that Adam Smith published his *An Inquiry into the Nature and Causes of the Wealth of Nations*, which fervently argued against governmental intervention in the development of the political economy. The most efficient economies, it suggested, are those which run themselves, without any public policy direction, and within which individuals enjoy a maximum liberty to pursue their own self-interest. The politics of liberty coincided with the economics of efficiency. In his *Theory of Moral Sentiment*, Smith aligned himself firmly with the dominant scepticism of Locke and Hume, suggesting that there was no such thing as innate ideas or 'moral judgment', merely sensational responses and reactions. Ultimately, the theory of 'moral sentiment' becomes a theory of individual response and self-interest. Politics, and law, is a matter of how individuals react with one another. It is not simply what is legislated by government. At the same time, Smith was not prepared to abandon the reality of a community. Free individuals still live in communities, but rather than being bonded together by love or reason or God, they are actually bonded by an empirical 'sensation of sympathy'. Any community must promote this 'sensation of sympathy', otherwise it will simply disintegrate. 'Humanity', he famously acknowledged, 'does not desire to be great, but to be beloved' (Smith, 1976b, pp 25, 85, 166; cf Ross, 1995, pp 98–194).

At the heart of Smith's theory of political economy can be found the key constituents of free market economics. First, derived from this theory of 'sentiment', and in the place of humanist theories of individual nature, there is a basic assertion that people do things in order to improve their lot in the world. Self-interest always precedes community interest. It 'is not from the benevolence of the butcher, the brewer, or the baker, that we expect our dinner, but from their regard to their own interest. We address ourselves, not to their humanity but to their self-love'. A free political economy runs itself because it expresses everyone's desire to be free to promote their self-interest. Smith terms this the 'invisible hand' of the market. Carried to its extreme, he suggested that a free market utopia would be free of any government regulation. In such a market, every man:

> ... as long as he does not violate the laws of justice, is left perfectly free to pursue his own interest in his own way, and to bring both his industry and capital into competition with those of any other man, or order of men (Smith, 1976b, Book 4, Chapter 9, p 51).

Paradoxically, for someone who was to end his working life as a customs and excise officer, Smith advocated that although smuggling might be unlawful it was not unjust. No form of economic exchange or trade of goods was intrinsically unjust. In a true free market, 'all duties, customs, and excise should be abolished' and 'free commerce and liberty of exchange should be allowed with all nations and for all things' (Ross, 1995, pp 318–22).

If this self-interest provides the ethic of the free market, the mechanics can be described in terms of prices, labour and competition. The value of something is never natural. In other words, there is no 'just price' for anything. Rather, the value of something is simply the price it can realise on an open market; the 'real price of everything, what every thing really costs to the man who wants to acquire it, is the toil and trouble of acquiring it' (Smith, 1976b, Book 1, Chapter 5, p 2). Values and prices can thus change dramatically from one situation to another. Labour and competition have an immediate effect on this theory of value. The wealth of a nation is written in terms of its industriousness. Smith was a confirmed Presbyterian, and clung to the idea that the godly protestant community is sealed by the participation of each and every citizen in promoting industry and wealth. Every 'man', he observed, 'lives by exchanging, or becomes in some measure a merchant' (Smith, 1976b, Book 1, Chapter 4, p 1).

Importantly, this wealth is immediately increased by a reduction in costs. The lower the costs, including wage and labour costs, the greater the profit. The ethic of self-interest demands an element of profit for the land or factory owner, and thus denies, once again, any more primitive notion of a natural price of something consonant with the value of the labour expended upon its production alone. There must always be a profit, otherwise no one will bother to invest either money or energy in the production of anything, and the common wealth of the nation is therefore realised by the competition of the individual rational economic actors who constitute it. Crucial to the competitiveness and efficiency of the individual, and thus the community, is the expedient distribution of effort. In a renowned passage in the *Wealth of Nations*, Smith recorded his impressions upon visiting a pin factory, realising at first instance the added productivity effected by the division of labour. Better that a worker should perfect one particular task on a production line of pins, than try to make the whole pin. The regimentation of the factory, in the cause of efficiency, is as acceptable as the regimentation of the economy by government is not. The factory will realise its own mechanisms for enhancing its competitiveness. It was the replication of this regimentation which, as we shall see in Chapter 6, has led the likes of Michel Foucault to describe the modern world as one large production unit. In the modern political economy, the market replaces the commonwealth and the factory the church.

Between the publication of the *Wealth of Nations* and the writings of John Stuart Mill in the mid 19th century, the idea of the political economy took centre stage in national intellectual life. In his *Essay on the Principle of Population*, Malthus warned that population increase threatened the social and economic fabric of the modern world (Galbraith, 1991, pp 77–80). A wealthy London stockbroker, David Ricardo, advocated the importance of free markets within which individuals, or at least a handful of them, could become wealthy London stockbrokers. Stripping away any vestiges of 'sentiment' from Smith's thesis, Ricardo's 'iron law of wages' determined that there must be a large surplus of people at the bottom of society who, through necessity, can be made to work for the minimum necessary wages, sufficient for subsistence and nothing more. Poverty and exploitation are natural, and indeed necessary in a competitive and free world. There will be no self-interest, or 'invisible hand', if everyone has all they want, for in such a situation, the supply would have exceeded demand, and no one would bother to produce anything at all. Ultimately, no one would need wealthy London stockbrokers, because everyone would have all they needed, and no one would bother to invest and speculate in markets. Extreme wealth, like Ricardo's, depends upon extreme poverty. The only thing which could disrupt this 'iron law' or 'natural price of labour' was ill judged governmental legislation, which, Ricardo emphasised, 'should never be tolerated' (Galbraith, 1991, pp 81–85).

Mill and the principles of political economy

As he emphasised in *On Liberty*, John Stuart Mill accepted both the inevitability and the desirability of a free market political economy. It was inevitable and necessary because it was the most efficient way of creating wealth, and it was desirable as the only way of preserving political liberty. Yet the purely economic resolutions suggested by such as Ricardo were wholly unacceptable to Mill. Exploitation, starvation and misery were not natural products of the free market but rather evidence of an immature market in need of further refinement. In the various editions of *Principles of Political Economy* and later in his *Chapters on Socialism*, Mill tried to accommodate the tension which lies between the need to permit the exercise of the free market and the demise of those who fail to compete effectively. Against Ricardo's suggestion that markets can be stabilised through the 'iron law of wages', Mill suggests that a reformist theory of political economy should be devoted to releasing the productive capacity of each individual. A process of natural evolution is inevitable in a free and competitive market. Standards will improve, and so, accordingly, will the productive capacity of the individual. Competition, rather than suppressing wages, will actually promote social and economic fluidity. If a market stabilises, capital will always gamble its investments in order to increase profit. At root, therefore, Mill was committed to the belief that a free market will always militate against stabilisation, and, moreover, that this is a good thing, because a free market secures individual liberty. The political economy is always a means to this particular political end, and it is this which makes the role of government in the economy the most 'keenly contested' question in the 'present age'.

Certainly, Mill appreciated the potential importance of law in a political economy, and followed Locke in affirming that it must protect the interest of the economic actor and property holder. At the same time, the political economy is a public activity in which everyone has an interest. Government intervention is, therefore, justified, but only if it is 'conducive to general convenience'. Obvious examples of justified intervention include: regulating monopolies and price fixing; acting against freeloaders in co-operative arrangements; ensuring basic subsistence for all; the financing of public goods, such as universities, the 'learned class', such as Mill himself, geographers and explorers, who can find colonies to be exploited, and public utilities, such as roads, hospitals and lighthouses. These examples of government intervention are 'necessary' or 'authoritative'. Other suggestions are merely 'advisory', and should be *prima facie* capable of dispute (Mill, 1994, pp 159–65, 311–16, 363–65). Whilst government can preserve the conditions in which a free market can flourish, it enjoys an even greater capacity to destroy both political liberty and economic efficiency. As Bentham had shown, English law has consistently erred on the side of excessive stability, reducing the capacity for property exchange in particular and restricting the market. The extent to which property was entailed through trusts was the most obvious example of the law acting against the interests of the free market, and thus the wider community interest. Similar examples of overprotective legislation included the laws of partnership, laws relating to commercial transactions and credit, and property contracts (Mill, 1994, pp 260–64).

Taxation was an area of particular sensitivity. Some degree of taxation is necessary for government to function and to preserve the conditions of a free market. But the degree of taxation will always be open to dispute. Mill personally favoured a proportional taxation, payable in accordance with income and capital capacity. Such a system is necessarily redistributive to some degree, and fulfils the ethical demand for 'redressing the inequalities and wrongs of nature'. So, as a particular example, property tax is desirable in order to mitigate the 'inequalities of wealth'. At the same time, however, government must guard against tax which is so punitive as to act to the detriment of the community as a whole. Thus, specific taxes on profits can be in no one's interest, and are 'extremely detrimental to the national wealth'. As an example, Mill used the corn laws, a matter of considerable contemporary political and economic debate. Excessive taxation on corn importation had merely resulted in the creation of artificially high prices, with the tax burden passed on to consumers. Accordingly, fewer farmers bothered to produce corn and fewer traders imported it because it was too expensive. The poor merely starved to death. Taxation, he concluded, must never discourage production or trade (Mill, 1994, pp 167, 265–93).

The uses of revenue raised leads Mill into the most politically controversial area: improving the condition of the workers through educational initiatives and supporting co-operatives. Both enterprises will better facilitate the ability of the individual to compete in the 'business of life' and to take responsibility for self-government and improvement. It is the basic fact of political economy that 'individuals are the best judges of their own interest' (Mill, 1994, pp 317–22, 332–52). Yet, at the same time as advocating the redistribution of resources in order to facilitate the better social condition and happiness of the majority, Mill is acutely aware that he is recasting the relation between the 'simple principle' of liberty from moral ideology. In retrospect, it can be seen that Mill's struggle with socialism is a defining moment in modern political thought. The free market is taken as inevitable, but there has to be some mechanism for preventing the fragmentation of communities and societies encouraged by open competition and exploitation. In his *Autobiography*, Mill aligned himself with the 'general designation of Socialists', whilst declaring himself against the 'tyranny of society over the individual'. Socialist 'combinations', such as unions, were a potential threat to freedom, not least because the workers themselves were 'generally liars' and not fit to participate actively in politics (Mill, 1989, p 209). Accordingly, Mill's socialism was subject to the overriding imperatives of individual liberty, and the object of social reform was not to do away with private property or profit, but to 'mitigate' the 'inequalities consequent' upon these various legally defined 'institutions'. A refined free market depends upon every market actor possessing the potential to engage in transaction, and the law must ensure against the situation in which some individuals are too impoverished to act effectively in the market.

Social reform and a utilitarian socialism 'looked forward to a time when society will no longer be divided into the idle and the industrious'. The 'social problem of the future we consider to be, how to unite the greatest individual liberty of action, with a common ownership in the raw material of the globe, and an equal participation of all in the benefits of combined labour' (Mill, 1989, p 175). In more practical terms, Mill became increasingly interested in the possibility of a radically decentralised political order. A utilitarian socialism could be founded on the libertarian principle of decentralisation, and the initial success of co-operative movements, such as that of Robert Owen in Lanark, was of particular interest. Mill, one of the intellectual heroes of liberal politics, was decidedly taken by the idea of a socialist utopia of decentralised communes, and this interest in political forms of socialism occupied him during the last years before his death. In the posthumously published *Chapters on Socialism*, he affirmed that the 'fundamental question' of 'liberty' had been transformed into the more pressing one of 'society', and revisions of the *Principles* during the late 1860s concentrated Mill's mind ever more on the means of reforming both individual and society. Mill's *Chapters* bear testimony to the 'wretched' condition of the majority of citizens in modern political economies; a condition caused not by indolence, but by inadequate government (Mill, 1994, pp 381–83). His earlier doubts with regard to whether the principle of liberty was better served by capitalism or socialism were answered, inevitably perhaps, by way of compromise. Capital could not be avoided, but its ethical foundation, utilitarianism, required an appreciation that the happiness of the greatest number necessitated a responsibility for government in designing the conditions of society.

The responsibility of law and government remained that of balancing the nature and consequences of intervention with an appreciation of the wider public interest. Mill suggested that the most pressing reform was for government to pass laws enshrining the public ownership of the means of production. Such ownership in no way militates against private property, but rather ensures against the accumulation of vital public interests in the hands of private economic actors. Only if these public interests are ensured can a free market economy hope to function in the interests of all its citizens (Mill, 1994, pp 414–15). As a more utopian ideal, Mill again cited the value of communes and co-operatives as the means to educating people in the duties of self-government and social participation. Such a system 'in which every person would have an interest in rendering every other person as industrious, skilful and careful as possible' would be a 'change very much for the better'. The relation between employer and employee, manager and worker, must be redefined as one of 'industrial partnership' where everyone is employer and employee, manager and worker. Such a social order is not a tyranny, or a threat to freedom. Rather it expresses the most mature form of economic freedom possible in a modern political economy (Mill, 1994, pp 420–36).

Reviving the good society

By the time of his death, the great prophet of liberty and the ethical value of a free market had abandoned the notion that a free market could ever be left entirely to its own devices. As we have already noted, Mill clearly agonised over the cruder aspects of classical utilitarianism, and desperately searched for something deeper and more ethical. Maurice Cowling has suggested that such an ambition led Mill back to a distinctly theological and conservative liberalism, whilst his later turn to socialism only emphasised a tendency to 'moral totalitarianism' (Cowling, 1990). John Gray has similarly described Mill as a putative 'market socialist' who increasingly adopted a utopian socialism, less because he knew precisely what should be done, but more because he realised that a pure free market economy simply could not work (Gray, 1989, pp 1–9, 217–38). The fact that Mill found himself trapped in a crucial ambiguity with regard to how far a free market should be regulated should not detract from the importance of refining the question. It is still the critical question in contemporary political thought, and remains essentially unresolved.

An attempt to redefine this essential tension has found expression in a distinctive school of what Amartya Sen has termed 'ethical economics', and what John Kenneth Galbraith has referred to as the 'good society'. The rational economic actor, it is suggested, is also a rational ethical actor, self-interested to some degree, perhaps, but not always exclusively so. Adam Smith acknowledged that individuals cannot be relied upon to act consistently as an analytical rational actor should. In every economic decision made, Sen asserts, there is a 'multiplicity of ethically valuable considerations involved', simply because every decision is made in a social context by economic actors aware that all decisions will have an impact upon others in that context. Economic activity is not individual, but 'mutually interdependent', and it is this interdependency which makes it always ethical to some degree (Sen, 1987, pp 62, 85–89). It is an approach which has recently been taken on by Martha Nussbaum in her analysis of the particular plight of women in the third world. As we shall see in the next chapter, Nussbaum recommends a kind of distributive justice based on the reciprocal 'capabilities' of respective market actors (Nussbaum, 2000).

Assuming the political and ethical challenge bequeathed by Mill, Galbraith suggests that the demise of pure free market capitalism actually lies with the inadequate moral philosophy of utilitarianism. Mill's turn to socialism, as he increasingly doubted the ability of the free market to evolve without some regard to the reality of society, was indeed prophetic. As the 19th century turned into the 20th, it became ever more obvious that the idea of free market economics could not resolve the problems of modern society, either in terms of pragmatics, in other words making society work, or as a matter of liberal principle, in terms of preserving the 'simple principle' of liberty. By the middle of the 20th century, Galbraith concludes, the idea of an unregulated free market was 'leading an increasingly esoteric existence, if indeed, any existence at all' (Galbraith, 1991, p 260). The need to reinvest economic analysis with its political and moral context has become ever more pressing. A 'political' economy is indeed political, for any economic exchange has political and social impact, and so economies must be regarded in terms of social responsibility. Without a degree of social and democratic control, the so called 'free' market simply becomes a market dominated by certain essentially bureaucratic economic interests, whether they be unions, multinationals, even high street banks. What the principle of liberty requires is not a 'free' market, but a democratic one; one that, as Mill noted, is not just a democracy of 'the fortunate' but of everyone (Galbraith, 1991, pp 282–300; 1996, p 8).

Of course, Mill's own utilitarianism anticipated the need for a more refined theory of utility that concentrated on more than simply the greatest happiness of the greatest number. Yet, the raw philosophy of utility, in which happiness is defined, not in terms of moral or theological philosophy, but in terms of making money and satiating self-interest, is condemned by its own success. We do, as Galbraith suggests, now live in an 'affluent society', characterised to a large extent by a 'culture of contentment'. This is not to deny the reality of poverty and misery which millions of people suffer around the world. Rather, the 'affluent society' describes a society in which the critical mass of people are sufficiently content with their economic condition that they do not feel the need to initiate a demand for the political or economic reform that would be necessary to address the disadvantages experienced by the exploited minorities. In other words, the happiness of the majority has been secured, and therefore, without any deeper ethical principle driving the need for reform, the utilitarian vision simply rests back and admires its success. It is precisely the kind of majoritarian tyranny which haunts liberal political theory.

Wealth, Galbraith affirmed, is 'the relentless enemy of understanding'. If the free market appears to work, there seems to be no need to think more deeply about its inadequacies. Capitalism is taken to be the norm, and the free market as a kind of sanctified regime which, if tampered with, might lead to the dissolution of the civilised world. In such a state of intellectual stagnation, we simply assume that poverty is the natural downside of market success. It was this 'truth' which Ricardo treasured, and Mill agonised about. The political economy is dedicated, in modern society, to satiating the demands of the consumer society: the credit card has become the new 'opium' of the masses, and providing it can continue to shop, the 'affluent society' feels little need for economic reform. In terms of economic theory, the only things which could disrupt this cosy stability are excessive unemployment and inflation, and modern government, therefore, sacrifices everything to controlling inflation and disguising unemployment. In this consumer society of unlimited credit and endless shopping, utilitarian happiness has been translated into the 'myth' of 'production'. We labour under the continuing illusion that this 'strategy of consumer debt' is somehow the result of natural market forces, rather than a consciously political condition (Galbraith, 1987, pp 215–22).

Ultimately, Galbraith suggests, we need to rethink what we mean by 'happiness'. The modern free market has 'privatised' happiness, so that it is defined by our relations with other private individuals as private market actors rather than with a community of individuals, as public market actors (Galbraith, 1987, pp 256–69). The withdrawal of public law from the sphere of economics both describes and prescribes the nature of modern political economy. The affluent society is not really a society at all, but rather simply a world of autonomous and atomised shoppers. A more inclusive society, one which Galbraith terms the 'good society', will only come about through the mechanisms of public law and government. Galbraith advocates an 'economic' communitarianism, founded on a revised idea of utilitarianism, and not dissimilar from Mill's later idea of happiness as being something which is always determined in relation, not merely to self-interest, but to respect for the interests of others. It is not a question of somehow destroying the free market, but rather of tempering its negative effects on the minority who lie outside the 'affluent society'.

Both as a matter of principle and of pragmatics, a strong market economy must be one which is constituted by all its citizens, for, as Mill suggested, the responsibility of government is to ensure that everyone enjoys the capacity to be a market actor. It is not merely a question of securing conditions for acting, but also fashioning the 'good society' in such a way that every actor is also secured against the calamity of absolute failure. Full employment is the most obvious example of a condition of the 'good society', and it is a condition which can only be secured by responsible government. Taxation policy is another. So is monetary policy, and public expenditure. Ultimately, the 'good society' is one which rids itself of the 'myth' of a 'free' market political economy, appreciates that any political economy is a 'political' entity, is always regulated to a considerable extent by government, and for the sake of democracy, must be recognised as such. Galbraith concludes by appealing for an economic world in which the 'affluent would still be affluent, the comfortable still comfortable, but the poor would be part of the political system'. The 'good society fails when democracy fails'. Conversely, in a 'true democracy', the constitution of which secures the participation of all in the political economy, the 'good society would succeed, would even have an aspect of inevitability' (Galbraith, 1996, p 143).

MARXISM, MATERIALISM AND DETERMINISM

The age of revolution

Writing in 1840, Pierre-Joseph Proudhon looked around and saw a continent that was no less polarised in terms of social and economic wealth than it had been half a century earlier. The revolutions of the 1790s had changed nothing. Above all they had not addressed the burning problem of property. 'What is property?', he famously asked in his essay of that name. The answer was simple: property 'is theft'. The idea of property, Proudhon alleged, offends the basic Aristotelian concept of equality. 'If man is made for society', he argued, then 'so is equality' (Proudhon, 1994, pp 13, 49,

178–83). And the canker of property, the 'origin of evil on earth', could be found in the institution of law. It is law which exists to secure property-holding in the hands of a select few, and which thus condemns the overwhelming majority to a life of want (Proudhon, 1994, pp 69–77). It would be a mistake to presume that Proudhon's contempt for the law presumed a similar contempt for the principles of fairness or justice. As we have already seen, a similar contempt for the institutions of law was voiced by William Godwin, and, for slightly different reasons, Jeremy Bentham. But both believed fervently in the idea of justice. And so did Proudhon. 'Justice', as he confirmed in his notorious essay, 'nothing but justice, that is the sum of my argument; I leave to others the task of governing the world'. And he then continued:

> Justice is the celestial body which governs societies, the pole around which the political world turns, the principle and rule of all transactions. Nothing takes place between men but in the name of right, nothing without the invocation of justice. Justice is not the work of the law: on the contrary, the law is only the declaration and application of what is just in all circumstances where men have relations with one another. If then the idea that we form of justice and right is badly defined, if it is imperfect or even false, it is clear that all our legislative applications must be wrong, our institutions vicious, our politics erroneous, and as a result there will be disorder and social chaos (Proudhon, 1994, p 23).

A presumed disparity between the institution of law and the ideal of justice emerged as a totem of mid 19th century radicalism; as of course it had during the 1790s. And, as the likes of Godwin had alleged, according to Proudhon, if there was a present danger of 'social chaos' it was advanced not by the absence of law, but by its presence. The suggestion would be aired once again towards the end of the century in William Morris's *News from Nowhere* (Morris, 1995, pp 83–86). Back in 1840, the suggestion was prescient indeed, for Europe was about to be engulfed in revolution.

And the great chronicler of this revolution would also turn out to be the most influential social and economic theorist of the following century and a half. This chronicler was Karl Marx. According to Marx, the freedom of the 'free' market was a hoax, a ruse put about by the interests of capital in order to finance their social and political authority, and the use of law and government as a means to securing capital provided incontrovertible evidence that the freedom of the market was indeed an illusion. Law in the capitalist State was the expression of political and economic power. As a student in Berlin, Marx had become fascinated by the historicism of Georg Wilhelm Friedrich Hegel, whose *Phenomenology of Spirit* described a process of co-determinate evolution for both individual and society. The human being can be perfected, and this perfection was premised on the congruence of individual and community development. The echoes, as Hegel acknowledged, were not just of Kant and the Enlightenment, but also of Plato and Aristotle. It was from Plato and Hegel that Marx inherited a belief in political and social revolution. The impact of the French revolution triggered a whole series of revolutions that pervaded mid 19th century Europe. The 'year of revolution', 1848, was of particular importance, because to many aspiring revolutionaries, it did indeed seem, at least for a fleeting moment, as if the collapse of the old order was imminent.

In the years immediately preceding 1848, Marx concentrated on the formation of a communist political movement which could complement the ideology of *The Communist Manifesto* and its famous call for the 'forcible overthrow of all existing social conditions' (Marx and Engels, 1985, p 120). The need to effect actual political revolution was central. As he commented in his *Theses on Feuerbach* (McLellan, 1995a, pp 127–28), 'philosophers have only interpreted the world in different ways; the point is to change it'. In 1846, Marx succeeded in refounding the Communist League, the first article of which announced that it 'aims at the abolition of man's enslavement by propagating the theory of the community of goods and by its implementation as soon as possible'. Situated in Brussels in 1848, as revolution broke out, Marx was ideally placed, or so he hoped, to oversee the first stage in the collapse of capitalism. The failure of the revolution was, accordingly, all the more unsettling. Yet Marx was never really daunted. Depressed certainly, indeed most of the time, but never to such an extent that he doubted the ultimate victory of the working classes. The 1848 revolutions in France, Austria, and particularly Belgium, had been betrayed by the 'treacherous' counter revolution of the bourgeoisie. When he was tried for incitement by the authorities in Cologne the following year, Marx berated them for their treachery and lectured the jury on the inevitable success of the working class enterprise. The foreman of the jury thanked Marx for his 'instruction' and duly acquitted him.

Seeking refuge in England, Marx duly embarked on his most productive, embittered and impoverished period, which lasted pretty much through to his death. There was a revolution to chronicle, and having acquired his reader's ticket for the British Library, he attended day after day, voraciously reading books on economics, history, politics, indeed everything necessary for the revolutionary intellect. Evenings were passed in the Rose and Crown in Soho, plotting revolution abroad and arguing incessantly over what sort of revolution it should be. Mill, who attended some of the meetings and became a friend of Marx, remained totally bemused, not merely by Marx's revolutionary politics, but by his seemingly bottomless anger. Even his ritualistic picnics on Hampstead Heath every Sunday afternoon were characterised by ferocious monologues, given to friends and family, on the nature of the impending social revolution. Between donkey rides and mouthfuls of cucumber sandwiches, Marx reassured his assembled audience that the privileges of the middle classes were about to be ended. The debates in Britain surrounding the 1867 Reform Bill, with which Mill was so involved, convinced Marx that revolution was imminent. Nothing, in fact, was further from the truth, for, as he subsequently came to realise, revolution had been avoided by the Bill, not ensured by it. Indeed, though an ardent historian, Marx was a peculiarly inept prophet. Not only did he misjudge the situation in 1848 and 1867, but he then announced to the world that the Paris Commune of 1870 represented the 'glorious harbinger of a new society'. The Commune was in fact crushed by the authorities, once the communards had eaten the Paris zoo and run out of alternative means of sustenance. Famously, Marx was to declare that the possibility of communist revolution remained everywhere imminent, apart from Russia, where there was no chance of any revolution ever succeeding. The Russian monarchy, he observed, was comfortably the most secure in Europe and would never fall to any insurrection.

Determinism and *The Communist Manifesto*

Much of Marx's work is historical. *The Communist Manifesto* opened by declaring that 'The history of all hitherto existing society is the history of class struggles'. *Capital*, particularly the first volume, contains copious accounts of the demise of custom and the evolving emergence of the modern political economy, much of which could be described in terms of diet. In one famously odd passage, he charted the demise of customary society by the eviction of Scottish shepherds who became 'amphibious' beach dwellers and whose diet was restricted to fish alone. Marx expressed a particular empathy with the 'brave Gaels', having already penned a vitriolic essay attacking the Duchess of Sutherland and her lawyers for making them eat nothing but fish. Detailed study of past political economies, particularly the process of their evolution and change, are time and again cited as illustrative of present conditions, and the relative possibilities of revolution and change. The rise in the number of vagabonds driven to crime by penury and desperation was always a reassuring sign for the frustrated revolutionary. In essays on the criminalisation of wood gathering or divorce laws, stages could be revealed in the alienation of modern humanity from society and the oppressive role of law. The fate of woodgatherers described the passage from the customary laws of feudal and pre-modern society to the impersonal alienating nature of modern positive law. Customary laws recognised that property was largely common, whereas positive law announced the sequestration of property by the privileged few. Law, like wood, became the concern of the few, not the many.

Marx's career can be charted as one which progressed from the esoterics of philosophy to the more practical analyses of politics and economics. Yet, throughout, Marx's methodology remained firmly that prescribed by Hegel. Marx was, first and foremost, an historian. Analysis of the present could only be made in the 'spirit' of the past. The opening passages of *The Communist Manifesto* continued by stressing the pervasive nature of class struggles as formative of contemporary modern society. The 19th century was determined by the prior historical struggles between 'freeman and slave, patrician and plebeian, lord and serf, guildmaster and journeyman, in a word, oppressor and oppressed' who 'stood in constant opposition to one another'. Indeed, modern humanity was caught in a state of perpetual tension described by the struggle between the active member of the community and the passive 'degraded' function of 'alien powers'. Modern humanity is in constant struggle to assert itself, and to come to self-understanding, and only when it overcomes this struggle can the community overcome its (Marx and Engels, 1985, pp 79–94).

'Man' cannot be envisaged outside of society and the modern State. He is not an 'abstract being squatting outside the world', and if 'man' was alienated from his world, it was because the capitalist expropriator intended that he should be so. The struggle is not resolved by a retreat into a private world demarcated by private rights, but rather to take control of the public world in which he lives. Freedom is something towards which humanity evolves, following the path dictated by history, and this process of evolving self-consciousness, Marx believed, had been expropriated from the people by bureaucracy. It was for this reason that the modern State was essentially false. Reactionary States, such as the Prussian, depended on stability and the suppression of change. Commonly, such reaction is founded on some sort of theology. Religion, Marx famously stated, was the 'opium of the people' (McLellan, 1995b, p 21). Even liberal States seek to suppress political change by suggesting that certain natural rights are inalienable and timeless. The great 'mythology of rights' had succeeded in convincing the French revolutionaries that their ambitions were satiated once individuals were invested with rights. In real political and economic terms, such rights are incapable of effecting justice or fairness, yet people remained deluded into thinking that they were free. The Enlightened State must be one which facilitates change and erases the institutional exclusion of the alienated worker. It is only within such a State that the individual can experience true freedom, and the revolutionary State, therefore, is the State of true freedom.

It was Marx's increasing belief that real social revolution must concentrate on dispelling false revolutionary doctrines that shaped his turn during the 1840s to theories of communes and communism, which could effect 'the positive abolition of property and thus of human self-alienation' and thus represented 'the real appropriation of the human essence by and for men' (McLellan, 1995b, p 24). A socialist revolution is a 'human protest against a dehumanised life, because it starts from the standpoint of the single, real individual, because the collectivity against whose separation from himself the individual reacts is the true collectivity of man, the human essence' (McLellan, 1995a, p 89). The alienation of the individual in modern society is central to Marx's history of the human condition. Accordingly, the situation and uses of law and the State became ever more important, and the influence of Hegel was once again crucial, for it was he who had emphasised that 'legal relations' and 'forms of State' were 'to be grasped neither from themselves nor from the so called general development of the human mind, but rather have their roots in the material conditions of life' (McLellan, 1995a, p 74).

The nexus between law, politics and ideology is crucial. In *The German Ideology*, Marx noted that 'the ideas of the ruling class are in every epoch the ruling ideas', adding that 'law, morality and religion are so many bourgeois prejudices, behind which lurk in ambush just as many bourgeois interests'. Law, in the modern political economy, 'can never be higher than the economic structure of society', and merely enacts the ideological interests of those that 'rule in these conditions'. The tragedy of modern law lay not just in its use as a weapon of class struggle, but in its ability to delude the oppressed into thinking that it enjoys some sort of natural authority. The 'imaginary authority' of modern law is constituted by both oppressor and oppressed. It is the 'specific illusion of lawyers and politicians' (McLellan, 1995b, pp 153, 160–62). Marx's theory of law was firmly premised on Hegel's idea of evolving self-consciousness, and so, in classically Hegelian terms, civil laws should reflect the mutually constitutive relation of individual and community as 'the inner, vital laws of human activity, the conscious mirror of human life'. Marx described his ideal modern State as a:

> … great organism in which juridical, moral and political liberties must be realised and in which each citizen, by obeying the laws of the state, only obeys the natural laws of his own reason, human reason (McLellan, 1995a, p 40).

Having prophesied the inevitable collapse of the capitalist State, Marx then proceeded to outline the means of effecting this collapse in the interests of the working classes. Central to the revolutionary programme of *The Communist Manifesto* is seizure of the State, and with it the means of production. Ultimately, and again echoing Hegel, Marx anticipated an 'end of history', or at least an end of the struggle which characterises modern contemporary history. The communist society will be perfected, and 'when, in the course of development, class distinctions have disappeared and all production has been concentrated in the hands of a vast association of the whole nation, the public power will lose its political character', for 'political power, properly so called, is merely the organised power of one class for oppressing another' (Marx and Engels, 1985, p 105). Thus, in 'place of the old bourgeois society, with its classes and class antagonisms, we shall have an association, in which the free development of each is the condition for the free development of all'. It has become popular to dismiss the

Manifesto as being itself an historical anachronism of limited relevance to contemporary life, if anything dangerously associated with communism and the totalitarian State. In fact, as Galbraith has suggested, the *Manifesto* can be far more readily aligned with the kind of liberal radical treatise articulated by the likes of Mill, advising the need for modern society to move to progressive taxation and make provision for public ownership of transport and communication, free education and full employment (Galbraith, 1991, p 137). The *Manifesto* was never intended to realise any sort of totalitarian utopia. Indeed, the desire to effect a genuine form of participatory democracy underpinned Marx's political visions throughout his life. Years earlier, in one of his journalistic pieces, he had emphasised that socialist revolution was only valid if it effected a democratic 'constitution' within which everyone could determine their own lives and realise their own potential. Democracy is the 'solution to the riddle of all constitutions', because only a democratic constitution is the 'free product of man' (McLellan, 1995b, pp 208–13).

Following the failure of the 1848 revolutions, Marx was ever more convinced that the success or failure of revolutionary activity depended upon seizure of law and State. In a commentary on the French Revolution, he emphasised that the slavery of the working class was ensured by the 'constitution', and that the overthrow of the bourgeoisie would only be ensured by a rewriting of that constitution. Centralised control was a prerequisite for the success of any revolution, and so the situation of law became increasingly important. Rather than society being based on law, as in a liberal philosophy, Marx reminded the Cologne jury that 'law must be based on society ... the expression of society's common interests and needs'. Using the classical base-superstructure argument, Marx emphasised that all legal institutions are built upon, and thus subsequent to, the economic base of society, and any 'attempted assertion of the eternal validity of laws continually clashes with present needs, it prevents commerce and industry, and paves the way for social crises that break out with political revolutions'. Law is a real political instrument, not a force of nature (McLellan, 1995b, p 194).

The liberal polity, with its concentration on rights to possession and privacy, as enshrined in the demarcated realm of private law and the necessarily limited sphere of public law, must be legally reconstituted. The socialist or communist constitution must erase the distinction between the public and private, because it is a distinction only justified by the needs of the political economy. A truly communist society has no need of private law, and so it must necessarily wither away. Moreover, a true citizen of a society can never retreat outside that society, or the world, but must remain, in all his or her being, a part of it. The individual is always public, because he or she, in a true society, is always a constitutive participating citizen. It is easy to see here, not merely the influence of Hegel, but also that of Aristotle. In *On the Jewish Question*, published back in 1843, Marx had emphasised that the idea of the citizen brings man 'back to himself', such that 'man must recognise his own forces as social forces, organise them and thus no longer separate social forces from himself in the form of political forces' (McLellan, 1995b, p 251).

Capital

Any legislation, as Marx continually emphasised, must be understood as serving no other purpose than to 'express in words, the will of economic relations'. The legal foundation of the modern political economy is provided by the laws of property. Competition, the 'war among the greedy', what he termed in *The Class Struggles in France*, the 'lust' for wealth 'where pleasure becomes debauched, where money, filth and blood commingle' is founded on the 'fact of private property'. Law must preserve property, so that it can then preserve that which is expropriated by the greedy, and successful, competitor. Marx turned to writing his monumental *Capital* following his arrival in England and researches in the British Library. Through the 'instruction' of history, Marx noted four vulnerable points in the political economy of capitalism: the distribution of power; unequal distribution of income; susceptibility to unemployment; and monopoly. The inability to resolve these issues led Marx to believe that capitalism was destined to crisis and collapse. The history of the emerging political economies had revealed the natural tendency of competitive interests to destroy one another. 'One capitalist', he affirmed, 'always kills many'. Capitalism tends naturally towards monopoly, and the 'monopoly of capital becomes a fetter upon the mode of production'. Eventually, the 'knell of capitalist private property sounds' and the 'expropriators are expropriated' (Marx, 1975, vol 1, p 763).

Aside from the contradiction within the capital process itself, it is worth noting in particular Marx's concentration on the development of a working class consciousness. Such a consciousness was vital, not just because it would furnish the community consciousness necessary to the Hegelian idea of human perfection, but also because it could facilitate the equally necessary overcoming of individual alienation. It was this alienation which secured the power of the capitalist exploiter. At the centre of *Capital* is the idea that the modern political economy has 'fetishised' modern man, so that, as a mere instrument of labour, he is defined in political economic terms, rather than essential human ones. The political economy has served to:

> ... mutilate the labourer into a fragment of a man, degrade him to the level of an appendage of a machine, destroy every remnant of charm in his work and turn it into a hated toil.

The worker and his family are accordingly dragged 'beneath the wheels of the juggernaut of capital' (Marx, 1975, vol 1, p 645). The value of the modern individual is not determined by moral virtue, but by value in the workplace. Marx referred to the 'objectification of labour' in the political economy as a 'loss of reality for the worker' and the foundation for exploitation.

The alienation of humanity is completed by money and by law. The 'working man' does not take home that which he labours upon, but a wage, an amount of money which is, necessarily in the political economy, less than the value of the product itself in the market place. It must be less, because the wagepayer, the capitalist who owns the means of production, demands a margin of profit. In *Capital*, Marx made the clear association of profit with rent levied by landlords. The capitalist levies a profit simply by the fact of the ownership of the means of production, the factory and tools. Marx frequently sought recourse to the metaphorical nature of the capitalist factory owner as a form of urbanised landlord who rents the means of production to the worker, not least because it better described the nature of the modern economy as one defined in terms of the contract. The employee is bound to the employer, through a contract of employment, just as the medieval tenant was bound to his manorial lord through his fee. The private law of contract sealed the fate of the alienated and exploited worker. Just as the 'Roman slave was held by fetters' so 'the wage labourer is bound to his owner by invisible threads'. The illusion is maintained by the *'fictio juris* of a contract' (Marx, 1975, vol 1, pp 88–89, 538). The law played a critical role in subjugating the worker to 'the material conditions determining their production'. The consciousness of the worker is described by the material conditions in which he finds himself, and these conditions are determined by the idea of private law; 'every form of production creates its own legal relations'. The political economy had created the mythical aura of the sanctity of private contract. In the preface to the *Critique of Political Economy*, written as a preparatory to *Capital*, Marx emphasised once more that:

> ... legal relations as well as forms of the State are to be grasped neither from themselves nor from the so called general development of the human mind, but rather have their roots in the material conditions of life (McLellan, 1995a, p 280).

The worker will only be liberated when public laws are passed which can protect against the need to alienate both self and labour. The worker must be protected against the oppression of the private contract:

> The bargain concluded, it is discovered that he was no 'free agent', that the time for which he is free to sell his labour power is the time for which he is forced to sell it, that in fact the vampire will not loose its hold on him so long as there is a muscle, nerve, a drop of blood to be exploited. For protection against the serpent of their agonies, the labourers must put their heads together, and, as a class, compel the passing of a law, an all powerful social barrier that shall prevent the very workers from selling, by voluntary contract with capital, themselves and their families into slavery and death. In place of the pompous catalogue of the 'inalienable rights of man' comes the modest Magna Charta of a legally limited working-day, which shall make clear when the time which the worker sells is ended, and when his own begins (Marx, 1975, vol 1, p 302).

Certainly the role of money and the market was important, but it was the role of law and State in fashioning the actual modes of production which resided at the heart of Marx's analysis of the modern political economy.

History and power revisited

It is difficult to overestimate the impact of Marx. And it is every bit as difficult to disentangle any species of 20th century left-wing ideology from the pervasive shadow of Marx's critique of capital. Socialism was to evolve in many shapes and sizes, and can still be found in the guise of European social democracy. In terms of intellectual critique, one of the most influential of neo-Marxist movements was a distinctive English school of economic historicism, which included the likes of RH Tawney, Christopher Hill and Edward Thompson. Adapting Max Weber's neo-Marxist thesis that capitalism and protestantism were mutually supportive, Tawney suggested that the social and constitutional order of 20th century England was fashioned during the 16th and 17th centuries by a particular alliance of protestantism, nationalism and the demands of the free market (Tawney, 1990). Hill applied a similarly Marxist analysis to the revolutions of the 17th century, writing a history that focused on the ordinary common folk of England. The revolutions, he suggested, were rooted, not in the politics of parliament, but in the politics of parish, in the social and economic, as well as theological, anxieties of a people who were no longer prepared to accept the specious presumptions of natural justice and natural law (Hill, 1996).

A similar approach was taken by Edward Thompson, who focused still more intently on the intrinsic relation between State and governance. The history of English law, according to Thompson, cannot be readily distinguished from the evolution of the free market and the fashioning of the society in which we currently live. In *Whigs and Hunters*, Thompson examined the application of the Black Act of 1723, a brutal law passed in order to suppress the pretended danger of 'wicked and evil disposed men going armed in disguise'. In fact, these men were engaged in a resistance movement dedicated to the preservation of ancient customary rights to forest, against the new drive by a number of park owners to enclose property. The suppression of the 'Blacks' represented an alliance of interests between Prime Minister Walpole's Whig government and the landed aristocracy and gentry upon which it depended for electoral support. Prime Minister was allied with park ranger to protect the interests of the landowning classes as they tried to capitalise property values in the increasingly competitive world of the free market. Legal and extralegal was blurred as legislator, executive and judicial institution combined resources to redefine the nature of English society. The Black Act was illustrative of the radical rewriting of English law necessary to complement the emergence of an ever more competitive free market ideology. As such, the Act reveals a whole new jurisprudential attitude. Law was no longer dedicated to the 'maintenance of order', but to the 'direct and personal interest' of certain economic actors in suppressing the liberties of others. Such were the stakes in this new economic world that the rituals of pre-modern punishment, the stocks and the ducking stool, were replaced by transportation and execution. This new world was one run, not by custom, by parish priests, or even by landlords as such, but by lawyers. When the going got tough, the whimsy of custom was replaced by a distinctive jurisprudential technology (Thompson, 1990, pp 188–97, 207–09, 262–65).

In a broad sense Thompson's work concentrated on the history of the working and artisan classes in 18th and 19th century England. *The Making of the English Working Class* suggested that the English working class was an interest fashioned by the emergence of the national political economy. Accordingly, the history of the working class reveals a critical and formative interaction between law, society and economics. Law is seen to be reactive to socio-economic pressures, and the increasing domain of private law, most obviously in contract and commerce, reveals the submission of law to the march of liberal, free market ideology. A working class consciousness emerged in response to this submission, and to the challenge of capitalism, and is, accordingly, defined by liberal legalism, even if it is a definition driven by hostility (Thompson, 1991, pp 9–10). At the heart of Thompson's thesis is a critical ambiguity in liberalism. Whilst championing the liberty of the individual within the free market, liberal legalism is keen to suppress the libertarian impulses of much working class ideology, dissenting movements such as methodism or, most particularly, the rhetoric of democratic populism. The law, then, which is supposed to guarantee freedom, is actually very selective with regard to the kind of freedom it protects. It protects the freedom of certain social interests to compete within a market, but suppresses any notion of democratic freedom for the working classes. It protects the right to own property, but not the right to eat.

Ultimately, the history of 18th and 19th century England reveals the impossibility of any whimsical notion of liberal neutrality. Liberalism is an intensely political philosophy dedicated to serving the socio-economic demands of a particular interest. Yet, the strength of this whimsy was considerable. Millions of starving peasants and exploited factory workers clung to the illusion that they were 'free born Englishmen', somehow privileged and protected by an ancient constitution which had been secured by their ancestors. To rebel against their masters would be to rebel against their own constitution and to jeopardise their own freedoms. Small wonder, perhaps, that Thomas Paine should have been harried into exile when, in his *Rights of Man*, he suggested that this was pure nonsense, that there was no such thing as an ancient, or indeed particularly modern, constitution, and that the 'free born Englishman' was a mythology put about in order to lend spurious legitimacy to the latent exploitation of one group of individuals by another. At the root of this exploitation, Paine perceptively noted, lay the power of the common law (Thompson, 1991, pp 85–106, 117–25).

Control of land was crucial to the development of the political economy. Between 1760 and 1810, 63 new capital offences were established as a response to what was perceived to be a growing lack of respect for property. In the final analysis, there was really only one 'offence against property' and that 'was to have none' (Thompson, 1991, pp 65–73). Millions did not have any land, or held the most limited of tenancy rights. By definition they were the designated 'delinquents' of the modern society. The need to compete within the new market economies had led to the breakdown of customary rights. The landowner no longer worried about his traditional paternalistic responsibilities, about the wellbeing of his tenants. Customary laws of land tenure and use were swept aside as the need to realise proper rental value become pressing. The most notorious result was the enclosure of common land, which resulted, first, in rioting by certain dispossessed tenant farmers, who lost the right to graze livestock on common, and then, secondly, in a brutal suppression legitimated by central government and executed by local landowners and magistrates, many of whom were one and the same. At the same time, working class organisations, from methodist chapels to putative trade unions, were infiltrated by government spies, and Whitehall was flooded with ever more hair-raising reports from increasingly zealous and panicky magistrates. The 'disciplinary gaze', as the French philosopher Michel Foucault was later to term it, was concentrated with ever increasing intensity into the provinces, parishes and factories of England. Eighteenth century England, Thompson suggested, was fashioned as one 'gigantic industrial panopticon' (Thompson, 1991, pp 237–39, 529–38, 859–61).

This destruction of traditional customs and customary laws defined the social and economic structures of modern society. Detached from their traditional allegiances with the land, the exploited working classes felt an ever greater affinity with each other. The destruction of customary law actually served to dispel the mythology of the ancient constitution and the common law. The juridical psychology which had served to stabilise class relations up to the 18th century was itself destroyed, and with it went the complementary myth of the rule of law. Law, too obviously, was not the same for everyone. It did not protect everyone alike. Law, it was increasingly clear, was an instrument used for political oppression and economic exploitation. The 'free born Englishman', precisely defined in jurisprudential terms, was an historical fiction. The law was not his, and never had been. It served the interest of someone else, and, accordingly, he no longer felt bound by it. It was not a sudden realisation, but by the mid 19th century, the stripping of the myth of a 'common' law led to a society in which there were insiders, for whom the law supported their status as competitive economic actors, and outsiders, who were designated by law as being economic delinquents. The law determined who was inside and who was outside the English political economy, and thus English society. That was the key function of law, and, Thompson implied, it still is (Thompson, 1993, pp 97–184).

NEO-LIBERALISM AND ECONOMIC ANALYSIS

Liberty and the nightwatchman State

The liberal counterattack against Marxism has been uncompromising. Karl Popper suggested that Hegel and Marx were the two great disciples of Plato's 'blueprint' for totalitarianism. It was Hegel, the 'source of all contemporary historicism', who resuscitated the Platonic illusion that society could somehow effect the perfection of the individual, and it was Marx who perfected this historicist 'nonsense'. The cause of liberty, Popper countered, must deny the mythical illusions of historicism (Popper, 1966, vol 2, pp 27–31, 118–29, 224–80). It was the cause of liberty which also underpinned Friedrich Hayek's critique. Like Popper, Hayek expressed a particular concern with Marxism and Nazism, which he termed a form of 'middle class socialism' (Hayek, 1962, pp 87, 123–34). Hayek spent much of his academic career arguing against the dominant post-war ideas of John Maynard Keynes, who advocated the role of central government in administering the national economy. As Hayek noted, although couched in the same intellectual tradition as Mill and radical English socialism, many of Keynes's ideas, including measures to nationalise key industries and utilities, and provide for comprehensive social welfare schemes, could just as easily be found in *The Communist Manifesto* (Gamble, 1996, pp 8–25). Keynes, he suggested, was a danger to democracy, and, in his polemical *The Road to Serfdom*, published in 1944, Hayek controversially suggested that England, under Keynes and the socialists, was headed for precisely the same totalitarian dictatorship as that experienced under Hitler. Socialism, the 'great utopia' of modernism, in reality 'meant slavery'. It was not, however, inevitable, and could be defeated, but to do so required the resurrection of classical English liberalism.

The virtue of this classical liberal tradition, as espoused by Bentham and Mill, was its appreciation that liberty is not natural or inevitable. Freedom must be worked for, and matters only in a real political sense, not as a mere philosophical expression. At the same time, it was Mill's great error to have confused this essential truth by advocating the need to reform society from without, rather than letting society reform itself through the wealth creating potential of the market. The free market is essential to Hayek, not just because it is the most efficient form of wealth creation, but because it encapsulates as well as preserves a moral order of freedom and responsibility. As he suggested in *The Road to Serfdom*, competition 'dispenses with the need for social control' (Hayek, 1962, pp 27–29). It is not, then, the market for its own sake. The free market is necessary as a means of preserving wider political liberties. If the market remains free then we can all continue to enjoy a greater measure of choice, and the responsibility that goes with it. In turn, political and legal institutions can only be legitimated if they preserve the free market and the moral order of liberty. Although democracy can be a virtue, it is merely a means, a 'utilitarian device for safeguarding internal peace and individual freedom', and Hayek preferred to concentrate on the greater importance of institutions of decentralisation which could preserve the freedom of the market. It is the market, not political institutions *per se*, which matter, and accordingly, the role of a legal system is to 'preserve competition and to make it operate as beneficially as possible'. The key characteristic of the liberal State is the rule of law. It may be that the rule of law 'produces economic inequality', but such 'inequality is not designed to affect particular people in a particular way' (Hayek, 1962, pp 28, 59).

In his subsequent *Law, Legislation and Liberty*, Hayek affirmed that the liberal community must be 'constitutional', and such a constitutionalism, once again, is never natural (Hayek, 1992, vol 3, pp 107–22). The process of constitutionalising liberty is subject in part to the 'inner dynamics of law', and once the principle of liberty is established as a constitutional principle, the writing of the law will be effected accordingly. The law will become 'infused' with the principle. Law does not naturally oscillate towards liberty, and can be just as easily sequestered by Marxists and used as a weapon to suppress individuality. By definition, then, a constitution that respects liberty will be a minimal one, itself interfering with the individual as little as possible. Whereas Marx advocated the abolition of private law, Hayek argues for the minimalisation of public law and the sanctity of the private (Hayek, 1992, vol 1, pp 65–66, 108–14, 124–33). The State is not the guarantor of freedom. It is its greatest threat and, accordingly, the principle of the rule of law must enjoy supremacy over any notion of sovereignty. It is for this reason that Hayek, despite a shared ideological belief in liberty, is caustic in his dismissal of legal positivism and its 'fetishising' of sovereignty (Hayek, 1992, vol 2, pp 19–23, 36–61).

In terms of legal philosophy, as opposed to merely legal science, the great ideological enemy is distributive justice, the common recourse of 'socialists' and 'totalitarian' apologists, from Plato and Aristotle to Marx and Hitler. There is no proper measure of 'worth', no 'principles of individual conduct which would produce a pattern of distribution which as such could be called just'. Justice is not a mechanism for trying to effect universal substantive fairness. Rather, it is a procedural device, legitimate only to the extent to which it effects the far greater good of liberty. Interestingly, as a matter of political expedience, in order to maximise the efficiency and liberty of the general community, Hayek is perfectly happy to advocate certain measures of distribution and welfare in order to support those in danger of being forced out of the market. Starvation leads to civil dislocation, which is in no one's interest. But it is important to recognise that such distribution is a matter of expediency, and not principle. Being poor and starving to death is a matter of political 'misfortune'. It is not a matter of 'injustice', and the idea that it might be is the crucial 'myth' of socialism. The principles of liberty, democracy and justice are preserved by the free market, not by the regulatory ambitions of a 'closed society'. The 'fight' against socialism and the 'closed society' is, he concludes, the 'last battle against arbitrary power' (Hayek, 1992, vol 2, pp 62–96; vol 3, pp 1–18, 43–60).

If Hayek's critique is largely written in response to Marxist theories of redistribution, a second, neo-liberal critique returns to Lockean first principles. The return to Locke in order to trace, and legitimate, neo-liberal theories of the free market has been recently advocated by Robert Nozick in his radical libertarian *Anarchy, State and Utopia*. For Nozick, the idea of a free market translates into the most minimal role for government in the ordinary economic and social activities of the individual citizen. Accordingly, the 'minimal State is the most extensive State that can be justified' and any 'State more extensive violates people's rights' (Nozick, 1974, p 149). It was Locke,

Nozick suggests, who first realised that all forms of government are parasitical – first, in that they exist subsequent to pre-existing natural political rights, to property most obviously, and secondly, in that they need constant justification. Nozick's ideal, his 'utopia', is a condition of anarchy. It is, of course, only a dream, like any utopia, but it remains a valid model for the political imagination. The natural State is one of no government, and this is an ideal only compromised for the most unarguable of political necessities. The 'fundamental question of political philosophy' is 'one that precedes questions about how the State should be organised'. It is a question of 'whether there should be a State at all'. If the State of anarchy is 'untenable' in political terms, and Locke had appreciated that civil government is a necessary supplement to the state of nature, then the Lockean 'nightwatchman' State is the only justifiable form of political supplement (Nozick, 1974, pp 4, 26–27, 298).

In jurisprudential terms, Nozick thus advocates the 'private' as opposed to the 'public' nature of law. Public law will be as minimal as government itself. Redistribution of goods will be effected by individuals in the form of compensation for the infringement of rights, rather than by government in the form of social benefits or taxation. Forms of public redistribution are nothing more than forced labour, 'seizing' the product of one person's labour for the benefit of someone else (Nozick, 1974, pp 149–72). Minimal government will oversee the administration of this private law, rather than impose itself in the form of public law. It will act as an 'invisible hand' to guide private relations between individuals. In such terms, Nozick follows a distinctively libertarian interpretation of Locke, diametrically opposed to any utilitarian alternative. There is never any justification for restraining individual liberty in the cause of any wider communal happiness. However, Nozick does recognise the need for certain 'moral side constraints'. Unlike utilitarians, who justify intervention on a purely pragmatic count of what will best effect the greatest degree of happiness, Nozick suggests that the 'morality' of these 'side constraints' is Kantian, in that it is founded on certain fundamental rights to freedom. In other words, they see individuals as ends in themselves, not as mere means towards some metaphysical notion of communal wellbeing (Nozick, 1974, pp 30–34, 65–87, 114–19). Ultimately, Nozick's is an intensely principled, even philosophical, defence of individual autonomy and the minimal State:

> The minimal State treats us as inviolate individuals, who may not be used in certain ways by others as means or tools or instruments or resources; it treats us as persons having individual rights with the dignity this constitutes. Treating us with respect by respecting our rights, it allows us, individually or with whom we choose, to choose our life and to realise our ends and our conception of ourselves, in so far as we can, aided by the voluntary cooperation of other individuals possessing the same dignity. How dare any State or group of individuals do more. Or less (Nozick, 1974, pp 333–34).

Of course, the difficulty for Nozick is precisely that which Locke encountered. If some degree of government is necessary, and indeed desirable in order better to effect such a moral philosophy, and moreover, that a strictly utilitarian definition of government is not acceptable, then precisely how can it be justified in terms of political principle? Government must constrain liberty, no matter how much we pretend to legitimate it as necessary for the protection of our natural rights, and no matter how loudly we proclaim fundamental natural rights. As a matter of crude political power, as both Hobbes and Locke appreciated, government does impose rights on both individuals and property, it does tax and it does sequester property if it sees fit. It is this realisation which has tended to favour alternative theories of government and economics, most notably the utilitarian and the Marxist. Ultimately, the more libertarian interpretation of Nozick, despite its anarchistic pretensions, is far more principled than practical, both in descriptive and prescriptive terms. It cannot, in practical terms, resolve a matter which, in purely principled terms, cannot be resolved, and it cannot defend the political restraints necessary to make a putatively free market work. The idea of the free market, or the political economy, only makes sense in purely practical political terms, and cannot be rationalised in terms of purely philosophical coherence or principle. The free market depends upon an imaginative feint that sees freedom as being something which is necessarily something short of free.

Economic analysis of law

Locke, Mill, Marx, Hayek; each wrote with the ambition of describing grand theories of politics, economics, law and so forth, fashioned from equally grand political principles, such as rights, liberty, social justice, equality. Although there is a core concern in the work of each to address real political issues, there is also present the grand theoretical narrative which comes of grand theoretical ambitions. The evolution of a distinctive economic analysis of law, often termed 'law and economics' scholarship, presents itself as a non-ideological alternative. Its origins are irreducibly pragmatic, even sceptical. At the heart of Richard Posner's influential economic analysis is an acutely pragmatic approach to matters of legal theory. Efficiency is not just of intrinsic value as a criterion for legal analysis. In a post-Enlightenment world, there is, quite simply, nothing else to which we can seek succour, nothing which can be agreed upon and used in the actual practice of law. So called principles of law, whether derived from metaphysics, theology or whatever, are of no practical use, and so offer no real alternative to efficiency and self-interest (Posner, 1995, p 403). The lack of either faith or interest in philosophical theories of law is fundamental to Posner's jurisprudence. 'Philosophers', he suggests, 'seem preoccupied with questions that no one with a modicum of common sense and a living to earn would waste a minute on', whilst pragmatism, in contrast, 'wants the law to be more empirical, more realistic, more attuned to the real needs of real people' (Posner, 1990, p 3; 1995, p 19).

It was Oliver Wendell Holmes who, at the turn of the century, wanted to introduce economic considerations into the practice of law. In the famous *Lochner* case, the US Supreme Court admitted that constitutional judgments must take account of the overriding interests of the free market economy. Early 'law and economics' concentrated on the principles of the free market, such as competition, monopolies and on those areas of law which most immediately address these principles, such as anti-trust law and corporate law. In recent decades, an alternative 'new' law and economics has emerged, determined to address the economic impact of all areas of law, from tort to crime to family and so on. The ambit of 'new' law and economics is pervasive: all law, it is suggested, has a potential impact on the free market. In his *The Economic Approach to Human Behaviour*, Gary Becker suggested that every aspect of life was economic to some degree, for everything we do has financial implications. Law, accordingly, is always economic to some extent. Of course, it is here that the determination to keep economic analysis purely pragmatic and away from the lures of grand theory becomes increasingly difficult.

In his seminal essay 'The problem of social cost', Ronald Coase addressed the matter of 'transaction costs', being such costs incurred during the passage of economic production or exchange which could otherwise be reduced, ideally to zero, without reducing the value of the goods produced or exchanged. The role of law, according to Coase's 'theorem', lies in analysing each legal situation in order to effect the maximum reduction in these costs. Under conditions of 'perfect competition', there will be no transaction costs. Coase's argument was a response to that of an earlier economist, Pigou, who suggested that all costs should be 'internalised', in other words incurred by those who create them. The principle is basically akin to the Aristotelian idea of corrective or rectificatory justice. Coase suggested that this was rather simplistic, perhaps right as a matter of principle, but not efficient in terms of the pragmatics of a free market economy. The courts must address, he countered, the overall 'social cost'. Using an example of a manufacturer who pollutes a river, Coase suggested that punishing the polluter, in other words 'internalising' the cost, may be counter productive. Any fine or damages levied against the polluter will simply be passed onto the consumer, and the efficiency of the enterprise will be reduced. In such circumstances, it might be in the wider community interest, and indeed in the interest of those who suffer from the pollution, who are themselves market actors in terms of being consumers, to move away or suffer the pollution (Coase, 1960). The theory was as prescient as it was simple, and its import threatened the very essence of liberal private law jurisprudence, which had committed itself to the notion that private individuals should be left to recompense one another for invasions of their privacy or property. In terms of economic theory, it suggested that the classical liberal tradition of Smith, Mill and Hayek, which saw the free market as expressive of a greater principle of liberty, was actually inefficient. What Coase announced was an alternative, acutely free market theory of neo-liberalism, wherein the pragmatics of efficiency overrode the principle of liberty.

Efficiency itself, however, is not an easy concept, and alternative theories of efficiency are often suggested by various economists. One is Pareto efficiency, which determines that an exchange is efficient if it makes one person better off and no one worse. The problem with Pareto efficiency is that, in the real world of economic exchange, when, as competitors, we are all trying to make a profit, someone must lose something. An alternative is Kaldor-Hicks efficiency, which suggests that an exchange is efficient if it makes one person better off, and that person who benefits is capable of compensating the disadvantaged. Kaldor-Hicks might seem to be more realistic, but it also introduces a principle of distribution, and this is a critical concession. Kaldor-Hicks efficiency, by definition, is not about pure efficiency at all. The difficulty of making sense of efficiency has asked all sorts of questions of neo-liberal economics. A pragmatic approach to the market is premised on the assumption that efficiency is the only criterion which a court should address, and that we know what it means. But if we do not know what it means, or if we are not entirely convinced that efficiency can always be pursued in the real world, then we can only fall back on alternatives derived from philosophical or political principle. In other words, we return to the classical liberalism of such as Mill or Hayek.

The most influential jurisprudential statement of 'new' neo-liberal economic analysis is Richard Posner's *Economic Analysis of Law*. Asserting a specific denial of deeper ideological ambition, Posner opens his 'analysis' of law by emphasising that 'economics is the science of rational choice in a world – our world – in which resources are limited in relation to human wants'. The rational economic actor is the essential construct of neo-liberal economics. It makes the crucial assumption, as Posner acknowledges, that man is a 'rational maximiser of his ends in life, his satisfactions' and 'self-interest'. Economic analysis is not, thus, about states of mind or any other kind of metaphysics. It is purely a 'model of rational choice' as empirically observed. To this extent, economic analysis observes the empirical spirit of Locke and Hume, though it refuses Adam Smith's complementary theory of moral 'sentiment'. Three fundamental economic principles underpin economic analysis: the law of demand dictating prices in a free market; the desire to maximise profit; and the tendency for resources to maximise their most valuable use in order to realise efficiency. Each can be found in Adam Smith, and none, in these terms at least, is controversial. To the extent that there is a political philosophy also underlying Posner's analytical theory, it comes in the form of a kind of raw utilitarianism. The market maximises the ability of the individual to pursue his self-interest. Posner makes much of an efficient market being of greater 'utility'. Moreover, the ultimate ideological justification for the free market lies with the danger that a 'legally coerced transaction is less likely to promote happiness than a market transaction, because the misery of the (uncompensated) losers may exceed the joy of the winners'. The justification for an overriding principle of wealth maximisation, accordingly, is that it is 'an important', perhaps 'conceivably the only', effective 'social instrument of utility maximisation' (Posner, 1986, pp 3–15).

A crucial distinction in Posner's economic analysis lies between 'positive' and 'normative' theory (Posner, 1986, pp 20–22). Whilst 'normative' analysis might attempt to prescribe mechanisms for maximising efficiency, 'positive' analysis merely describes the process by which courts have and do operate to refine the market. A substantial part of Posner's thesis is historically descriptive, suggesting that the courts have shaped the common law in order to serve the best, meaning most efficient, operation of the free market. The role of policy in normative analysis is not denied. Indeed it is, by definition, intrinsic. Positive economic analysis, however, remains a pure science, dedicated to the economic principle of efficiency. The distinction between the two, as we will see shortly, has become ever more important to Posner as he has attempted to deflect political and ethical criticism, and the distinction is emphasised in the opening passages of *Economic Analysis*. Since:

> ... economics yields no answer to the question of whether the existing distribution of income and wealth is good or bad, just or unjust ... neither does it answer the ultimate question of whether an efficient allocation of resources would be socially or ethically desirable.

The positive economic analyst, the only one with whom Posner is really concerned by the time of the third edition of his book, in 1986:

> ... can predict the effect of legal rules and arrangements on value and efficiency, in their strict technical senses, and on the existing distribution of income and wealth, but he cannot issue mandatory prescriptions for social change (Posner, 1986, p 13).

Economics, ethics and selling babies

Since the original publication of *Economic Analysis* in 1973, Posner has refined his position to take account of various critiques, both political and ethical, and in response has underlined the distinction between 'normative' and 'positive' economic analysis. However, at the same time, he has been drawn deeper into political and ethical terrain. Although Posner has tried to maintain the integrity of a 'positive' economic analysis, the weight of criticism has forced concessions. The move away from the tricky issue of determining efficiency and towards the more principled idea of distribution in economic analysis was initially made by Guido Calabresi, who conceded that economics can never be purely a matter of efficiency. Economic theory 'cannot tell us how far we want to go to save lives and reduce accident costs'. Decisions which balance 'lives against money or convenience cannot be purely monetary ones, so the market method is never the only one used' (Calabresi, 1970, p 18). Law is not purely a matter of economics, and economic theory does not exist in a rarified world apart from matters of politics or ethics.

An illustration of the difficulties that Posner has encountered in his attempt to demarcate the economic analysis from the ethical is described by the controversy surrounding the idea of selling babies. In a controversial article entitled 'The economics of the baby shortage', Posner advocated the creation of a market in babies in order to facilitate adoptions. The regulation of adoptions by public authorities resulted in an inefficient and severely restricted market, inherently a public monopoly, which was indefensible in terms of the interests of either putative adopting parents or putative adoptive babies. Most particularly, it denied the 'potential gains from trade from transferring the custody of the child to a new set of parents'. One of the central planks of Posner's criticism was the regulation which the authorities maintained so as to 'sell' each baby to adoption at the same 'price'. So, even though the public adoption agencies enjoyed a monopoly which prevented competition, they were not able to extract a profit margin. The market was doubly restricted. Moreover, as a matter of political pragmatism, public regulation has not prevented the selling of babies. Instead, it has merely consigned the process to a black market, which being itself unfree, is hedged by various monopoly interests and therefore wholly inefficient. The 'social' or 'transaction' costs of such a process, including the search for babies, and time wasted trying to conceive naturally, as well as the price fixing of the black market, are considerable. Statistics suggested that a black market baby could cost anything between $9,000 and $40,000, whereas the actual compensatory cost to natural parents who wish to relinquish a baby should come to no more than $3,000. The practical results of the regulations, aside from the inefficiency and moral dubiousness of a black market, is a shortage of babies for parents who wish to adopt and a 'glut' of children maintained at public cost in foster homes and the like. Furthermore, as a matter of public policy, if a free market was allowed to operate, Posner suggested that the price of babies would almost certainly fall, allowing those less well off to adopt a baby which they could not afford on the black market, as well as providing legal protection against fraud or misrepresentation in the 'contractual' situation (Landes and Posner, 1978, pp 323–41).

Much of the controversy was stirred by the language used in the article, the 'glut' of children, whose situation in regulated homes was described as resembling an 'unsold inventory stored in a warehouse'. There was also the implication that children, even if they were intrinsic moral selves, could be rationalised as marketable commodities. In a market environment, financial values would be attached to children, and it was clear that this value was bound to vary from one child to another. Posner's response to the idea that buying babies might be ethically undesirable was again acutely pragmatic. If a parent is prepared to spend money in purchasing a child, then there is an intrinsic reassurance that he or she will protect that investment. Few people he observed 'buy a car or a television set in order to smash it'. To be bought by a parent should be a matter of reassurance to a child. As a related public policy argument he suggested that, for a number of foetuses, the only way in which they could avoid being aborted would be if their parents could be assured that they could be sold (Landes and Posner, 1978, p 343).

Although Posner had tried to preserve the 'positive' nature of his analysis, it could not do otherwise than open up deep ethical issues. The most common critique rejected the idea that human life could be commodified. Life is an end in itself, not a means to constituting a market. Children are not like cars or television sets (Cass, 1987, p 89). The scientific rules of economic analysis simply cannot be applied to matters of intrinsic human worth. Certain things cannot, and should not, be valued. A related argument suggested that not all children are anyway alike, and so cannot be generalised. Some babies are male, some female, some white, some black, and so on. It would be wholly undesirable if a market was allowed to operate which would then value these characteristics differently. It may be better to have lots of children parentless rather than just lots of girls or lots of black children without parents, even if the total number was fewer. In such situations, inefficiency is more desirable than the alternative (Frankel and Miller, 1987). Jane Maslow Cohen voiced a popular feminist critique of Posner's analysis. Because only women give birth, only poor women can be exploited in the market place. By 'treating the babies of poor women as a form of readily convertible asset' Posner 'renders such women even more vulnerable to a politics of disinvestment'. Not only will such a market exploit poor women, it will also afflict the young, the inexperienced, the anxious, the fearful – in short, all those least capable of operating rationally in a market. Young, scared, poor women are not likely to fulfil the ideal aspirations of the rational economic actor (Cohen, 1987).

Pragmatism, utility and the limits of economic analysis

Economics, in a sense, merely fills an intellectual vacuum. As Posner readily admits, the current vogue for contextual and interdisciplinary studies of law, of which 'law and economics' is one of the most 'prominent', is 'rooted in skepticism'. The 'foundations' of any comprehensive moral philosophy of law 'have been kicked away', and now today 'we are all skeptics', and it is in this sceptical situation that we must seek recourse to a 'critical pragmatism'. It is common sense which suggests that individuals are rational maximisers of self-interest. Even Mill's defence of the free market in *On Liberty* was as much driven by pragmatism as principle. Rational wealth maximisation provides the 'instrument rather than the foundation' of liberty (Posner, 1990, pp 353, 382–87, 452–53). Free market liberalism 'creates the conditions that experience teaches are necessary for personal liberty and economic prosperity'. Because it is experience which teaches us the virtue of liberty, the 'case for liberalism is pragmatic'. Moreover, it is the 'fit' between liberalism and pragmatism which can 'transform legal theory' (Posner, 1995, pp 23–29, 263–68).

Unsurprisingly, in the attempt to justify his determinedly pragmatic defence of economic analysis, Posner has been irreducibly drawn into deeper jurisprudential waters. Thus, in *The Problems of Jurisprudence*, he confessed to favouring a kind of pragmatic utilitarianism, citing Bentham as the first of the economic 'scientists', and aligning himself with an 'activity theory of law'. Such a pragmatism is devoid of principled basis, but that does not matter. The scientific approach which is applied in 'positive' economic analysis provides the only jurisprudence in such a non-foundational world. In more general jurisprudential terms, it describes a form of practical reason which Posner terms a 'grab bag' of precedents and common sense. Economic analysis is itself a form of practical reasoning, founded on the wider pragmatic assertion of social science, that law is a matter of politics and that legal theory is an expression of a given political ideology. In the modern world, the situation of legal theory is 'one of practical indeterminacy'. Necessarily, therefore, judges, and Posner is one, are 'policy makers', and legal institutions, such as courts, are policy making forums. It is wholly 'unrealistic', he adds, 'to believe that our judges can render objective decisions' particularly in 'difficult cases' (Posner, 1990, pp 14–26, 73–100, 132–33, 221–40).

Just as the argument with regard to adoptions lured Posner into the realm of law and morality debates, so too his contribution to the debate on sexuality has drawn him into the world of politics. In *Sex and Reason*, Posner presented a history of sexuality as a history of pragmatic self-interest rather than the evolution of moral principle. As a pragmatic and self-interested theory, it is an 'economic theory of sexuality', which describes the continuing final victory of the free market over theology (Posner, 1992, p 3). Whereas 'social constructionists' concentrate on sexuality as a matter of power, the economic analyst concentrates on incentive and desire. Accordingly, Posner proceeds from a basis of 'morally indifferent sex', which results in a defence of acute sexual freedom. To deny sexual predilection is to deny desire, and to create 'social cost'. The reason for advocating such a liberated approach is not because Posner is particularly interested in permissiveness, but rather because he is keen to effect the 'satisfying' of 'preferences'. Sexuality and economic analysis are precisely about 'satisfying preferences' whilst minimising cost (Posner, 1992, pp 85–87). Thus he defends the liberalisation of sodomy and homosexuality laws because they do not actually effect the suppression of such acts, but simply make them more expensive, and ultimately, such an expense is one which, following Coase's theory, is passed on to all of us. He defends the legalisation of prostitution for precisely the same reason. The attempt to prevent prostitution by making it illegal is wholly unpragmatic. Prostitution does not disappear, because sexual desire cannot be suppressed by law. It merely moves to a black market, rather like illegal adoptions, and becomes so much less efficient. The same arguments, against the inefficiency of the black market, are also used to support the legalisation of abortion (Posner, 1992, pp 111–41, 206–07, 299–311).

Whilst homosexuality, prostitution and abortion might be said to open moral arguments, they also address political concerns and the use of law as a mechanism for exercising power over a sectional interest. Posner dismisses both. The regulation of sexuality is only defensible in the cause of promoting efficiency. Thus the central organisation of sex education is defensible, because it will reduce the social costs of unwanted babies and sexual diseases. So, too, government must continue to support abortion clinics, as well as permitting, of course, private clinics. An unwanted baby always levies considerable social costs, as the baby selling arguments suggested. The licensing of prostitution is an acceptable form of regulation, because it will serve the better interests of both prostitutes and clients, most obviously in reducing sexually transmitted diseases. Accordingly, once again it will also minimise wider social costs in treating such diseases (Posner, 1992, pp 181–215). There is a coincidence between the interests of women and efficiency. Indeed, Posner makes much of the argument that the economic approach, rather than being against the interests of women or other disadvantaged groups, will actually assist the cause of liberation. The relation between liberalism and free market economics, he advises, always serves such causes. Only a free market, to echo Popper, will remain 'open' and accessible to all. It is the free market which has liberated women in modern society, and so, rather than fighting the principle of liberalism, feminists should treasure it and defend it against any communitarian challenge. An example, he presents, is the use of contraceptives. Once the contraceptive market was opened up, against the wishes of moral interest groups such as the Catholic church, the price of contraception was reduced, enabling more women to experience sexual freedom, and in turn exercise greater control over their own lives (Posner, 1992, pp 151–80).

Posner's discussion of sexuality, like that of adoptions, has opened up a fierce dialogue with a series of critics. Feminists have decried the alleged benefits of the free market approach, countering that the arguments for sex equality are a matter of political principle and best realised through legislative enforcement. Communitarians see economic analysis as ethically nihilistic and a denial of social values, whilst those liberals who argue from a more principled position suggest that pragmatic liberalism denies the intrinsic value of the individual. Justice, according to Ronald Dworkin, cannot be 'traded off' with wealth maximisation. Rights rest with the moral individual, as Kant suggested, and cannot be bartered away (Dworkin, 1985, pp 237–89). Similarly, Robin Malloy has used Adam Smith as the resource for illustrating precisely the errors of Posner's neo-liberal analysis. Whereas Smith's market was nurtured as part of a 'social order', which was itself the 'outcome of innumerable self-directed actions and reactions taking place within an everchanging socio-economic environment', Posner's analysis is concerned solely with 'conceptions of wealth maximisation, efficiency, and neutrality'. Underpinning Smith's classical tradition was a desire to 'balance the greatest possible protection' of 'liberty against the justice of imposing limited restraints for a greater social good', and so efficiency was never a determining criterion, merely a constitutive factor in any rational decision making process. Pure efficiency presumes that all decisions are made in splendid isolation, but practical efficiency must always recognise that any economic decision is always affected by a number of social factors, many of which militate against pure efficiency. As Hayek noted, the role of government is primarily directed towards preserving individual freedom, not making, or redistributing, money (Malloy, 1988; 1990).

From the more radical perspective of critical legal studies, Mark Kelman aligns law and economics scholarship with all the other jurisprudences which seek to establish some sort of scientific rationale and determinacy. Law and economics denies the real political impact of law and, despite its protestations of pragmatism, is founded on model actors and markets which simply do not exist in the real world. Posner and his colleagues are engaged in creating 'visions' of 'wish fulfilment' framed in terms of a particular conservative ideology. Neo-liberal economic analysis accounts for the politics of the 'selfish' over that of the disadvantaged outsider and the idea of the inclusive community. Selfishness is not a natural force but an attitude stimulated by a market environment, and so any attempt to describe it as being some sort of non-political dynamic is disingenuous (Kelman, 1984, pp 606–18; 1987, pp 114, 126, 151–52, 173–76). Economic analysis denies the very essence of humanity as difference. People are not all alike and cannot be presumed to be so just for the sake of analytical convenience. Posner, according to Kelman, displays a 'powerful urge to flatten human experience and deny complexity in the service of a desperate Panglossian optimism about the straight world of middle class barter' (Kelman, 1987, pp 114–18). Decisions within a so-called 'free' market are never anyway free, and so, accordingly, the:

> ... theory of individual will that identifies chosen positions with desired positions is primitive at the individual psychological level, unable to cope with regret and ambivalence, and primitive at the sociological level, unable to deal meaningfully with the omnipresence of constraint and duress or to define when constraint is legitimate (Kelman, 1987, p 129).

All choices are context specific responses to the constraints operating within the market and upon the particular chooser. In such terms, economic analysis cannot properly distinguish between giving money to a mugger and paying taxes, and the notion that economic decisions are made, and economic analysis possible, separate from real political conditions is a 'pernicious myth' (Kelman, 1987, pp 131–34, 150). The fundamental refusal to appreciate the essential unpredictability of human beings serves to limit any pragmatic value in an economic analysis of law.

CHAPTER 6

POLITICS, POWER AND PRAGMATISM

THE POLITICS OF DECISION

Decisionism and the return to Hobbes

Thomas Hobbes should not be remembered solely as one of the progenitors of English legal positivism. He was also, as the German political theorist Ferdinand Tonnies suggested, the original 'philosopher of power', and therefore the great prophet for modern theories of the relation between law, government and the modern political State. Accordingly, Hobbes was also proclaimed, by the likes of Tonnies, as well as Leo Strauss and Carl Schmitt, as the intellectual authority behind a distinctive 'decisionist' theory of law and government which emerged in late 19th and early 20th century Germany. Strauss concentrated on Hobbes's movement, from a residual interest in natural superiority to a more pragmatic appreciation that power follows politics (Strauss, 1963, pp 44–56). Hobbes represented a seismic shift in legal and political philosophy, because he wrote, not for the sake of the individual, but to legitimate the State, and thus Strauss could place Hobbes at the very beginning of a tradition in political philosophy which progressed through Hegel to Marx and beyond. At the same time, echoing the argument that Hobbes also provided the theoretical foundations for utilitarianism, Strauss argued that the theory of the State, the Leviathan, is supplemented by a particular moral philosophy of self-interest. Hobbes, he suggested, provided a crude 'utilitarian morality', which was itself the 'morality of the bourgeois world', the morality of possessive individualism (Strauss, 1963, pp 108–28).

It is no coincidence that Strauss shared his interest in Hobbes with the contemporary German legal theorist, Carl Schmitt, who subsequently aspired to be the intellectual force behind National Socialist jurisprudence. It was Schmitt, Strauss suggested, who realised the internal, deeply fascistic, logic of Hobbesian positivism (Strauss, 1976, p 105). During the 1920s, before Hitler's accession to power, Schmitt wrote a series of books and essays in which he repeatedly urged a series of weak and incompetent Weimar governments of the need to take firmer political control, precisely in order to pre-empt any radical revolution. Schmitt had no faith in democracy, and like Hobbes was concerned to warn of the danger of social and political unrest if external revolution was not forestalled by internal constitutional reform. From his very earliest writings, he revealed a pragmatic contempt for liberalism and its presentation of abstract 'romantic' concepts such as rights and freedom. In *Political Romanticism*, Schmitt attacked two centuries of 'romantic' philosophy, which included Kant, for trying to replace theology with a new philosophy of 'human passions and metaphysical abstractions'. In place of 'romantic conversation', Schmitt craved political 'decision'. The modern 'legal order rests on decision and not on a norm' (Schmitt, 1985, pp 10, 31–32; 1986, pp 24–29, 137).

In *The Crisis of Parliamentary Democracy*, Schmitt refocused his attack upon the idea of democracy. Democracy, he suggested, is inherently impossible because it is premised on a homogenous society, cast in liberal ideology in terms of formal equality and freedom. But history revealed that such a society could never exist, for in practice, democracies are always ruled by certain political interests. Freedom, in a liberal democracy, just becomes 'freedom of the ballot winner'. Fifty-one per cent represents dictatorship and, Schmitt added, can write any law it likes. Consciously echoing authorities such as Hume and Mill, Schmitt concentrated his fire against the tendency of liberal democracies to slip into narrow, internecine party politics. Prophetically, he warned that modern liberal democracies, such as Weimar Germany, would destroy themselves in precisely this way (Schmitt, 1988, pp 32–39). In simple terms, liberal democracy does not work, and against the abstract philosophy of liberal democracy, Schmitt countered the need for a political theory that fastened onto 'concrete existential reality'. Moreover, that reality was expressed, not in the cosy friendliness expressed by one right thinking liberal to another, but in the altogether more brutal Hobbesian world of the 'friend' and 'enemy'. All human, and thus political, relationships could be analysed as being with a 'friend' or an 'enemy'. There is no middle ground. Moreover, your enemy is a threat to you and must be exterminated. In the same terms, if you are a contented member of a State, then the enemy of the State is also your enemy, and must be likewise exterminated. Schmitt's advice to the Weimar Republic was explicit: either it destroyed Nazism, or Nazism would destroy it (Schmitt, 1976).

In the end, it was Nazism that destroyed the Weimar Republic. Rapidly converted to Nazism, Schmitt immediately proclaimed himself 'crown jurist' of the new order, and set about outlining a Nazi theory of law explicitly founded on Hobbes's theory of the State (Bendersky, 1983). The resonance with Hobbes's experience is clear. Schmitt moved as easily from working for the Weimar government to working for Hitler as Hobbes moved from his allegiance to the Stuart monarchs to his pragmatic allegiance to Cromwell. Schmitt's 'friend-enemy' distinction, and its associated contempt for liberal ideas of a community of equals under law, was expressly based on Hobbes. The National Socialist State was to be designed around the blueprint of *Leviathan*. Most immediately, in his *State, Movement, People*, written and published within six months of Hitler's rise to power in 1933, Schmitt approved the idea of 'total' politics, the entire community described by and dedicated to politics. The strength of such a politics lay in its denial of the fictional liberal distinction between realms of public and private interest. The everyday life of every German could not be distinguished from the overarching ambition to perfect the Nazi political State as the expression of essential German-ness. The irony, of course, was that, by 1933, Schmitt had himself sought recourse in precisely the same romantic vagaries which he had consistently attacked during the 1920s.

Schmitt's justification was entirely pragmatic. Hitler was the effective power in post-1933 Germany, and so it was to Hitler that political allegiance must be given, regardless of the perceived political morality of the regime. Politics is not a matter of morality, but of effective government. Schmitt again returned to Hobbesian positivism as authority for the affirmation that any law, to be law, had to be effective, and moreover, any law to be effective had to be enforced by a unitary sovereign body, unlimited by any abstract liberal notions of the rule of law. It was Hobbes who advised that 'making a decision is more important than how that decision is made' (Schmitt, 1985, pp 55–56). There must always be an identifiable body which can be relied upon to make the ultimate political 'decision' and then to enforce it. An analysis of power, moreover, must always concentrate on the 'exception', the difficult 'decision' which cannot be easily reached by courts of law. Interestingly, as early as 1921, Schmitt advised that dictatorship was the most efficient form of political government in times of crisis. As a matter of jurisprudential analysis, the 'Sovereign is he who decides the exception', and the veracity of a political and legal system can only be assessed with regard to who makes this decision, and how effective it is (Schmitt, 1985, pp 5–13). Political authority, ultimately, lies with those who can enforce legal decisions.

Pragmatism and realism

At the same time as German political theorists, such as Leo Strauss and Carl Schmitt, were concentrating on acutely pragmatic theories of law and power, so, too, in North America there was a comparable movement away from classical philosophy and towards an experiential pragmatism and its distinct jurisprudential complement – legal realism. One of the leading figures in late 19th and early 20th century pragmatism was John Dewey, who, rather like Schmitt, concentrated his critique against the 'essential' liberal 'fallacy' of certain fundamental political truths, such as freedom, equality and 'rights' (Dewey, 1963, pp 271–98). Influenced by Darwin's theory of natural evolution, Dewey suggested that history testified to the fact that any so called 'absolute' truth is always superseded by a new 'absolute' truth. Truths are merely 'classes of meaning', pronounced by particular groups of historically situated ideologues. In his *The Meaning of Truth*, fellow pragmatist William James had emphasised that truth is simply a matter of 'opinion', legitimated if those who hold that opinion can convince others, by fair means or foul, that their opinion should provide the basis for laws, either moral or civil. As Dewey concluded, the only free man in a liberal society is one who enjoys this degree of 'power' and influence (Dewey, 1963, pp 13–35, 282–83).

At the same time as levelling a critique against liberal political philosophy, pragmatism also concentrated on the possibilities of social and political reform. In many ways, the political agenda of pragmatism, particularly Dewey's, is strikingly communitarian. It was Dewey the educationalist who convinced the US government to restore civic studies to US classrooms, and as we shall see in Chapter 7, Richard Rorty has reinvoked Dewey's spirit, precisely because it is one which represents a critical elision of pragmatic liberalism and the idea of political community. According to Dewey, in the final analysis, regardless of metaphysical disputes regarding the veracity of 'truth', in practice it does not really matter whether something is true or not, for what really matters is whether something is functionally useful or not, and whether it can facilitate social and political reform. Freedom means nothing if it is not experienced by each and every citizen (Dewey, 1963, pp 294–98). As he concluded in his *Philosophy and Civilization*:

> Better it is for philosophy to err in active participation in the living struggles and issues of its own age and times than to maintain an immune monastic impeccability, without relevancy and bearing in the generating ideas of its contemporary present (Dewey, 1963, p 55).

The affinity between such an approach and related theories of utilitarianism and positivism is clear, though paradoxically often denied by pragmatists themselves, who mistrusted the attempts of such as Bentham and Mill to fashion some kind of internal logic from empirical observation.

The similarities with Schmitt are just as striking. In 'Logical method and the law', Dewey affirmed that law is about making 'decisions' and enforcing them. As such, the key figures for jurisprudential analysis are judges, whilst jurisprudence itself must be understood as an 'empirical and concrete discipline'. Dewey specifically approved the pragmatic approach of Oliver Wendell Holmes, who admitted that whilst legal formalism might 'flatter the longing for certainty' in the jurisprudential mind, in reality it is an 'illusion'. Judges, as Holmes affirmed in his *The Common Law*, can rarely furnish decisions driven by internal logic, but instead have to balance immediately political accommodations of interest. The 'actual life of the law', as Holmes admitted, is not 'logic' but 'experience'. Loose 'intuitions of public policy', together with personal 'prejudices', inform judicial decision making, not 'prevalent moral and political theories'. Dewey shared this fundamental pragmatic appreciation that legal formalism sought only to provide an 'illusion of certitude'. In reality, a judicial decision rarely conforms to any internal logic, and theories of law are better directed to the politics of legal adjudication than the metaphysics of right. Significantly, he further suggested that this pragmatic insight means that law should not be seen as possessing any especial timeless legitimacy. In practice, the political morality which judges seek to locate within the common law and then express in immediate political decisions is rarely appropriate to contemporary society. A pragmatist theory of law, then, is one which readily appreciates the constant need for legal reform, and social progress must never be retarded by any mythical notions of formal legalism (Dewey, 1924).

Dewey's pragmatic theory of legal decision making, as indeed his approval of Holmes suggested, bore striking affinities with legal realism. It, too, challenged metaphysical notions of law and legal rights, not just on the intellectual grounds that such theories were abstract and indeterminate, but more immediately because they represented barriers to the reform of society and the possible restoration of a sense of community, civic duty and public responsibility. As a professional educationalist, and echoing the concerns of earlier humanists such as Erasmus and Bacon as well as Bentham and Mill, Dewey was convinced that the first step towards social reform lay with universal education in civic responsibilities. It was also a concern that was central to legal realists, and remains, as we shall shortly see, a driving force in contemporary critical legal scholarship. Indeed, aside from the pronouncements of judges such as Holmes, the prime impulse for legal realism lay in US law schools and their perceived need to reform legal education so as to make it more practically useful in contemporary society (Duxbury, 1995, pp 72–93). Law students, it was thought, should be taught more about the practice of law than the theory of it.

Legal realism should not be seen as representative of any one particular ideology or even methodology. There were various realists with various individual agenda, from the most sceptical such as Holmes, for whom law was not 'a brooding omnipresence in the sky', but simply that which a judge says it is, through the educationalists, to whom we shall return shortly, and on to the more philosophically inclined such as Felix Cohen, who attempted to restore a distinctly utilitarian ethics in realist jurisprudence. Cohen was acutely concerned that bald pragmatism, of the kind advocated by the likes of Holmes, in its refusal to acknowledge that legal validity depended upon anything more than judicial authority, could fail to withhold legitimacy from all kinds of undesirable laws. According to Cohen, whilst legal pragmatics did indeed mean that law depended on judicial authority, there were certain constraints or 'rules of adequacy' with which law must be in accordance. Such rules included consistency, precision and, perhaps most controversially, if confusingly, a moral 'neutrality' which does not deny the reality of a 'political morality' which defines and describes every political community. In other words, whilst recognising that all laws are products of political morality, in individual cases judges should refrain from infecting their decisions with their own ideas of morality and instead look to the morality of the community itself. Of all the legal realists, Cohen came perhaps closest to reinvesting a normative legal ethics. As a matter of jurisprudence, there are bad decisions and bad laws. Such laws are not bad because they are somehow untrue, but because they fail to promote the corporate 'happiness' and 'goodness' of the political community. Ultimately, for Cohen, a realistic jurisprudence was one which appreciated that law is a mixture of principle, pragmatism and utility (Golding, 1981).

Llewellyn and the law job

Perhaps the most influential of the later realists was Karl Llewellyn, who further intensified the turn towards practical utility in legal theory. Llewellyn was particularly concerned with legal institutions and what he termed the 'law job'. Such an approach chimed with the particular evolution of realist 'functionalism'; something which, in turn, focused attention on legal instituitons, such as courts and law schools. In *The Bramble Bush*, a text designed to serve as an introduction to legal studies, Llewellyn affirmed that law does not create social order in a community. It is the study and application of law which fulfils that 'function'. At the same time, he immediately sought to dispel from students' minds the notion that they should be concerned with such things as rights. Rights, unless they can be realised in a court of law, are 'worse than useless'. Affirming the injunctions of both Holmes and Schmitt, Llewellyn premised his study with the observation that what matters is the 'concrete instance' of the legal case and the measure of what institutions and judges 'do about disputes'. The study of rules and rights can never itself be enough to address this question, for, as he shrewdly observes, if law was no more than the application of rules to fact situations, then there would be little mystery and even less need for trained lawyers. It is the inconsistency of legal decision making in hard case scenarios which is the subject for legal study. How do judges deal with the 'exceptional' legal case, the dispute upon which various lawyers and litigants disagree? (Llewellyn, 1960a, pp 11–24, 29–35, 58–60, 110–12.) The resonance with Schmitt's theory of sovereignty, determined by the resolution of exceptional cases, is striking.

The degree to which Llewellyn was committed to this functionalist approach can be seen in his comparative anthropological study, *The Cheyenne Way*. The extent to which political theory should be seen as a relative cultural phenomenon was fully appreciated by Dewey, and a number of legal realists increasingly turned to comparative legal studies, rather than legal philosophy, in order to discover functionalist truths (Dewey, 1963, pp 7–9). The Cheyenne, Llewellyn noted, identify precisely the same question as US courts of law – the resolution of hard case legal disputes through the mechanism of certain established juristic institutions. However, what is also clear is the sense of community which remains pervasive in a society which has not succumbed to the fragmenting impulses of liberal ideology. There is no divide between spheres of public and private interests, and legal disputes amongst the

Cheyenne were always characterised as both. Accordingly, there was no question of individual rights held against other individuals, or by implication the rest of the community. At the same time, and in considerable part because of the former conclusion, the 'Cheyenne way' assumes that all laws and rules of conduct are contextually and socially situated. In turn, therefore, the settlement of disputes, the resolution of the 'law job', is guided by the pervasive desire to effect justice in the particular situation, and is not constricted by any countervailing anxiety about conformity to formal rules (Llewellyn and Hoebel, 1941, pp 41–63).

This is not to deny the presence of historically determined notions of political morality. Indeed, the narrative tradition of the 'Cheyenne way' placed considerable stress on the validity of historical principle, which served as something of an alternative to a system of case law precedent. However, such a principle only served as a tool, itself an institution, dedicated to the greater concern for justice. At all times, implicit in the 'Cheyenne way' is the assumption that the realisation of individual justice is congruent with the wider interests of the community, and therefore its promotion cannot be counter to the social purpose of law itself. As a closing and perceptive observation, Llewellyn noted that, whilst Cheyenne jurisprudence might seem to be rather primitive in comparison with US law, its ability to resolve disputes to the satisfaction of all parties, and the extent to which it continued to enjoy the widespread confidence of its community, was something which contemporary Americans, lawyers included, could only look upon with envy. Regardless of its idiosyncrasies, the 'Cheyenne way' gets its 'law jobs' done with a degree of efficiency and popular acceptance far greater than that achieved by more modern and supposedly sophisticated jurisprudences, and it does so because it focuses upon the function of its legal institutions and does not permit itself to be deflected by any unfounded metaphysical distractions (Llewellyn and Hoebel, 1941, pp 273–340).

According to Llewellyn, then, all cultures deal with the same basic problem of attempting to effect justice by establishing certain institutions and mechanisms for getting the 'law job' done. The precise description of these institutions and jobs, and the way in which they are conducted, might vary from one culture to another. But, at root, all communities seek to deal with legal issues and to legitimate legal decisions through institutions. The form of law becomes not the form of rules, but the form of institutions. This conclusion was developed further in his *The Common Law Tradition*. The value of legal precedent, Llewellyn suggested, lay in the extent to which it invested the institution of law with a degree of consistency and predictability. It informs the 'craft' of decision making and expedites the completion of the law job. To a certain extent, in his support for what he terms the 'grand style' of legal decision making, by which he meant an appeal to immanent reason, as opposed to the countervailing 'formal style' of rule based legalism, there is much in Llewellyn's mature theory of law which, rather like Cohen's, seeks to reinvest a measure of philosophical, even ethical, stability. At the same time, this adherence to the stabilising qualities of an historical reason is generated purely by a desire to facilitate the 'functions' of the legal institutions, and not by any more metaphysical aspiration (Llewellyn, 1960b). Indeed, as he observed in *The Bramble Bush* and a series of later essays, Llewellyn, perhaps more than any other of the realists, shared a burning desire to use law to facilitate social reform. Society is always changing, always in need of reform, and the legal realist must share the critical appreciation that law, as a 'living' entity, dependent upon the life blood of the community, must be responsive to social change rather than set itself as a bulwark against it. The ultimate 'purpose' of legal theory can only be legal 'reform' (Llewellyn, 1960a, pp 65–81, 117–18, 145–51; 1962, pp 3–41).

HISTORY, KNOWLEDGE AND POWER

Foucault and the culture of modernism

When Michel Foucault died of AIDS in Paris in 1984, he was pronounced the 'most famous intellectual in the world' (Miller, 1993, p 13). Such claims normally attract an appropriate degree of scepticism, but in Foucault's case, it is just possible that this was true. Exploiting a culture of technology which he consistently denounced, Foucault fashioned for himself a position as the intellectual chronicler of the modern world. If every teenager's wall had a poster of Che Guevara stuck on it, every self-respecting middle class intellectual had a copy of Foucault's *History of Sexuality* or *Discipline and Punish*. The fact that hardly any teenager really knew that much about Guevara, or that anyone bothered to slog through the three volume *Sexuality*, hardly mattered. Foucault was an icon, and this was precisely what he set out to be. At the root of Foucault's personal and intellectual philosophy was a determination to uncover the suppression of individualism and to reverse it. It is this suppression which characterises modernity. As we will shortly see, in a more obviously juridical sense, this suppression of individuality is evidenced by the establishment of prisons and police forces. But it can be seen throughout modern society. It is why we are all encouraged to diet, or to jog, or to own 'our' own houses, so that mortgage houses and building societies can be kept in business, as well as health gurus and sportswear manufacturers. We aspire towards the body beautiful, just as we aspire to be model citizens and householders. At all times, we are presented with ideals and instructed that we really ought to be like everyone else in aspiring to realise these ideals. This is Plato's legacy. It is why we need laws to encourage us to conform, and exercise manuals to encourage us to jog. These are what Foucault terms the 'disciplinary processes' of the 'body'. Modern society controls us by encouraging us to constrain ourselves. It determines the lifestyle decisions which we think we make, by controlling the alternatives from which we have to choose.

With his denunciation of the culture of modernism, Foucault expressed the anxiety and rebellion of a generation. He was hugely influenced by the populist political movements of the late 1960s and early 1970s. Moreover, he lived that rebellion, actively supporting a series of politically sensitive issues, including the liberalisation of drugs legislation and reform of laws relating to sexual practices. He consistently advocated civil disobedience and in later years made a series of controversial comments suggesting support for international terrorism against imperialism and capitalism. Freedom must always be seized, for it is never given willingly by those in power. The relative merits or demerits of each of the causes Foucault supported perhaps matters less than the fact of his consistent determination to rebel and, most importantly, to inspire others to question the established 'facts' of their lives. If Foucault achieved anything, it was to get ordinary people, or at least ordinary middle class intellectuals, to think hard about their situation in modern society; to question who has power to determine what they do, and why they have that power.

Of course, the intellectual context goes much deeper than popular protest, drugs and sexual practices. Or at least it is historically deeper, even if thematically consistent. William Connolly has suggested that the sado-masochism of the Marquis de Sade provided the literary equivalent of Hobbes's *Leviathan* (Connolly, 1988, pp 68–85). Whereas Hobbes wrote to rid us of any illusion that law or politics was anything other than an expression of power, so too de Sade wrote to convince us that moral nicety was simply an excuse for one particular ethical vision to be enforced against individual desire. De Sade's *Philosophy in the Bedroom* urged us to express ourselves through the most acute forms of passion, because only through the intensities of passion can modern men and women react against the suffocating dominion of modernist ethics and its universalising ambitions. De Sade removed God from the bedroom, just as Hobbes removed him from politics. Foucault was the natural successor to both, living the philosophy of de Sade whilst chronicling the politics of Hobbes. The radical and liberating potential of this critique is at the centre of Foucault's politics. A critique which advocates the experience of individuality necessarily demands the possibility of experiencing political power. It was the desire to emancipate the individual from the strictures of institutionalised power, from schoolroom to prison to parliament, which underpinned Foucault's determination that we should choose for ourselves whether to take drugs, whether to indulge in sado-masochistic sexual practices, or whether to go on strike. Modern government is equally keen that our decisions should be constrained by a higher authority. We take drugs which government sanctions, such as nicotine or alcohol; we indulge in sexual practices that government permits; we withdraw our labour only under the statutory conditions determined by 'our' parliament. Everything, of course, hangs on the spurious legitimacy of the 'our'. There is no 'our', but somehow, and this is the great secret of modernity's success, we are deluded into thinking there is.

In the final chapter we will encounter a series of theories which can be loosely termed postmodern, and which attempt to redefine philosophy in terms of literature and the politics of writing. Although the precise nature of Foucault's relation with an identifiable postmodernism remains controversial, certainly, as its chronicler, he tried to place himself outside modernism. Most obviously he can be situated within a particular tradition of 20th century French intellectualism which sought to redefine modernism by turning towards literature, art and emotion. In *Being and Nothingness*, Jean-Paul Sartre emphasised that there is lived experience and nothing. These are the only two alternatives. The irony, of course, which Sartre noted, is that we spend most of our lives desperately looking for a third alternative which we hope might provide some sort of deeper metaphysical meaning to life. Although there was much in Sartre that Foucault was keen to dismiss, the urge to get us to take responsibility for our own existence, rather than hide behind such metaphysical guises as reason or nature, was very much a shared one.

Ultimately, the essential figure against which this intellectual critique was directed was Immanuel Kant. As his career progressed, Foucault increasingly situated himself in a particular 'discourse' with Kant who, he asserted, was the last great champion of modernist philosophy. Foucault saw his particular duty as one of taking Kant's critique of reason to a logical conclusion which lay beyond modernism itself. This discourse with Kant became ever more dominant towards the end of Foucault's career. In asking the question 'what is Enlightenment?', Kant had abandoned history in an attempt to investigate the present. He had posed modernism as an ultimate condition, described by pure reason. Yet he had also posed modernism as being something that was intrinsically different. Kant's critical project was geared to the ultimate realisation that even reason could not be sheltered from the contingencies of history and politics. Thus, for Foucault, Kant's critique represented the final realisation that any philosophical universalism is defeated by the contingency of the self, and by locating reason within the self, Kant at once destroyed the possibilities of pure philosophy. It is Kant's critique which announced the limits of reason and after Kant, therefore, everything is political to some degree (Foucault, 1984, p 32).

History and knowledge

The engagement with Kant was critical, not just because it signalled the demise of philosophy and the emergence of politics, but because it also privileged another discourse, that of history. The Enlightenment, Kant realised, was incapable of interrogating itself without recourse to history. It is the essential discipline for the contextual understanding of anything. A pure science, of politics, philosophy or whatever, is never actually pure, and things only make sense and can only be explained within their historical context. Politics is a necessarily historical discipline. Most important of all is the control of knowledge, a control exercised by history for the benefit of political power. History has fashioned both the society in which we live, and the knowledge which that society uses and by which it defines itself. Knowledge, like science, is never independent or pure. It is always historically and socially situated (Hunt and Wickham, 1994, pp 6–13).

At the core of Foucault's thesis is the assertion that power and knowledge are intimately complementary and reinforcing. Those with power control the 'conditions of the possibility' of knowledge. What we know is knowledge we are allowed to know. If this was not true, there would be no need for any form of censorship, for judicial protection for certain government documents which can be kept out of court proceedings, for cinema censorship, for national curricula in schools, for university law syllabuses prescribed by The Law Society. Law is both an element and an expression of power. Because knowledge is itself produced by history, and by the dominant discourses of history, the ability to write history, to tell us what happened in the past and therefore why things are as they are today, is the greatest power of all. Our present law, and our knowledge of it, is the product of an historical evolution, more precisely the various struggles between various historical discourses. Already in this book, we have encountered alternative theories of law, from Plato to Aquinas to Kant to Hobbes, each of which is the product of immediate historical circumstance. We never exist purely in the present, but are always to some degree determined by our history, and the same is certainly true of law.

The realisation that our own situation, and that of our political institutions such as law, is historically situated is a defining characteristic of modernism. In Chapter 4, we witnessed Thomas Hobbes signalling the end of natural law theory and heralding the emergence of a legal positivism which aligned law with politics rather than metaphysics or moral philosophy. It was Hobbes who announced the arrival of a distinctive modern modernism, sceptical of any metatheory and determined to analyse law and politics in terms of its real empirical impact upon the lives of men and women. Michel Foucault emerged as one of a series of major intellectual figures of the 20th century who determined to understand better our present society by chronicling its historical evolution. Foucault did not write 'history' in the sense of traditional progressive history, and he frequently denied the appellation 'historian'. Yet his ambition, to explain the evolution of modernism, was certainly historical in the broader sense. Modernist history assumes some sort of narrative function, with a beginning, a middle and an end. Foucault, crucially, denied any such 'metanarrative', and in its place described first an 'archaeology' and then a 'genealogy'. An 'archaeology' helps us to understand better our real political existences as a product of various histories particular to us. So history for men is different from history for women, just as the history for Americans might be different from history for Japanese. It does not carry with it the ideology which, Foucault suggested, lies behind modern history. An archaeology describes why things are. It does not seek, as does modernism, to prescribe how they also should be. It acknowledges the different histories of each person, and does not seek to locate some sort of fabricated shared allegiance in the past.

Foucault's first major publication, *Madness and Civilisation*, was a study of the techniques, strategies and discourses which effected the marginalisation of those considered to be 'mad'. Madness was 'invented' by a modern society keen to establish certain norms of behaviour. No one in the pre-modern age had thought fit to incarcerate anyone who acted out of the ordinary, unless they actually committed some criminal act. But in modern society, those who do not seem quite right are imprisoned in asylums. The study was the first in a series which have been termed structuralist. In other words, they are studies of how knowledge is prescribed through forms of language and description. The people who enjoy power in society are those who can persuade us, through various media, that they are somehow right and can describe norms of behaviour. At the same time, accordingly, they can persuade us that certain others are wrong and abnormal. The mad were described as those who did not engage in rational discourse. Their exclusion from society, like that of any other marginalised group, is effected by their being excluded from normal political and social discourse. Today, it is an exclusion suffered most obviously by women, ethnic minorities and the poor. It was this essential thesis which also underpinned his *The Archaeology of Knowledge*, published in 1969. In both *Madness* and *Archaeology*, Foucault aspired to discovering 'truth', in so far as was possible, in methodology. The methodology of archaeology could reveal the truth of things, including our particular situation in society. However, such a truth, even if descriptive rather than prescriptive, was still a 'meta-history'. It sought to provide a final absolute history, and following the events of 1968–69, and the student riots with which he was closely associated, Foucault recoiled from such a temptation.

Foucault's turn from structuralism to post-structuralism was a turn away from any vestiges of 'truth'. Instead, Foucault embraced a radical contingency which was demanded by any politics which sought to be genuinely radical. Rather than archaeology, which presumed certain facts which could be objectively presented, Foucault turned to 'genealogy' as a methodology of purely subjective interpretation. There are no facts, merely interpretations of other interpretations. Politics is about the relation between alternative interpretations, and whoever's interpretation is legitimated enjoys power. Politics becomes a 'strange contest, a confrontation, a power relation, a battle among discourses' (Sheridan, 1980, p 134). His work during the 1970s evidenced a determination to subvert the modern rationalist discourses of history, and their implicit claims to describing 'truth'. In 'Truth and power', he suggested that truth 'is not outside of power', but rather 'is of this world'. In other words, truth is not given by God or nature. We create our own truths, and if we are powerful enough we make others believe it is some sort of metaphysical truth. Each society, he concluded, 'has its own regime of truth, its general politics of truth' (Foucault, 1980a, p 121). It was precisely the conclusion reached a century or so earlier by William James and John Dewey.

His later work, including that on governance and punishment which we shall consider shortly, concentrated increasingly on the methods for legitimating the exercise of power under the spurious authority of 'truth'. *The History of Sexuality* sought to explain the narratives of power and 'normality' which surround sex. It was not merely an account of sexual behaviour, but rather sought to explain which discourses of sexuality enjoyed dominion in our lives. What is described as 'normal' sexual behaviour is simply that which is prescribed by those who control the discourse. The sexually deviant have been 'invented', just as were the 'mad'. Sexuality has not been repressed *per se*, though there are certain laws which have sought to proscribe certain sexual activity. Rather, the discourse of sexuality has been controlled by certain political interests, primarily as a means of reinforcing the moral authority of those interests. We talk about sex more than we ever have before, but what we say is closely controlled, both by legal and extralegal authorities. Accordingly, for example, homosexuality has not been proscribed because it is a certain type of physical act, but because that proscription is demanded as part of a moral philosophy which is used by certain political interests, at a particular time, as a means of legitimating political dominion over a society. The discourse of sexuality is a 'disciplinary technology' geared to the subjugation of an entire society.

Law, governance and discipline

Law, according to Foucault, is simply the expression and exercise of power. If you can get someone to do what you want, then you can prescribe a rule of behaviour. Whether or not it is universal is irrelevant. The exercise of any rule is always in the particular, obeyed or not in a particular instance. All law is thus particular, merely aspiring to universal application in an attempt to justify itself as being somehow normal or right or natural. According to Foucault, the very 'idea of justice in itself is an idea which in effect has been invented and put to work in different societies as an instrument of a certain political and economic power or as a weapon against that power' (Foucault, 1984, p 6). Furthermore, developing his work on claims to 'truth', Foucault suggested that the particular characteristic of modernism is the claim that law somehow expresses, even preserves and secures, certain truths. Law has become consonant with truth. If something is the 'law', it is supposed to be right. In a 1976 lecture, he aligned law, truth and power:

> The system of right, the domain of law, are permanent agents of these relations of domination, these polymorphous techniques of subjugation. Rights should be viewed, I believe, not in terms of a legitimacy to be established, but in terms of the methods of subjugation that it instigates (Foucault, 1980b, p 96).

In other words, the study of law is not a study of philosophy or ethics, but of politics and power.

The suggestion that law is merely an expression of power was emphasised in Foucault's lectures on 'governmentality' and liberalism. The exercise of government is facilitated by employing certain 'techniques' and strategies whereby the freedom of individuals is constrained in order to service a particular moral and political vision, and law is the mechanism by which these constraints are effected. But this law is more than merely the rules and regulations laid down in statute or case law. It is an entire disciplinary process, part of which is certainly legalistic, but part also is governmental. We are not ruled simply by laws, but by an entire governmental process. It was this process which was established in the early modern period of European history, and described most effectively by Hobbes's *Leviathan* (Hunt and Whickham, 1994, pp 52–56). Thus, in 'Politics and the study of discourse', Foucault suggested that the study of politics should not simply be the study of the official 'institutions' of power, such as parliament or the courts of law. Rather, radical politics must address the 'networks of power' that control society (Foucault, 1991). The relation between the preponderance of lawyers in the House of Commons and the practice of government would be one obvious example. Another would be the related preponderance of wealthy people in public life. Law, money and politics time and again forge a particular 'network of power'.

The particular characteristic of modernism, then, is governmentality. It describes the process by which society is governed by administrative bureaucracy, and the way in which the governed are convinced by certain truth claims that this is necessary and expedient. The complexities of modern life, we are told, make it inevitable that a measure of freedom must be sacrificed so that the government of our lives can be efficient. As Galbraith suggested, our expectations are carefully controlled by the 'consumer society' in which we live, and which has emerged as a classic example of 'disciplinary technology'. Bureaucracy has become part of our lives. We are told it is necessary, so we think it natural. Modernism is characterised by a 'science' of government concerned solely with expediency, which no longer aspires to realise perfect justice or save men's souls, but which simply seeks to govern society in such a way as to maximise its own efficiency and to maintain social stability. It is the government which complements the driving demands of the modern political economy. Accordingly, modern government concentrates, not on the moral or spiritual improvement of the individual, but on governing the relationships between individuals as economic actors (Foucault, 1991, p 93). The 'technologies' of government have thus changed. No longer are we governed by Westminster or our parish church, but by our banks and insurance companies, our doctors and solicitors, teachers and lecturers. These are the effective 'micro-centres' of power in modern society, the 'technologies' which govern the modern individual. In such terms, the traditional concern of jurisprudence with identifying sovereignty in Parliament or the courts or wherever, is a myth designed to keep law students amused and the general public obedient. Sovereignty is now radically dispersed in a myriad of these 'micro-centres'. Law is simply the ultimate, most obvious, of these 'technologies' of power, directed to 'arrange things in such a way that, through a certain number of means, such and such ends may be achieved' (Foucault, 1991, p 95).

Jurisprudence, Foucault suggested, is simply an attempt to legitimate the exercise of power through the use of mythology. This imaginary juristic 'relationship of domination' is 'fixed, throughout its history, in rituals, in meticulous procedures that impose rights and obligations' (Foucault, 1977, p 150). This idea was expressed most strongly in his *Discipline and Punish*, a study of the 'birth' of the modern prison. At its heart is the suggestion that the move from the public spectacle of torture and execution to imprisonment and surveillance reflects the administrative 'technologies' of the individual body which defines modernism. The responsibility for punishing the individual has passed from the public spectator and executioner to a 'whole army of technicians' (Foucault, 1979, pp 10–11). Criminals are no longer hanged, drawn and quartered, but are 'scientifically' killed by lethal injection. Punishment has always been a simple matter of exercising control over the bodies of others, and the way people are punished is dictated by the political interests of those who have the power to punish. It is part of the same essential nexus, of politics, power and knowledge (Foucault, 1979, pp 27–28). In past centuries, that power was, in large part, exercised through theatre and ceremony. The ritual of power was pervasive, from the coronation of God's anointed to the public torture and execution of the criminal. There was no question of execution being hidden away behind prison walls. The execution of a criminal was a theatrical experience, a day out for the locals, often with a customary holiday thrown in. The theatre needed its audience, and the ceremony of torture and execution served to confirm once again the immediate authority of the sovereign (Foucault, 1979, pp 32–69).

As we have already noted, reform of the disciplinary processes of punishment was part of the pervasive ethic of efficiency which spread through 19th century Europe. The demand that prisoners should be made to labour hard to purge their guilt satisfied both the demand to discover easily exploitable labour and the desire to educate the recalcitrant in their duties to the wider capitalist community. Prisoners could be readmitted to society only when they had proved that they were indeed willing to sacrifice their lives to the greater cause of the free market, and the modern prison was designed to develop the 'habit' of work (Foucault, 1979, pp 104–31). The design of the modern prison was an essential ingredient of this 'disciplinary process'. Prisons, factories, hospitals, military camps, were all built to 'permit an internal, articulated and detailed control'. Bentham designed his Panopticon in such a way that every prisoner's cell was constantly open to the 'gaze' of a central tower. Though none of the prisoners could see one another, they were constantly viewed by the prison authorities. Though Bentham was inordinately proud of his model prison, Foucault termed it a 'cruel, ingenious cage', designed to subjugate the individual to the pervasive demands of the modern political economy. It represented a 'disciplinary gaze', and this obsession with surveillance reflected a society which no longer trusted people to live in accordance with social norms, or to work hard enough. Modern society needed to 'see' that people were obedient and industrious. Similarly, the invention of 'police' forces in the 19th century in many European countries reflected an ideology of government that was determined to institute an 'indefinite world of supervision' (Foucault, 1979, pp 205–14). The purpose of prisons or police forces has never been to eliminate crime. Crime will never be eliminated in modern society. Their purpose is to control individuals, either directly, by incarcerating them, or indirectly, by threatening to (Foucault, 1979, p 272).

Prisons are only one example of this tendency to employ 'strategies' of control. Factories and schools are designed in precisely the same way. The factory floor and the schoolroom were designed in such a way that the individual worker or student could be surveyed at all times. Each physical movement was monitored in order to improve, not merely efficiency, but control. Each aspect of modern life was fashioned by the various institutions in which people live their lives in order to enhance political control. This 'micro-physics of power' was pervasive, affecting every aspect of life. It introduced timetables into the schoolroom, gymnastics as a form of exercise, every physical movement of which was directed by a school teacher, even good handwriting. Children who wrote with their left hands were brutally punished. The central concern, common to school teachers, doctors, army officers and prison authorities, is to suppress individuality. Children must be educated to be good citizens, patients to be healthy ones, soldiers to be responsive to orders, and prisoners to be all three. It was a 'disciplinary process' first advised by Plato and Aristotle. Ultimately, each of these institutions was, and still is, designed to produce 'individuals mechanised according to the general norms of an industrious society' (Foucault, 1979, pp 139–53, 200–01, 235–42). In the final analysis, the law, prisons, police, delinquency, each constitute a mutually supporting industry. These various 'juridico-political' institutions serve to categorise society. There are criminals and good citizens, just as there are poor and wealthy, good free market competitors and bad ones.

At the heart of Foucault's thesis is the assertion that there is a clear affinity between the criminal and the poor. Moreover, this is an affinity actively supported by the structures and morality of modern society. The modern political economy needs an identifiably exploitable class. It needs failures, just as much as it needs success. Law and its associated 'disciplinary processes' play a crucial and active role in categorising society. Law ensures that there will be an element of society that will fail to compete, that will seek recourse to means outside the law in order to survive, and which can then be punished in such a way as to enhance its exploitability. The criminal delinquent is 'an institutional product', the product, indeed, of the 'new economy of power'. Today, the extent to which poverty is seen as being a cause of crime is a matter of political controversy, but it is worth noting that when the institutions of modern juridical and political power were established, it was universally accorded that crime was predominantly the preserve of the impoverished delinquent classes. Moreover, this was a necessary and good thing, a signal that the political economy was working as it should, identifying an exploitable class of individuals, and controlling them (Foucault, 1979, pp 272–304). It is here that the clearest echoes of Marxism can be discerned, in the suggestion that modern law is merely an instrument of economic ideology. The role of law, and the 'disciplinary processes' of prisons, police and so forth, are all dedicated to promoting the ethic of the modern political economy. In a very real sense, law is the handmaiden of politics.

CRITICAL LEGAL THINKING

Critical legal studies

During the 1970s, a self-styled 'Critical Legal Studies' movement (CLS) emerged, primarily in North America. To the extent that it enjoyed a formative aspiration, it was to demolish the presumed pretences of liberal legalism, and its associated jurisprudences. Coining a particularly resonant phrase, one leading 'crit', Mark Kelman suggested that critical legal thinking is dedicated to 'trashing' the various mythologies of liberal legalism, particularly notions of adjudicative neutrality. Every judge, Kelman arued, is a political actor effecting a particular political agenda, in its broadest sense, free market liberalism (Kelman, 1984; 1987). The intellectual roots of CLS are various, but the most common attributions are to realism and post-structuralism. Foucault is a common idol. Much early CLS writing concentrated on the social dimensions of legal history, and the relativist critique of liberal legalism emerged from these essentially empirical studies (Tushnet, 1991; Gordon, 1982). There is also a pervasive interest in the politics of legal education; something to which we will turn shortly. At the same time, as we have already noted with Unger's particular type of reconstructive legal thinking, there are immediate affinities between ideas of radical participatory democracy and more classical communitarian ideology. An example of how all these intellectual strands elide can be seen in Karl Klare's critique of labour law; empirical and historicist in methodology, radical communitarian in prescription. According to Klare, the critical weakness in 'liberal rights consciousness' is its inability to conceive of 'human freedom as self-expression and growth in and through community' (Klare, 1981, p 479).

The critique of rights is a central theme of much CLS writing. Mark Tushnet denounces rights as 'illusions' and 'myths' designed to mask fundamental social, political and economic inequalities (Tushnet, 1984). Rights merely enact fictional divisions within communities, separating individuals and thus diminishing the potential for collective political action. The need to recast critical legal thinking in terms of communities of active political interest was emphasised by Joseph Singer. The first step, and it is one which can be facilitated by critical lawyers, is to 'retake' legal theory and to resituate it within a larger political enterprise. 'Theory', Singer emphasises, 'expresses our values; it does not create them'. The reclamation of theory is both a prerequisite of political power, and an exercise of it. In words which again bear striking comparison with various communitarian theses, Singer suggests that, 'Like law, consensus must be made, not found'. It is the emphasis 'on the creative, communal nature of common understanding' which 'creates an appropriate relationship between thought and action', and once 'we have envisioned how we would like to do things, we can then use the principles and counterprinciples in legal discourse to describe what we value about these alternative arrangements' (Singer, 1984, pp 60–65). As Radbruch suggested, social revolution is premised upon critical legal thinking.

It is sometimes suggested that the CLS movement has fallen into decline (Duxbury, 1995, pp 426–28). It is perhaps better to suggest that it has evolved in more directed fashion, and three particular directions warrant especial note. The first is the kind of reconstructive liberalism of Roberto Unger which we encountered in Chapter 3. A second is in the particular areas of feminist and race theory, to which we shall turn shortly. The third direction is towards theories of language. This latter development has grown apace in recent years, and can be aligned, at least to some degree, with the kind of postmodern legal writing that we will encounter in the next chapter.

One of the most strident of this latter breed of linguistically-inclined 'crits' is Allan Hutchinson. According to Hutchinson, political reform must be a linguistic enterprise, for we all 'live' in language in so far as we express ourselves and our politics through language. Therefore, politics must become a more conversational enterprise, and a radical politics must, accordingly, be dedicated to facilitating wider dialogue between citizens. Language, he suggested, 'must be recognised as both the prize of political conflict and the arena in which the conflict takes place'. Because 'language and imagination are inextricably linked, the complex interface between individual consciousness and social systems of meaning is the crucial phase of political engagement'. 'We are never not in a story', Hutchinson affirmed, because 'History and human action only take on meaning and intelligibility within their narrative context and dramatic settings'. We are all living our lives like actors in a performance, and lawyers are merely trained to play a particular role. Once we understand this theatricality or pretence, then we can indeed 'debunk the elite fables of law', realise our constitutive role in the actual performance and play a more assertive role (Hutchinson, 1988, pp 13–14, 21–22, 148).

Another of the linguistically-inclined 'crits' is Gerry Frug. Invoking a specifically Arendtian idea of permanent social revolution, Frug also tended towards reconstructive theories of localised participatory democracy (Frug, 1980, pp 1068–74). More precisely, the triumph over the countervailing forces of 'administrative bureaucracy' will be effected by a 'rewriting' of the 'language of democracy'. Our legal contexts are conversationally created, through the interaction of all of us in the social situation, and there is no 'foundation' outside this dialogic relation (Frug, 1988). Alan Hunt has suggested that CLS must embrace the textual insights of postmodernism, not because there is an intrinsic merit in uncovering linguistic indeterminacies, but because such insights can legitimate wider critical political agenda. The appreciation that law is textual serves to emphasise that it is a purely social and contingent construct, and deserving of no deeper intellectual reverence. In the final chapter, we will return to the idea of a postmodern jurisprudence, and its potential as a critical legal theory. According to Hunt, writing in 1990, CLS scholarship was riven by a particular tension, one which was, in large part, generated by an uncertainty as to how far it should evolve towards an identifiable postmodern agenda (Hunt, 1990). For a number of the more radical political critical legal scholars, certainly those associated with the earlier socio-legal critiques, the turn to textuality threatened a return to grand, and obscure, philosophies of law; a foundation in language was a foundation like any other. For others, such as Hutchinson or Frug, the turn towards language was the only direction which could be pursued by anyone seeking to suggest a more reconstructive vision of law and society.

Legal education and the limits of critical legal studies

A particularly notorious debate between Peter Gabel and Duncan Kennedy, entitled 'Roll over Beethoven', which was published in 1984, provided a vivid illustration of the rival positions which emerged within CLS and which remain largely unresolved, perhaps by definition unresolvable (Hunt, 1990, p 521). Gabel and Kennedy assumed these very different, indeed polar, positions within CLS scholarship: whilst Gabel advocated some form of reconstructive enterprise, Kennedy maintained a more radical and uncompromising position determined to concentrate on 'trashing' liberal legalism. Thus, as the debate revealed, for Gabel the critical project was directed towards making law better approximate 'experienced reality'. The 'human condition' is one of 'fundamental contradiction', and law must acknowledge this whilst reflecting the need for individuals to 'overcome alienation' from society. The sense of community which must be inculcated into previously alienated individuals will be realised by a crucial moment of connectedness, a 'moment of describing existential reality at the level of reflection', which Gabel termed 'intersubjective zap'. At the same time as reinvesting a philosophy of self, Gabel, like others such as Roberto Ung...., wanted to effect a complementary revision of legal theory and practice. However, unlike Unger, Gabel's revised theory is premised on moving beyond the 'illusion that there is an entity called the State' and 'that people possess rights'. 'Exactly what people do not need is their rights', but rather 'actual forms of social life' which are not shrouded in liberal myths of formal equality. Moreover, the ultimate responsibility lay with lawyers, to appreciate the irreducibly political nature of their enterprise and to use the law to reform 'their own political aims' (Gabel and Kennedy, 1984, pp 2–4, 10–15, 34–35).

Whilst approving the appeal to political action, Duncan Kennedy dismissed all this talk about 'experienced reality' and 'intersubjective zap' as 'abstract bullshit'. Philosophy does not provide the answer to the real political problems experienced by modern men and women. Rather, it turns people into 'pods', incapable of thinking for themselves, and merely the voicepieces of someone else's ideology. Instead of philosophy, Kennedy suggested that critical lawyers must operate through more familiar media, such as 'soap opera, pop culture, all that kind of stuff'. Such an approach, Kennedy alleged, was intellectually and appropriately ironic. Critical lawyers must proceed by being ironic, and will operate more effectively by 'communicating' with 'jokes' than they ever will with 'abstract formulation' (Gabel and Kennedy, 1984, pp 3, 8–11). This, of course, was the original fear shared by Plato and Aristotle, and as we shall see in Chapter 7, it is the strategy stridently recommended by Nietzsche and latter-day Nietzscheans such as Richard Rorty. The determination to undermine the pretensions of law and legal language is a crucial attribute of Kennedy's more immediately radical approach. So, too, is his determination to instrumentalise actual political change, by organising resistance groups within all institutions, universities, law firms and so forth. The radical intellectual must learn the art of revolution, the 'skill of workplace organising'. Revolution will not just happen. It must be made to happen (Kennedy, 1993, pp 25–33).

One of the most intriguing areas of debate in critical legal studies relates to legal education. And it could be found at the very heart of the Gabel-Kennedy debate. Gabel noted that law students tend to distance themselves from reality. Because they are going to 'become lawyers', law students 'think they have to transform' their 'feelings' into 'good legal arguments'. They start talking about unconscionability or rights to privacy, or any of the myriad of legal technicalities which pervade lawyer-speak. In effect, 'without realising' the fact, 'there is a weird dissociation taking place', between the human being and the lawyer. Law students are co-opted into a particular 'ideological framework', without even noticing the fact (Gabel and Kennedy, 1984, p 26). Because law is a political expression, so too legal education is irreducibly political. This is not a good or a bad thing. It just is. But it also needs to be appreciated both by law teachers and law students. Every textbook, every lecture, and every tutorial is a political exercise, and those law teachers who pretend not to be political are simply more dangerous, not less political. Again, it is not the politics of law that matters, but the denial of it. So much was accepted by both Gabel and Kennedy. It was the question of how to deal with the problem which, once again, revealed critical differences. Gabel wanted to inform law students of the alienated condition and the potential of 'intersubjective zap'. Kennedy preferred direct action and encouraged students to picket supermarkets. If society is to be reformed, such a reform must begin in the legal profession and thus in legal education. What law teachers should be doing is worrying less about teaching legal minutiae and more about instilling a social conscience in their students.

Much of Kennedy's most challenging work has been concentrated on legal education. In a series of controversial essays, he has consistently asserted that law school is a 'training for hierarchy' (Kennedy, 1990). Law professors, overwhelmingly white, middle class and male, train law students, themselves disproportionately white and middle class, to take up positions in society of enormous and disproportionate political and economic power. Yet, at all times, legal education denies this truth and fails to equip students with a proper sense of responsibility for the exercise of this power. At the same time, by the very fact of their own structure and organisation, university law schools are intensely hierarchical. By studying in a law school, students are inculcated with an unhealthy and undeserved respect for the authority of institutions and academic staff. They accept what professors tell them and that lectures somehow describe the legal 'truth', when the real truth is that most of what is told is an unhealthy mixture of political ideology and personal prejudice, tempered with a not-uncommon dash of opinionated nonsense. Kelman rightly noted the tendency of most law professors to spend their time engaged in 'patently unstable babble' (Kelman, 1984, p 322). In order to counter this mythology of 'hierarchy', Kennedy advised that all university workers, from professors to janitors, should be paid the same salary, and indeed should exchange jobs for a while. In more immediately practical terms, he argues the case for affirmative action in university faculties, so that they better represent the social, ethnic and gender proportions of society. An appointment to a law faculty is a political appointment, because to teach law is to engage in a process of 'cultural and ideological development in a situation of contest, of domination and subordination'. Law professors are political actors, like it or not (Kennedy, 1993, pp 34–82).

In his more recent writings, Kennedy has advocated a rather quieter strategy, preferring to 'undermine and entice', rather than engage in anything more confrontational (Kennedy, 1997, p 340). It is certainly true that much of the zeal that so fired the 'crits' during the 1980s appears to have passed. As Peter Goodrich suggests, the critical strategy now appears to be one of nurturing intellectual 'sleepers' in law schools, subversive radicals, who 'await the twenty-first century night when under cover of darkness they will crawl out of the belly of the beast' (Goodrich, 2001, pp 974–75, 982). There is an ironic edge to the observation. But it remains an intriguing thought, and it might just prove to be the more effective strategy after all. For it is certainly true that law schools retain their enormous, and disproportionate, influence in modern society.

And it is just as true that they presently remain every bit as discriminatory and unrepresentative of that society. We will investigate further the extent of gender discrimination in the final part of this chapter. The extent of racial discrimination is every bit as corrosive. Two recent, and vivid, examples of racial discrimination in the modern law school are striking. The first is the *Quereshi* case, in which the University of Manchester Law School was held by an Industrial Tribunal to have discriminated against and 'victimized' one of its own coloured members of staff. The second example is given by the visceral reception reserved, in some quarters, for the work of the coloured American law professor Patricia Williams. We shall investigate this work in greater depth shortly. As Peter Goodrich and Linda Mills have recently revealed, it confirms that the modern law school is an overwhelming male and white 'space', one that actively seeks to exclude both women and members of ethnic minorities (Williams, 1991; Goodrich and Mills, 2001). Because of this, the composition of these schools in no way reflects the composition of society itself. Law schools, and their inhabitants, are alienated and distant from the real world, and the process of legal education does its level best to exacerbate this. As Jules Getman has affirmed, law schools tend to train the law student to be a lawyer instead of being a real person. It is because of this that so many lawyers, though they may 'know' the law, are quite incapable of providing a legal service that is of any real value to society as a whole (Getman, 1988). It is small wonder, given the nature of legal education itself, that the composition of the legal profession and the nature of legal practice should also be discriminatory and wholly unrelated to the real needs of the real political world it so often and so patently fails to serve.

Critical legal feminism: strategies of sameness

One of the most acute forms of discrimination, felt not just in the law school, but in society as a whole, relates to gender. It is probably true to say that the advance of gender theory, along with that of race, represents the most exciting development in contemporary CLS, or perhaps post-CLS, scholarship. Of course, feminist theory is not new. On the contrary, a 'first wave' feminism is commonly traced back to the likes of Mary Wollstonecraft writing at the end of the 18th century. In her *A Vindication of the Rights of Women*, Wollstonecraft railed against the patriarchal nature of late Enlightenment political society and the presumed gender characteristics upon which it was based. A particular idea of womanhood, she suggested, had been forged by men. She 'was created to be the toy of man, his rattle, and it must jingle in his ears whenever, dismissing reason, he chooses to be amused' (Wollstonecraft, 1995, p 38).

This assumption, that men must abandon reason when dealing with women, was a particular focus of Wollstonecraft's *Vindication*. The faculty of reason, she countered, is not gender specific. Both men and women are equally capable of reason. The problem is that society trains the reason of men, whilst endeavouring to keep women in a state of 'perpetual childhood'. Precisely the same approach was taken by John Stuart Mill in his *The Subjection of Women* published in the mid 19th century. And it was for this reason that both Mill and Wollstonecraft concentrated on the need to improve the education of women, as a precursor to their taking a more active role in both public, and personal or private, government. Rather than treating women like 'slaves' or 'beasts', Wollstonecraft urged, society should endeavour to 'cultivate their minds, give them the salutary, sublime curb of principle, and let them attain conscious dignity'. It is, finally, 'the right use of reason alone which makes us independent of every thing' (Wollstonecraft, 1995, pp 40–41, 136). For this reason, Wollstonecraft famously concluded with an appeal to women's rights:

> Let woman share the rights and she will emulate the virtues of man; for she must grow more perfect when emancipated, or justify the authority that chains such a weak being to her body (Wollstonecraft, 1995, p 222).

In its more contemporary guise, feminist legal thought has tended to attach itself to the broader debate regarding 'sameness' and 'difference'. In simple terms, is there something that defines a 'man' or a 'woman', some essential 'sameness', or is there just a myriad differences between all men and women, with gender being merely one of a mass of characteristics that contribute to a distinctive human personality? There is no definitive answer to this question, of course. But the debate has been vigorous, and, as Deborah Rhode noted, paradoxical too. For it is the strength of this debate which has also evidenced the fragility of any supposedly identifiable feminist critique of law. The more women have talked about 'sameness' and 'difference' the more obvious it has become that feminist theories of law can be very different indeed (Rhode, 1990).

The most obvious argument in defence of 'sameness' is rooted in biology, rather than culture or experience, and tends to oscillate around the concept of gender rather than sex. Thus Robin West argues that biology describes a 'gender' distinction that is 'essential' rather than somehow nurtured (West, 1993, pp 179–249). To an extent, such an approach echoes Carol Gilligan's original, and controversial, suggestion that women 'speak' in a 'different voice', articulating in terms of 'care, connection and context' (Gilligan, 1982). For others, there is an essential woman defined by the experience of political exclusion. Diane Majury thus emphasises that critical legal feminism must ally intellectual and political strategies. There is a value in creating a norm of disempowerment, regardless of intellectual niceties. Women must define themselves in order to identify their oppression and the nature of feminist politics (Majury, 1991).

It is along these lines that one of the most influential of feminist 'crits', Catherine MacKinnon, has enjoined the wider CLS critique of liberal legalism. MacKinnon suggests that the kind of formal rights-based idea of equality favoured by liberal jurists ignores the deeper political and social disadvantages experienced by women. Pornography is an obvious example. The ability to publish pornography is defended as a liberal right of 'free' speech. Yet that right directly discriminates against the 'right' of women to 'equal' respect, because pornography exploits one particular gender (MacKinnon, 1989, pp 195–214, 247–48). Liberal legalism, MacKinnon affirms, is a 'medium for making male dominance both invisible and legitimate by adopting the male point of view in law at the same time as it enforces that view on society' (MacKinnon, 1989, p 237). Inequality is a 'collective condition', and it is a political condition, the product of a particular political ideology that diminishes the female experience. As she stated in *Towards a Feminist Theory of State*:

> Inequality because of sex defines and situates women as women. If the sexes were equal, women would not be sexually subjugated. Sexual force would be exceptional, consent to sex could be commonly real, and sexually violated women would be believed. If the sexes were equal, women would not be economically subjugated, their desperation and marginality cultivated, their enforced dependency exploited sexually or economically. Women would have speech, privacy, authority, respect, and more resources then they have now (MacKinnon, 1989, p 215).

Accordingly, MacKinnon recommends a radical democratisation which will empower women in a real political sense. This could include quota systems, of a certain properly representative number of women admitted to law schools, recruited to the academic professions, promoted to senior positions within university departments or law firms, even to the bench. Law cannot be left to perpetuate a myth of supposed neutrality, which in reality merely reinforces the disadvantage and effective political oppression of women. Law must instrumentalise a more equal society. And to do this, in practical terms at least, is must presume a common degree of discrimination and disadvantage. The practical argument is compelling. Despite the criticism which has increasingly been levelled at the theoretical presumption that all women share the 'same' gender experience, the idea of a 'strategic essentialism' can still be justified in terms of necessity (Conaghan, 2000, pp 367–73). Indeed, in its absence there is the ever-present threat of an 'utter paralysis of political reflection' (Barron, 2000, p 276).

In this context, the advance of a strategy of 'gender-mainstreaming' is striking. Gender-mainstreaming attempts to cut a compromise between the two positions; respecting the reality that female experiences can be different, whilst also recognising, and trying to address, the very obvious and fundamental gender-based discrimination that operates in our society. According to proponents of 'gender-mainstreaming', a 'systematic integration of respective situations, priorities and needs of women and men in all policies' with the purpose of effecting real equality' can affirm the 'equal valuation of different characteristics among and between women and men' (Bretherton, 2001, p 61; Pollack and Hafner-Burton, 2000, p 434). In practice, gender-mainstreaming policies are supposed to effect the 'integration of gender equality considerations in all activities and policy levels'. It implies a considerable reach, and requires a considerable commitment. And whilst it might seem rather aspirational, even allusive, it is worth noting that the European Union, for one, has explicitly committed itself to a wide-range of mainstreaming policies over the next decade (Bretherton, 2001, pp 60–61).

The need for practical measures also underpins Martha Nussbaum's idea of a 'capabilities' approach to female disadvantage; an approach which enjoys an obvious consonance with the strategy of gender-mainstreaming. Basing her argument on the premise that a 'capabilities approach' better focuses on 'what people are actually able to do and to be', Nussbaum reinvests a differentiated 'political liberalism', one that attempts to liberate the disadvantaged in terms of ensuring their equal capability to act in the various political and economic spheres that define their lived experience. The facility of this equal 'capability', she alleges, is a 'necessary condition of justice', and it should be the prime aspiration of any liberal public policy (Nussbaum, 2000, pp 5–6, 71–72, 81–82). In making this argument, Nussbaum aligns the practical, and 'essentialist', with the principled, and liberal. Such a political liberalism, she argues, insists on a necessary 'separateness of one life from another, and the equal importance of each life, seen on its own terms rather than as part of an organic or corporate whole'. It is a liberalism, she contends, that places irreducible importance on the idea of 'equal worth and respect'; a concession that is resonant, as we have already seen, of Dworkin's most recent writings on liberal jurisprudence. It is a liberalism that recognises the realities of 'collectivity' and shared experience, whilst also admitting that such collectivities 'are made of individuals who never fuse, who always continue to have their separate lives' (Nussbaum, 1999, pp 9–11, 62–63). In this sense, of course, Nussbaum's liberalism is also a liberalism of 'difference', even if it is premised on a political philosophy that has been ritually accused of diminishing the female experience. It is, as she concludes, a philosophy of 'difference', even if it is one that centres on the particular 'capabilities', or lack of them, enjoyed by one identifiable, and identifiably female, section of society (Nussbaum, 2000, pp 302–03). Above all, perhaps, it underlines one particular conclusion, that the lines between the 'sameness' and 'difference' can never be clearly drawn; something which probably militates towards the latter being more credible than the former, even if the former is of rather greater strategic use than the latter.

Critical legal feminism again: narrativity and difference

But is there something that defines a 'woman', even a distinctive female experience? An increasing number of feminist commentators have begun to doubt the possibility. The presumed 'woman of feminism', as Therese Murphy put it, now stands 'accused' (Murphy, 1997, p 39). Joanne Conaghan spells out the problem, and the threat, that strategies of essentialism pose. Once 'feminists invoke the experience of women to challenge the dominance of male points of view, they risk falling into the same trap: to claim to speak for "all" women is, inevitably, to exclude the voices and experiences of some while privileging those of others' (Conaghan, 2000, p 367). The invocation of 'voice' is intriguing. An alternative feminism, one that stresses 'difference' rather than 'sameness', has deployed a distinctively more narrative strategy. It finds a strong expression in Maria Aristodemou's suggestion that women must retrieve a distinctive voice with which they can then tell their own 'stories'. At present, she alleges, 'women's origins, women's achievements, women's justice continue to inhabit a silent dark continent'. If the condition of women is to change, this paradigm must be shifted. 'Writing', she confirms, 'is not a substitute for living, but living itself' (Aristodemou, 2000, pp 57, 200).

To a considerable extent this narrative turn in critical legal feminism resonates with the *ecriture feminine* associated with the likes of Luce Irigaray and Helene Cixous. According to Cixous, a 'feminine writing' will be revolutionary in so far as it will create a 'place' which is 'not economically or politically indebted to all the vileness and compromise' implied by essentialist strategies (Cixous and Clement, 1975, p 72). It also resonates with the kind of postmodernism that we will encounter in the next chapter. In this context, it underpins Judith Butler's suggestion that the female identity should be determined by its discursive nature, by the fluid and constitutive 'process of signification' (Butler, 1990, pp 141–45). It is in this same narrative spirit that Drucilla Cornell marries the assertion that the law is a matter of rhetoric and language with a politics which demands social reform and the democratisation of political processes. Cornell's community is a fractured one, which inheres multiple identities and in which power is dispersed in a radically plural manner. Cornell's particular political concern lies with the disadvantages experienced by women, both in the legal profession and at the hands of the legal process. In order to address these disadvantages, a sophisticated postmodern legal feminism must identify the singular woman. Women are not of an essential type, and neither are women lawyers, but should rather be seen as part of a 'choreography of difference'; a choreography, indeed, which defines humanity itself (Cornell, 1992; 1998).

The turn to postmodernism and narrativity does not require the abandonment of political morality, but it does necessitate acknowledgment of fundamental difference, together with a willingness to concede the autonomy of other feminist legal theories. The raising of a female 'consciousness', as Carol Smart emphasises, cannot itself legitimate any particular political ideology. Because morality is only one determinant of women, it cannot prescribe the whole of a feminist agenda (Smart, 1995, pp 171–78, 186–99, 211–20). Mary Jo Frug similarly stressed that questions of gender are not just questions of politics, or just of biology, but of economics, ethics, culture, art and so on. Thus, to pursue some particular identifiable model woman is to pursue a certain preordained and objectified ideal; most importantly, someone else's ideal (Frug, 1992). In the attempt to try to accommodate the alternative strands of critical legal feminism,

Kathleen Bartlett has invoked an idea of 'positionality'. Rather than conceding fundamental indeterminacy, Bartlett suggests that a female identity can be stabilised by the very act of acknowledging the contingency of truth. Truth is 'situated and partial' and derived from human relations across gender. Indeed, truth is defined by such relations. Positionality, thus, 'can reconcile the apparent contradiction within feminist thought between the need to recognise the diversity of people's lives and the value in trying to transcend that diversity'. To 'understand human diversity' is 'to understand human commonality' (Bartlett, 1991, pp 392–401). Such a conclusion resonates with Rhode's assertion that the key for a reconstructive critical legal feminism is to fashion 'understandings that can resonate with women's shared experience without losing touch with our diversity' (Rhode, 1990, p 626).

It is precisely in this spirit that Patricia Williams has related her personal experiences, as a black woman law professor, with the wider travails experienced by blacks and women in contemporary North America, and particularly its legal institutions (Williams, 1991; 1995). The tone of her writings is distinctively confessional. The experience of a black woman, she rightly argues, is very different from that of a white one; just as the experience of a rich woman is very different from that of a poor one. It is for this reason that she adopts a consciously legalistic strategy for reform. Rather than railing against liberal legalism from the sanctuary of the law school campus, feminist lawyers should seek to effect genuine political reform through the institutions in place, namely constitutions and courts of law. For black people, during the 1960s through to the present day, the exercise of rights in courts of law has been a vital means of effecting political emancipation. Reform may have been slow, requiring sacrifices of life and liberty, but without rights, that emancipation would never have been achieved. In the real political world, short of full scale social revolution, it is the only hope that any disadvantaged minority enjoys. Better to effect incremental reform from within the existing system, than to dream whimsically about the possibilities of radical reform at some unknown point in the future (Williams, 1991, pp 146–65).

The confessional tone of Williams's writing, dovetailing the personal and the public, illustrates the strategic potential of feminist narrativity. It is, indeed, one of the reasons why her work has attracted such opprobrium from the conspicuously male and conspicuously white intellectual establishment, particularly in the UK. The argument for reforming legal institutions is framed within a wider argument that challenges the very nature of what law is, and how its experience should be chronicled (Goodrich and Mills, 2001, pp 26–31). Perhaps the most compelling insight of feminist critiques of law, whether they be nominally essentialist or narrative or postmodern, is that they impress this confessional, experientialist context. Law is not an abstract conception. It is something experienced, something lived; by all of us, male and female, black and white. As Ngaire Naffine has recently observed, the study of law is, or should be, a 'study of life', of real personal experiences, not abstract rules and doctrines (Naffine, 2002, pp 73, 82). It cannot be otherwise. What matters is the readiness to admit this subjectivity, to champion it, and to use it.

CHAPTER 7

POSTMODERNISM AND DECONSTRUCTION

THE POLITICS OF THE ABSURD

Nietzsche and the crisis of modernism

The crisis of modernism was signalled by the popularity of the turkey trot, and confirmed by the senseless slaughter of the First World War. The turkey trot swept across Europe during the first decade of the 20th century, replacing the respected traditional dances such as the waltz and the quickstep. A Prussian general was so incensed by seeing junior officers abandoning traditional German dances for bastardised American jigs that he shot one as an example. Rather than prosecuting the general for murder, the Kaiser issued a decree banning the turkey trot in the German army. To dance the turkey trot was to disrupt order, simply by asserting choice against tradition. The same context surrounds the periodic anxieties caused by rock and roll, punk rock and rap. Gustav Radbruch thought that revolution is effected by philosophers. Hobbes aligned revolution with politics, whilst Marx suggested that its conditions were prescribed by political economics. The Russian composer Stravinsky thought that revolution, at least social revolution, was described by dance. In Paris in 1913, he presented a ballet, *The Rites of Spring*, for which the music was deliberately disruptive and the dancing consciously clumsy. It challenged the received wisdom of harmony and beauty. The idea for the ballet, Stravinsky recorded, was that of a 'ritual' slaughter in which a 'sacrificial virgin dances herself to death'. It was a metaphor for modern Europe and a striking prophesy (Eksteins, 1989).

The turkey trot and *The Rites of Spring* provide the context for the postmodern and the turn to language. In methodological terms, postmodernism seeks to 'deconstruct' the 'metanarratives' by which those with power seek to prescribe or 'write' the conditions by which the rest of us should lead our lives. In its place, it advocates a politics of radical contingency, founded on the respect for 'difference', from one situation to another and from one individual to another. An appreciation of the textual nature of our lives, that we express ourselves through language, and are described by others on these same terms, can better equip us to appreciate the dominion which text enjoys in our existences. At the same time, it can also encourage us to seek to retake control of our lives, by raising our voices and reclaiming the language by which we can describe and express ourselves. As Foucault noted, language, accordingly, both constrains and empowers. The intellectual torch has thus passed from the philosophers to the poets. Whereas Plato and Aristotle feared poetry for its disruptive potential and challenge to the sovereignty of reason, postmodernism has returned to the aesthetic in an effort to reinvest some sort of intellectual unity. If reason cannot found everything, and provide a reason for existence, then maybe art and poetry can. At the same time, by concentrating on art rather than a metaphysics of reason, this foundation is a foundation in the self and the ability of the self to perceive and to judge. As Iris Murdoch has emphasised, the immediate echoes of Kant's idea of judgment are resonant. When we prescribe what is right, as a matter of morality or law, we are, in the very process of doing so, imagining what is right. We create images of ideal behaviour, as indeed Plato suggested. But this imagining is an aesthetic act, as well as a moral or political one (Murdoch, 1992).

Of course, this approach to normativity and aesthetics had been most recently revisited in the great defining struggle of the Enlightenment, what Samuel Taylor Coleridge termed the 'rage of metaphysics', the struggle between sense and sensibility, reason and romance. It found a famous expression in William Wordsworth's retreat from politics and ideology in his vast confessional account of the French Revolution, 'The prelude'. It found a similar expression in Shelley's version of the same historical events, the *Revolt of Islam*; a poem which, its author declared, was written with the hope of 'kindling within the bosoms of my readers a virtuous enthusiasm for those doctrines of liberty and justice, that faith and hope in something good', and above all a belief in 'growth and progress' and its capacity to enhance a universal 'love of mankind'. According to Shelley, such a love, ultimately, could only be achieved by poets drawing a 'succession of pictures'. After all, as he famously said in his essay 'A philosophical view of reform', poets are the 'unacknowledged legislators of the world' (Shelley, 1990, pp 29–84; Ward, 2003, pp 61–62).

It was an insight fervently adopted by the 19th century American philosopher, Henry David Thoreau. In *Walden and Civil Disobedience*, Thoreau described his self-inflicted exile from society, a retreat to the backwoods of Massachusetts. As we shall see, such retreats are, in many ways, a hallmark of the tortured romantic and existentialist. Here Thoreau mused on poetry and nature and the meaning of a 'more ethereal life'. And he came to a striking conclusion. The good life is not accessed by rules and regulations, anymore than it is by prescribed moralities, whether they be Socratic or Kantian or whatever. A good life, and a good politics, is a matter of sensibility. In a famous passage in *Walden* he observed:

> Once or twice, however, while I lived at the pond, I found myself ranging the woods, like a half-starved hound, with a strange abandonment, seeking some kind of venison which I might devour, and no morsel could have been too savage for me. The wildest scenes had become unaccountably familiar. I found in myself, and still find, an instinct toward a primitive rank and savage one, and I reverence them both. I love the wild not less than the good (Thoreau, 1986, p 257).

Ultimately, Thoreau's acute romanticism took him, as it took Shelley, to the very edges of radical libertarianism. Indeed, in his observation that 'law never made men a whit more just', in his later essay *Civil Disobedience*, he took it to the edges of romantic anarchism (Thoreau, 1986, pp 385–89, 395–96).

Someone else who was fascinated by the power of language, and its relations to feelings, by all the travails of Enlightenment romanticism, and more particularly by the ability of language and feeling to destabilise as well as stabilise meaning, was Friedrich Nietzsche. Central to Nietzsche's thought is the desire to disrupt order and cherish inconsistency. It is only in conditions of disorder that the creative will can flourish, and we, as individuals, can only assert ourselves against the prescribed order if we can create conditions of disorder. Here, Nietzsche identified with Dionysus and the Bacchanalian cult of orgy and indulgence, individual experience and extremes of aesthetic and emotion. In a notebook of 1888, the last year before he descended into a permanent insanity, Nietzsche wrote about the importance of overcoming order and reasserting the 'Dionysian spirit', the 'awareness that creation and destruction are inseparable' (Hayman, 1995, p 7). Much has been written about Nietzsche's insanity, and the extent to which his writings should be read within this particular context. No one was more aware of the frailty of mind and body than Nietzsche, and his notebooks record wild fluctuations between periods of self-approbation and self-loathing. As a university teacher, he was convinced that teaching strained the brain and led to madness, and it is perhaps characteristic that Nietzsche should pursue a vocation that he was convinced would ultimately hasten his own destruction. As he suggested in *Ecce Homo*, the ultimate expression of self-assertion is self-destruction.

Undoubtedly, Nietzsche saw his own physical sickness and deterioration as a metaphor for that of the modern world. In 'Beyond good and evil' (Nietzsche, 1979), he suggested that Karl Marx had effected the ultimate demise of the 'modern' world, replacing the 'herd mentality' of Christianity with that of socialism. The Europeans of the 20th century would be 'talkative, weak willed, and highly employable workers', fooled by an illusion of 'democracy' which is 'conducive' only to the 'production of a type' prepared for economic 'slavery'. Ultimately, he predicted, Europe would refashion its morality so as to accommodate the demands of a common market. The epitome of this demise was the idea of a German State, an entity demanded and effected by politics rather than culture. Such a yearning for affirmation reveals a lack of self-confidence and necessarily denotes disease. Nietzsche despised nationalism, which he ascribed to male impotence, and suggested that the nationalism which characterised the idea of the German State was a contagion which would spread across Europe.

The only recourse for modern man, Nietzsche asserted, was to rebel against the inexorable logic of modernity, and to seek recourse to poetry and art. Art is everything, and man only exists as an artistic reflection. The genius of Byron and Wagner, and by implication Shelley and Thoreau too, was to appreciate that tragedy, as the most acute form of emotional experience, was also the highest form of art. Only art deserved study, because only it could provide the mechanism by which modern men and women could overcome the constraints of modernity. In *The Birth of Tragedy*, first published in 1872, he blamed Socrates, not just for advocating the illusory power of reason, but most importantly for the complementary rejection of tragedy. In contrast to this illusory power, Nietzsche countered that it 'is only as an aesthetic phenomenon that existence can be justified'. *The Birth of Tragedy* was written in this spirit, and most immediately in praise of Wagner who, better than anyone, appreciated the empowering potential of art. It was Wagner who realised that 'art – and not morality – is presented as the properly metaphysical activity of man' (Nietzsche, 1993, pp 7, 60–72).

Life, as prescribed by Socrates and reason, is futile and absurd. It is a life devoted to an illusory form of perfection which flies in the face of our inevitable physical and mental demise. Socrates cannot explain death, but art and Wagner can, or at least they can describe it, and, in so doing, fashion our reconciliation with it and thus our overcoming of it. Life has no meaning in the sense that Socrates would have us believe. Seeking recourse to a contemporary event which shook Europe, Nietzsche observed that the senseless slaughter of the Paris Commune of 1871, and the demise of its revolutionary ideals, cannot make sense. Things happen; they do not need to have reasons. Prophetically, Nietzsche suggested that the 20th century would be increasingly characterised by such slaughter, and our inability to rationalise it. Instead of agonising over its apparent futility, the modern world must learn to laugh in the face of tragedy (Nietzsche, 1993, pp 11–12). Later he was to suggest that the hero of the postmodern world would be the comedian. If Byron was the hero of the past, Charlie Chaplin was to be the Nietzschean hero to come. In a typically inconsistent fashion,

Nietzsche then added that too much happiness and fun merely makes you ill. The inconsistency is, of course, vital. Comedy, as a mechanism for describing misfortune, is both necessary and destructive, desirable and undesirable. Comedy is the essence of life, and of death, and is itself an expression of inconsistency. He referred to art as the 'healing enchantress' who:

> ... alone can turn these thoughts of repulsion at the horror and absurdity of existence into ideas compatible with life: these are the sublime – the taming of horror through art; and comedy – the artistic release from the repellence of the absurd (Nietzsche, 1993, p 40; Ansell-Pearson, 1994, pp 45–54).

Truth is not fixed, in reason or God, or anything else. Rather, truth is situated, in a fluid sense, in language, in a 'mobile army of metaphors'. Truth is an illusion created by language. It is the Dionysian who appreciates the 'illusion of illusion' which is described by language, that any objectivity is an illusion effected by language, an apparent truth masking an irreducible subjectivity. The Dionysian celebrates this irreducible subjectivity, appreciates the 'pain and contradiction' of 'primal oneness', and is reconciled to the fact that we are ourselves 'images and artistic projections'. We are all readers of others, and read by others, but the gap between readers remains bridgeable only through language. The illusions of truth exist in this gap, and so, accordingly, does metaphysics. In *The Birth of Tragedy*, Nietzsche referred to the 'ecstasy' of this 'Dionysian State' challenging the 'habitual barriers and boundaries of existence' (Nietzsche, 1993, pp 29–39). The recasting of philosophy as a matter of art and language was not a rejection of metaphysics, but a rewriting of it. Philosophy was redefined by the limits of language.

The politics of Zarathustra

Nietzsche became increasingly interested in the idea of developing the political and ethical implications of this insight. Most importantly, the postmodern must be sceptical. An appreciation that the only truth, a necessarily insufficient one, lay in language, required an ethical scepticism which could complement an appreciation of aesthetic absurdity. The truly 'heroic' man, such as Wagner or Byron or Napoleon, is a sceptic; an insight famously shared by the mid-Victorian melancholic Thomas Carlyle. His subsequent works reinforced the virtue of the heroic sceptic, someone who denies absolute moral values. A postmodern political morality would be a sceptical morality. At the same time, it repeated the assertion that only the poet, or one who appreciates poetry, can be a heroic sceptic; someone indeed, like Nietzsche. In the final pages of *The Birth of Tragedy*, Nietzsche emphasised the all consuming power of language. The reciprocal relation of self and audience, text and reader, defines the limits of moral and political philosophy. There is nothing else, merely us and others, all engaged in a theatre of illusion which is described exclusively by this relation. The political 'ethic' of *The Birth of Tragedy* lies in reinvesting the importance of audience; the 'rebirth of tragedy also means the rebirth of the aesthetic listener'. A sceptical politics, a distinctively postmodern politics, will be founded on this ability to reinvest power in the subjective other, the audience. This is a challenge directed at the heart of modernism and the modern State founded on the illusory justification of Socratic reason. It will reveal the 'mythology' of modernism, those 'unwritten laws more powerful than the mythical foundation that guarantees its connection with religion and its growth out of mythical representation'. It is these myths which 'check' the artistic imagination, the subjective self. Political empowerment in a postmodern world must be premised on the appreciation that politics is always an aesthetic engagement (Nietzsche, 1993, pp 107–10).

Nietzsche was convinced that the civilisation of the 'modern' world is in irreversible decline. The emergence of the political economy, in which we are all active participants, either as tax collectors or shopkeepers, has merely confirmed our decaying state. In *Thus Spoke Zarathustra*, he would refer to 'our howling and cries of distress' (Nietzsche, 1969, p 314). Rather than trying to support modernity, the true poet should devote himself to hastening its demise. From the ashes of the modern world would come a new postmodern world defined by a reinvigorated aesthetics. In this sense, this concern with art and the absurd was not merely a concern with aesthetics. The challenge of art was an intensely political challenge. In unpublished notes, made just a year after his arrival at Basle, Nietzsche recorded that 'the task of art is to annihilate the State' (Hayman, 1995, p 124). Just as he rejected his Prussian upbringing and its values, almost despite himself, so Nietzsche despised the Prussian State – indeed, any State. Government, if it is not self-government, is slavery, the enforcement of the absurd. Laws exist to prevent self-expression, and it is reason which provides an illusory justification for this suppression; an opinion which very obviously echoed the romantic anarchism of Shelley or Thoreau. It is only when we come to appreciate that all laws are simply a jumble of words, coined by someone else, and which we can recast in our own image if we have the courage, that we can become truly free. The ultimate role of the aesthetic experience is, in this sense, an acutely jurisprudential one. Humanity's potential for self-overcoming is irreducibly aligned with the fate of law, and the first step towards this self-assertion lies with retaking and rewriting this law. Zarathustra was to be the great destroyer of laws and, accordingly, the liberator of modern humanity.

Zarathustra is part Nietzsche, part Dionysus, at once real and illusory, a figment of literary imagination, and yet, as a form of autobiography, an expression of the most intense reality. Contradiction lies at the heart of *Zarathustra*. The historical figure upon whom Nietzsche based his fiction, the 7th century BC Persian, Zoroastres, founded a religion based on the fundamental contradiction which exists in everyone, between good and evil. Whereas Christian theology sought to overcome evil, Zoroastrianism acknowledges the everpresence of contradiction, and champions it, for in contradiction lies alternative and the potential for creation and change. The essence of life is contradiction and choice. It is, of course, the conclusion that Heraclitus reached over two millenia ago. It has also found a more recent echo in Chantal Mouffe's assertion that liberty and democracy are 'agonistic' concepts. In other words, the sign of a healthy democracy is the presence of constant political struggle, the positing and counter-positing of different political opinions and beliefs by 'friendly enemies' in a spirit of mutual reciprocity; an insight which, as we shall see, is strikingly post-modern in its tone (Mouffe, 2000, pp 13–15, 101–07).

And, of course, strikingly Nietzschean. The 'happy certainty' of Zarathustra, Nietzsche declared, is to 'dance on the feet of chance' (Nietzsche, 1969, p 186). Such a happiness is the comedy of *The Birth of Tragedy*, a reconciliation with absurdity. In the final passages of *Zarathustra*, Nietzsche emphasises that an absurd world, a world of choice and contradiction, is a world without truth. Zarathustra knows that 'the world is deep: deeper than day can comprehend' (Nietzsche, 1969, p 330). But this does not bother him. It is not a reason for anxiety. It just is. And we too, by following

Zarathustra's lead, will come to reconcile ourselves with this, our unavoidably bottomless existence.

As far as the distinction can be made, *Zarathustra* is a work of fiction rather than a philosophical tract. As a fiction it can achieve a sense of unity. Zarathustra effects self-overcoming, yet can only do so as fiction, in the imagination. Most famously, Zarathustra is the anti-Christ. As Nietzsche had suggested in 'The gay science' (Nietzsche, 1979), ours is a world in which 'God is dead. God remains dead. And we have killed him'. It is not a world in which God never existed. As a textual expression, descriptive of an intense, if illusory, belief system, God existed. But it was only as a textual expression. The postmodern, appreciative of the futility of existence, and no longer dependent on illusory hopes of eternal blessedness, can cast aside this God, just as it can cast aside various previous incarnations of God, such as Socrates, Plato and Aristotle. In its place, in a suitably paradoxical fashion, is the new anti-Christ, Zarathustra. God is replaced by an anti-God god. Ultimately, God is replaced by us: 'Away with such a god. Better no god, better to produce destiny on one's own account, better to be a fool, better to be God oneself' (Nietzsche, 1969, p 274). As the anti-Christ, Zarathustra is, at once, the representation of anti-Christian morality. Nietzsche wrote *Zarathustra* in the immediate aftermath of sexual rejection by the only women to whom he ever expressed his love. The task of Zarathustra is to destroy Christian morality by destroying the myths of 'conscience', the 'spittle licking and fawning' of piety and love, and thereby severing the illusory bonds which are said to universalise humanity. As the prologue emphasises, 'man is something to be overcome', and Zarathustra is dedicated to this task of self-overcoming. Modern man, in his 'decadent' and 'decaying' condition, needs a superman to engineer this overcoming, to show him the way to self-assertion and re-empowerment, so that he, too, can 'dance on the feet of chance'. With Zarathustra will come a new age of supermen, Dionysian heroes, who will cast out 'popes, sorcerors, kings, ugly men and wanderers', all the inadequates who sat in Plato's cave (Nietzsche, 1969, pp 41–52, 196, 290).

This overcoming is an innately jurisprudential matter. Zarathustra is the all destroyer of 'modern' law, the law of God and 'universal' man. In its place there must be a law of self. The 'way of the creator' is to create one's own laws. There are two tired 'old men' who must be cast aside – law and virtue. Both are illusory. Virtue 'is a sort of pose', whilst Nietzsche warns us to 'mistrust all those who talk much about their justice'. The justice of modernity, of Socrates and God, is always 'their' justice, not ours. Law must be rewritten so as to overcome the illusions of universalism with which Socrates had tried to justify its existence, and the bastardised idea of virtue which Aristotle and Christianity had then developed. Repeating his earlier accusations, Nietzsche challenged the myth of the modern legal State, the 'new idol', founded on this illusion of law and virtue: 'I call it the State where everyone, good or bad, is a poison drinker: the State where everyone, good or bad, loses himself: the State where universal slow suicide is called – life.' The concept of virtue was invented as an excuse for police forces, tax collectors, shopkeepers and kings, and all the other officers of the modern political State (Nietzsche, 1969, pp 63, 76–77, 89, 119–24).

Such distractions as law and justice, love and morality, must be destroyed; the 'good and just call me the destroyer of morals'. Zarathustra appeals to the melancholic masochist:

> For the sake of those who may one day become companions and collaborators ... I must perfect myself: therefore I sidestep happiness and offer myself to every adversity – for my ultimate trial and judgment.

This is the martyrdom of the anti-Christ, and every martyrdom is a jurisprudential expression. To embrace such misfortune is to deny the illusion of community and its morality. Self-overcoming is founded on tragedy and the play, or aesthetic, of the trial. The idea that the legal trial is a piece of theatre, merely descriptive of the human condition and nothing more, is acutely perceptive. It implies that law is itself an illusion, something which exists in our aesthetic imagination, and nowhere else. Its authority, as symbolised by the court is, accordingly, equally illusory. For Nietzsche, the court is the literal mouthpiece of the State, and it is through the court that the State articulates its 'lies' and 'illusions' (Nietzsche, 1969, pp 65–67, 76–77, 93).

Life and the absurd

Nietzsche's intellectual legacy is founded on the concept of the absurd. In *The Will to Power*, Nietzsche suggested that his legacy to the modern world was its pointlessness, the nihilism which appreciates 'the long waste of strength' that characterises modernism. To a certain extent, any intellectual movement which has determined to move beyond modernism, to embrace postmodernism, is Nietzschean. Much of the contemporary Critical Legal Studies movement (CLS) writing owes its intellectual heritage to Nietzsche (Singer, 1984). Conservative counter reaction tends to level accusations of nihilism against Nietzsche's challenge. Yet, Nietzsche is a prophet, someone who seeks to describe a present condition. He does not prescribe nihilism, and as we shall see in the remainder of this chapter, the postmodern thesis has concentrated on the possibility of reconstructing a political morality through language and poetry.

The absurd is the first step towards ethical reconstruction, a narrative mechanism for understanding the nature of our private and public existences. There is no question of anarchy. The politics of the absurd advocates a reconstruction founded on the destruction of the modern State and the consequent empowerment of the individual through language. The attempt to reduce the role of the State, and to empower the individual by increasing the potential for conversational participation in the creation of communities, has been cited by both Juergen Habermas and Richard Rorty as the 'turning point', from which a postmodern philosophy emerges (Habermas, 1987). In similar terms, William Connolly has situated Nietzsche at the end of a series of political philosophers who concentrated their critique on the metaphysics of power. Power describes political reality, not reason, and, as we have repeatedly noted, a consistent critical tradition has sought to reform modernism from within, by concentrating on the dispersal of power from the public sphere of the modern State to the private sphere of the modern individual. Nietzsche's critique is original in that it moves outside modernism in order to radicalise this critique of power from the perspective of language and art, rather than political morality or political economy. Nietzsche casts the social sciences into the same intellectual outer darkness into which modernism had already thrown metaphysics and theology (Connolly, 1988, pp 137–67).

The single most influential Nietzschean of the 20th century was the great philosopher of the absurd, Albert Camus. Sometime professional goalkeeper, bestselling novelist and cultural icon, Camus is himself an almost mythical figure, whose early flirtation with communism and passionate concern for the rights of immigrant minorites – of which, being an Algerian, he was one – tapped a particularly acute political sensitivity in the postcolonial intellectual world. Active resistance against Nazi occupation during the war, and equally active and vociferous denunciation of French colonial policy, enhanced Camus's political reputation as the advocate of the oppressed and marginalised in modern society. This concern with the 'outsider' became a centrepiece of his writings, and, in many ways, Camus's politics can be closely aligned with that of Hannah Arendt. The experience of Nazism convinced both of the need for 'democratic rebellious politics' dedicated to empowering the individual against the totalitarian impulses of the modern political State (Isaac, 1992). But whereas Arendt devoted herself to political philosophy, Camus turned to language itself. The movement from modern philosophy to postmodern language is undoubtedly the great contribution of Nietzsche, and it was Camus who appreciated, better than anyone perhaps, that the philosophy of the absurd is a philosophy of art and language. The theme is pervasive in Camus, but two texts warrant our particular attention, *The Myth of Sisyphus* and *The Outsider*. In both, the philosophical idea of the absurd is tied to the notion of existentialism, the suggestion that the metaphysics which defines the intellectual heritage of modernism denies the creative potential of the individual. By searching for metaphysical justifications for our existences, it refuses to acknowledge the full import of Descartes's *dictum* 'I think, therefore I am'. Only the self is authentic; everything else is an impression made by the self. As Camus says, 'I understand only in human terms' (Camus, 1975, p 51).

Sisyphus is a muse on suicide. Camus opens by suggesting that 'There is but one truly serious philosophical problem and that is suicide' (Camus, 1975, p 11). Suicide is the essential philosophical problem because it questions the very meaning of life. Life is absurd because reason is limited, as Kant had suggested and Nietzsche had confirmed. When Camus suggests that life is meaningless, what he means is that there is nothing metaphysical which can give it reason. If life has a purpose, we cannot look to philosophers to provide it. We must take responsibility for justifying our own existences. Nietzsche, of course, had advocated our recourse to art and tragedy in order to reconcile ourselves to this responsibility, and *Sisyphus* revisits the Dionysian realm of *The Birth of Tragedy*. According to Camus, when faced with our 'absurdity', we have three possible options: philosophical suicide; physical annihilation; and revolt. Only the third option, revolt, is authentic, because it prescribes our living with absurdity and reconciling ourselves to it: 'I draw from the absurd three consequences which are my revolt, my freedom and my passion ... But the point is to live' (Camus, 1975, pp 62–63). There is no point to life other than life itself. Camus illustrates this by the myth of Sisyphus. Condemned by the gods to the ultimately absurd life, the execution of a supremely pointless task, Sisyphus conquered his fate by reconciling himself to its futility. Camus presents an evocative conclusion:

> I leave Sisyphus at the foot of the mountain! One always finds one's burden again. But Sisyphus teaches the higher fidelity that negates the gods and raises rocks. He, too, concludes that all is well. This universe henceforth without a master seems to him neither sterile or futile. Each atom of that stone, each mineral flake of that night-filled mountain, in itself forms a world. The struggle itself towards the heights is enough to fill a man's heart. One must imagine Sisyphus happy (Camus, 1975, p 111).

The question of the absurd is not, of course, a merely ethical or literary one. It is also an intensely jurisprudential one in that it threatens the very basis of modern legal philosophy. The absurd challenges the classical orthodoxy that life must be pursued towards some virtuous ideal, and that the idea of justice and concept of law can be justified in terms of this ideal. If life is absurd, then why should we live our life in line with any particular moral philosophy? Why, indeed, should we live it line with laws and legal theory which can only be justified in terms of this illusion? The most potent forms of postmodernism train their assault on the idea of justice, and Camus enacted this assault, in literary form, in his novel *The Outsider*. The novel relates the story of a young man, Mersault, who kills an Arab on a beach for no 'apparent' reason. Murder is the fundamental challenge, just as suicide is in *Sisyphus*, and Mersault is the classic 'absurd hero' (McBride, 1992, pp 8–13; Ward, 1996, pp 142–44). The jurisprudential crux of the novel occurs in Mersault's trial. The trial is a piece of theatre. It is not 'real', or at least it is real only as a piece of theatre or illusion. At the same time, Mersault is not tried for the murder of an Arab, but rather for challenging the political morality of his community. By murdering the Arab because he seemed to be an 'outsider', Mersault too has become an 'outsider'. The depiction of the trial scene concentrates on Mersault's isolation. The law is clearly not his, and never has been. Ultimately, he realises, we are all outsiders, and the political morality which binds the community is itself an illusion. The trial, and the laws which it effects, are the semiotics of this illusion. Law is an illusion, which exists only so long as we live our lives inauthentically, by submitting ourselves to a mythological idea of morality. Camus challenges the science, the rationality of law, by using literature as a means to uncover the illusory nature of modern legal philosophy. Law is not Mersault's, and it is not ours. But literature is. Law certainly cannot provide a justification for life, or community, but literature might.

Literature, then, is power and empowerment. Camus's equally iconic contemporary, Jean-Paul Sartre, suggested that writing is a revolutionary enterprise. In *What is Literature?*, Sartre emphasised that the search for truth is indeed an exercise in linguistics and, in these terms, any political or philosophical enterprise is in large part a literary one. Indeed, the literary text, the novel, the play, the poem, is better suited to furthering political debate than the political treatise or philosophical tract. Literature empowers because it is open to all. We may not all be able to pen treatises in jurisprudence, but we can all write stories and read novels, attend theatres or watch television. Reading a text is a 'dialectical going and coming' between author and reader, and by recognising that the reader contributes to political meaning, such a form of 'praxis' is necessarily liberating and revolutionary. A postmodern political theory will be founded on this understanding of the creative reader. It will be fashioned, Sartre concluded, by a 'total literature', a 'concrete and liberated literature', a literature of 'praxis'. In the final analysis, such a literature, as a political exercise, is also an ethical exercise, for the 'situation' of the postmodern writer is one which stands 'for an ethics and art of the finite' (Sartre, 1967).

In recent years, a distinct law and literature 'movement' has emerged, emphasising the extent to which law is a textual enterprise and to which legal theory must be an exercise, to some degree, in literary criticism. The extent to which this 'movement' operates in the shadow of Nietzsche and Camus can be seen in the work of Richard Weisberg. Citing Nietzsche's depiction of 'crisis' in the modern world, Weisberg uses a series of authors and texts, including Camus as well as Kafka and Dostoevski, Dickens and Melville, to uncover another jurisprudence which exists in literary texts. The modern novel, from Kafka's *The Trial* to Dostoevski's *Crime and*

Punishment, from Dickens's *Bleak House* to Melville's *Billy Budd*, is an exercise in legal thought, and Weisberg suggests that the law and literature 'movement' must seek to write a new 'poethics', to reinvest ethics as a form of literature rather than science. 'Poethics', he maintains, 'in its attention to legal communication and the plight of those who are "other", seeks to revitalise the ethical component of law' (Weisberg, 1992). In these terms, law and literature represents an acute form of postmodernism in that it seeks not merely to stress the linguistic form of all law, but also to move beyond 'legal' texts towards alternative forms of discourse, beyond texts written by lawyers for lawyers, to texts written by anybody for everybody.

THE TURN TO DECONSTRUCTION

Auschwitz and the end of philosophy

In *The Postmodern Condition*, Jean-Francois Lyotard challenged what he perceived to be the 'metanarratives' which dominate modern western philosophy, the grand universal theories of Plato, Aristotle, Kant and so on. At the same time, he stressed that postmodernism, whilst founded in a reorientation of philosophy towards language, is, ultimately, an exercise dedicated to social and political reform (Lyotard, 1984, pp 71–82). Lyotard introduced the idea of a 'differend', as an essential difference between individuals, a difference preserved by language, and the creative political potential which language preserves. The world is a world of irreducible particulars, of differences between individuals, situations and so forth, which cannot be erased by universal moral theories. It is this which makes the 'differend' a textual construct with an intensely political import (Lyotard, 1988, pp 118–23, 130–41). The spur for a rewriting of philosophy which denied the 'metanarrative' was Auschwitz, the symbol of the ultimate attempt to deny humanity. Nazism represented the attempt finally to realise the dream which lies at the foundation of modernism, a homogenous utopia of white, able, wealthy, industrious Europeans. As Nietzsche had prophesied, the ultimate expression of the modern State lay in the attempt to enforce a uniformity on its population. A marginalised 'other' was identified, excluded and silenced. George Steiner famously referred to the Holocaust not as a peculiar incident in modernism, but as something intrinsic to it. The extermination of the Jews was the realisation of a 'long and precise imagining' (Steiner, 1971). The exclusion of the Jews was a 'silencing', a removal from political and intellectual discourse. Silencing represents the ultimate injustice, because it denies humanity.

After Auschwitz, according to Lyotard, there could only be 'silence'. The great intellectual apologist for Nazism, Martin Heidegger, famously refused to condemn the gas chambers. His 'silence' on this score, Lyotard suggests, is indicative of the sudden, striking 'silence' of modern philosophy. Modernism has 'silenced' itself, and has nothing else to say (Lyotard, 1990). It cannot justify, and it cannot rationalise. As Nietzsche suggested, some things are beyond rationalisation. Now there can only be 'sentences', and a theory of 'sentences', rather than a philosophy of metanarratives. Such a theory will respect the individual as a contributor to this discourse, rather than paying obeisance to the metanarratives articulated by philosophers, politicians and other apologists of modernism (Lyotard, 1988, p 169; 1992). One of the supreme ironies of postmodernism is that a movement which is so much an intellectual reflex action against the gas chambers was, in large part, fashioned by a man who notoriously refused to condemn them. Heidegger's *Being and Time*, certainly one of the most influential philosophical treatises of the 20th century, was completed at a breathtaking rate during a frenzied three month period, during which time its author kept his sanity by indulging his favourite pastime of chopping wood. The choice of hobby is of enormous significance. At the core of Heidegger's personal philosophy was a deep reverence of the country. The countryside represented nature and authenticity, and provided an environment of self-expression against the scientific urban environments which symbolised the dehumanised modern world. Whilst the city enslaved the individual, engagement with the country, such as growing food or chopping trees, represented a concrete example of self-expression. When Heidegger chopped trees, he felt that he was striking out against Socrates by refusing to submit to science. He could have got a machine to chop them, but he chopped them himself.

Whenever he was faced by a major intellectual or personal crisis, Heidegger always liked to say that he had resolved the issue by returning to the Swabian hills, where he was born, and listening to the trees and rivers. Unfortunately, it seems that the Swabian trees and rivers convinced Heidegger of the wisdom of supporting Adolf Hitler, and he joined the Nazi party in 1933. This fact alone does not condemn. Millions of Germans, many of whom despised Nazism, did the same. It was the fact that Heidegger so enthusiastically wore Nazi insignia, made Nazi salutes and sang raucous Nazi songs that is more revealing. However, the most damning evidence is supplied by his notorious rectorship of Freiburg University. Heidegger accepted an invitation to govern the university as a model establishment of National Socialist learning, and he accepted with alacrity. In his rectoral address, 'The self-assertion of the German university', he advised his students, and pretty much every student in Germany, that their entire lives must be dedicated to fashioning an intellectual complement to the political reality of Nazism. At the core of this philosophy must be a new jurisprudence, for 'To give the law to oneself is the highest freedom' (Heidegger, 1985, p 476). At the same time, in a subsequent address to the 'students of Germany', he reminded them:

> Do not let principles and ideas be the rulers of your existence. The Führer himself, and he alone, is the German reality of today, and of the future, and its law.

In other words, the law of National Socialism must be a law of its people, as expressed by its Führer, and not one fashioned by Socratic metaphysics. It is no coincidence that at the time of the address Heidegger was immersed in a decade long study of Nietzsche.

Following the war, Heidegger strenuously refused to clarify his relationship with Nazism, and when later asked to condemn the gas chambers, refused, suggesting that they were simply another manifestation of modern technology, akin to tractor factories. Though there may be some insight in the general comparison, which in some ways echoes much of what Lyotard has suggested about the mechanised forms of modern life, the failure to appreciate the degree of distinction is shocking. Yet, it does appear that the experience of Nazism had a considerable effect on Heidegger's intellectual approach. The Heidegger of *Being and Time* sought the 'essence', or foundation, for our existence, our 'Being', in pre-Socratic philosophy. Just as they had sought 'essence' in water or the stars, so Heidegger sought it in chopping wood and talking to rivers. He was convinced that Hitler would provide the purifying fire that

Nietzsche had recommended, and return the 20th century to the naturalistic ideals of the pre-Socratics.

It is fashionable amongst Heideggerians to talk of a Heidegger I and a Heidegger II. The post-Nazi Heidegger II is a different, chastened Heidegger, and it is this Heidegger who effects the famed 'turn' from philosophy to language. The affinity with the authentic, the natural, is still central. Indeed, Heidegger remained obsessed with the need to go back to building houses out of wood (Heidegger, 1977a). However, the house in which we live, in intellectual terms, is one made of language. Language 'is the house of being'; we only live in language. The 'essence' of Heidegger II is no longer metaphysical, pre-Socratic, National Socialist or otherwise. It is language. One of his very final essays, written in 1962, was suggestively entitled 'The end of philosophy and the task of thinking' (Heidegger, 1977b). Like Nietzsche, Heidegger saw himself as the philosopher who had finally ensured the 'end' of philosophy. Beyond philosophy as metaphysics lies infinite possibilities. Heidegger repeatedly used a metaphor of a forest, at the centre of which lies a clearing. Our lives, he suggested, are pathways upon which we travel in darkness seeking this clearing. The similarity with Plato's cave metaphor is, of course, striking. The 'end' of philosophy lay in appreciating that these pathways are defined by language. We cannot 'know' what the clearing is, whether it is virtue, justice, harmony, or anything else the metaphysicians have told us. It is the pathways that ensure our progress, and they alone, and 'thinking' stripped of metaphysics is a purely linguistic engagement.

Derrida and the jurisprudence of deconstruction

Someone who recognised the error of Heidegger I, and who recognised that it was intrinsic to his thinking, is the French deconstructionist, Jacques Derrida (Bennington, 1993, pp 16–20). Just as Heidegger suggested that Nietzsche was in fact the last philosopher, Derrida suggests that Heidegger I is the last philosopher and Heidegger II the first post-philosopher. His engagement with Heidegger's legacy, and Nietzsche's, is expressed most intensely in his critique of Heidegger's rectoral address. What fascinates Derrida is Heidegger's use, in the rectoral address, of the concept of *geist* or 'spirit'; a concept which has a particular resonance in the tradition of modern German philosophy, emanating from Hegel's use of 'spirit' as providing some sort of metaphysical 'essence' of the community. According to Derrida, Heidegger's address is an 'interrogation' of 'spirit', and thus, of modernity itself. In *Being and Time*, spirit was 'spirit', in Derrida's words 'guarded' by inverted commas. But in the address, in the context of providing an intellectual foundation for Nazism, Heidegger 'releases' spirit from its commas. This might all seem rather cryptic. But what it means according to Derrida is that in the rectoral address, the early Heidegger realises his critical error, so critical indeed, that he never repeats it. Indeed, Heidegger II is dedicated to correcting and erasing it. The error was to essentialise *geist*, to use it as some sort of metaphysical foundation upon which an entire political philosophy could be based. Heidegger II breaks with the Hegelian tradition by placing the word spirit, once more, in inverted commas. *Geist* again becomes '*geist*'. It is no longer an essential metaphysical concept, but rather a rhetorical expression, a simple word and nothing more. Heidegger II realises that any concept, even that most central to modern philosophy, is merely a word. It is the reconciliation to a fundamental philosophical indeterminacy demanded by words, and according to Derrida, it is this realisation which provides the intellectual foundation for the Heideggerianism which underpins so much contemporary postmodern thinking. Heidegger, he suggests, provided the 'deconstructing strength' necessary for a postmodern politics (Derrida, 1989; cf Cummings, 1981).

The 'Question' that Heidegger asked is a simple one: 'what is humanism?' – and the answer, Derrida suggests, is that it is a question. But there is also a deeper, and perhaps more unsettling, answer. It is also the realisation that anti-humanism is a humanism. The denial of humanism, of metaphysics, is also an expression of humanism and metaphysics (Derrida, 1989, pp 47–55). To deny an answer is to provide an answer, even if it is to say that there is no answer. In other words, there is no such thing as 'I don't know', but only 'I know that I do not know'. Language is always determinative. Every sentence provides an answer. It is determinative as a sentence, but that is the only determination it provides. Language is the only limit, but it is a limit to meaning. Indeed, it is the crucial limit. It is this insight which convinced Derrida that Heidegger's rectoral address, and the realisation of its failure, led Heidegger inexorably towards deconstructionism and the politics of language. It is the engagement with Heidegger, then, which demands Derrida's engagement with politics and ethics, but before we address the particularly jurisprudential nature of this engagement, we must better understand what is meant by deconstructionism.

Deconstruction uncovers the politics which underpins philosophy, and by concentrating on language seeks to reveal how this politics is secreted away. The politics of philosophy lies in language. This is the core of deconstructionism, at least to the extent that deconstruction can admit a core. Derrida's increasingly vociferous assertions about what deconstruction is and is not have been criticised as being essentialist, but if we take Derrida at his word, that any definition of something is as valid as any other, at least as a textual exercise and expression, then the levelling of any definition can be said to embrace the spirit of deconstruction (Bennington, 1993, pp 8–13). The justification for my suggesting a 'core' of deconstruction lies in the fact that I am a reader as well as an author. We all are. The hysteria which deconstruction has caused in university philosophy departments around the world is a reaction to the responsibility this realisation entails. We are all readers and we are all entitled to our opinion. But this is not a negative factor, and to deny specific incontrovertible meaning to any text or idea is not nihilist. Indeed, quite the reverse is true. It is precisely because of this entitlement that text can empower us as readers. The creative potential, established by the power to read and interpret, is the important insight that deconstruction presents (Gasche, 1986). Deconstruction is the recognition that there is always more to the text than what the author has written. This 'supplement' is provided by the context of the text, and by the context of the reader, which is itself a constituent of the context of the text. It is the acknowledgment that text cannot close off possible interpretations or understandings, because the reader will always introduce context, and, in doing so, rewrite that text. At the same time, there is only the text, because what the reader brings to the text is text itself (Mortley, 1991, pp 96–97, 107). Meaning can never be 'closed off' by context. No context is ever fixed, just, indeed, as Heraclitus had noted that no river is ever fixed. Deconstruction's context is Heraclitus's river.

Deconstruction is a jurisprudence because at its centre lies a determination to readdress the question of justice. For the same reason it is also an ethics. In its simplest form, deconstruction urges us to look to justice in the particular rather than the universal. Justice is realised, not in universal absolutes, but in particular situations. Individuals experience justice and injustice. It is a real experience, not something that can be determined in the abstract. Like Camus, being of north African and Jewish descent, Derrida shares a similar sensitivity to the plight of the 'outsider', and the situation of the individual is the dynamic behind the politics of deconstruction. More particularly, it is the situation of the 'marginalised' or excluded 'other'. Derrida refers to this politics as the politics of 'difference' which respects difference. The deconstruction of text reveals the politics of language, and the deconstruction of the legal text, accordingly, reveals the politics of law. It is in this way, as sketched by Nietzsche, that jurisprudence does indeed become an aesthetics as much as an ethics. The modernist suppression of the aesthetic was a conscious attempt to suppress the political, and it is for this reason that an aesthetics of law can better express the politics of law. Deconstruction denies the political neutrality necessary to universal moral philosophies, and the politics which constitutes the context of language denies the pretended absolute value of such concepts as virtue or justice. Virtue and justice are 'virtue' and 'justice', particular words with particular political import, created by certain individuals in certain situations and contexts. The irreducible contingency of such contexts forbids any absolute stable meaning to the expressions 'law' and 'justice', just as it does to any words.

In 'The force of law: the mystical foundations of authority', Derrida stresses that the 'force' of law is the product of the necessary 'difference' in the relationship between the self and 'other'. Law is a 'differential force', an expression of power relations. Justice is not. Justice is a matter of ethics once it is understood that it refers to this relation, between self and 'other'. Justice has no abstract meaning and it is not an absolute. It only 'exists' as an expression of this relation, and is particular to it. There is no absolute justice, merely an infinity of justices particular to each situation and relationship between individuals. It is this which describes the ethics of justice and, as a descriptive ethics describing relations between individuals, it is at once an aesthetics as well as an ethics. A postmodern jurisprudence forever deconstructs the pretended universalism of any 'philosophy' of 'law' because it reveals the particular politics which constitutes the contexts within which that particular philosophical 'discourse' has been made. Jurisprudence, accordingly, becomes the legal relation between particular individuals in a particular context. Because postmodern jurisprudence recognises the reality of particular relations over abstract metaphysical concepts, it is a more precise jurisprudence, and provides a more particular and precise 'justice'. A real political and legal situation can only be resolved justly by taking account of its particularity. Justice is particular to the 'self' and 'other', and in this sense, of course, it becomes our justice, described by us and our particular context (Derrida, 1990, pp 925–33).

At the same time, a properly postmodern jurisprudence, by acknowledging contingency, recognises also the 'openness' which lies 'beyond' the text, and which has yet to be realised. This 'openness' is essential. If it is denied, justice is lost and becomes stabilised by the 'force of law'. The 'openness' of a postmodern ethic of justice maintains the everpresent potential of change by recognising the everpresent reality of our contingent existence. Our lives change, and so do our values, as individuals and as societies. If this were not the case then the police would still be occupied preventing people carrying bows and arrows in a threatening manner, and marital rape would still be lawful. Deconstruction does not prescribe change. Life does that. Rather, it recognises that situations change, and that this is a good thing, and that a postmodern jurisprudence can best accommodate, indeed celebrate, this fact. In comparison with the modern tradition, as exemplified by the common law, which displays an almost obsessive concern with the past, a postmodern jurisprudence has the confidence to embrace the future, and to cherish the creative and empowering potential of change (Derrida, 1990, pp 945–47, 959–61, 969–73).

The politics of friendship

Deconstruction is not, then, a challenge to ethics, or morality, or justice. Rather, it challenges any abstract universalist notion of 'ethics', 'morality' or 'justice'. It cannot be against ethics, because ethics simply is. But it is against any attempt to foreclose what ethics might become. It is the 'beyond' of ethics, the future writing of ethics, not ethics itself, which matters to Derrida (Derrida, 1985). A postmodern ethics is one that maintains the possibility of freedom. If the concept of 'freedom' lies at the centre of any ethical philosophy, and it certainly does in that of such as Kant, then deconstruction, by emphasising the textuality of our existences, preserves a space for freedom in the 'beyond', that which is not yet prescribed and within which we can assert our own understanding of justice (Derrida, 1978). The ambition of Derridean deconstruction is to reinvest the 'moral law' by rewriting the ideas of freedom and equality in the particular.

The ethical dimension of Derrida's writings became dramatically more apparent during the later part of the 1990s. Of course, as we have already noted, there was a very obviously ethical import to essays such as *Of Spirit*. And it finds a clear reaffirmation in his later and concentrated study of Marx which develops the same essential metaphor, *Specters of Marx*. *Specters* is an essay about 'ghosts, inheritance, and generations, generations of ghosts', the ghosts, above all, of 'justice'. In essence, as Derrida affirms from the outset, it is an essay about 'ethics itself', about how to 'learn to live – alone, from oneself, by oneself' (Derrida, 1994, pp xviii–xix). The most mischievous of the spectres that haunts modern Europe, Derrida declares, is humanism; most immediately the Marxist variant of humanism. The failure of Marx has allowed the likes of Francis Fukuyama to claim the triumph of liberalism and the 'end of history'. This assertion must be challenged. There must be an alternative, a reinvested humanism. With a suitably Nietzschean flourish, Derrida suggests that the supposed 'end of history' is merely a 'disjunction', one that heralds the reassertion of an original ethics and the 'possibility' of a resurrected idea of 'justice'. A 'new' age of enlightenment, a postmodern age, he suggests, will be defined by this jurisprudential 're-naissance', a justice and a democracy 'to-come' (Derrida, 1994, pp 14–15, 27–28, 36, 169).

As ever, the fate of the 'other' is uppermost in Derrida's ethics; it defines the very idea of justice. Thus, when he talks about retrieving a sense of humanity it does so at the point where 'a certain determined concept of man, is finished', where there can, once again, be discerned 'the pure humanity of man, of the other man and of man as other' (Derrida, 1994, p 74). This ethical imperative is revisited in Derrida's more recent *Politics of Friendship*; a muse, as its title suggests, on the Aristotelian idea of friendship. Amidst the wastes of Enlightenment political morality in our post-Holocaust and post-Marx age, Derrida urges a return to these classical conceptions of friendship and community. Of course, there is a danger here: the various lures of Socratic virtue, and law, that Nietzsche so despised. And Derrida is fully aware of this.

But he is retrieving a rather different Aristotle, the one, he suggests, who described justice, not as a matter of moral or jurisprudential absolutes, but as an expression of inter-personal friendship and commonality. According to this Aristotle, Derrida affirms, 'the very work of the political ... amounts to creating (producing, to making, etc) the most friendship possible' (Derrida, 1997, pp 7–8, 198–99). The critical alignment here is justice and democracy, the morality of 'truth' and the 'politics of fraternity'. There can be 'no deconstruction without democracy, no democracy without deconstruction'. In the final analysis, where there is true friendship, there is no need for 'law' (Derrida, 1997, pp 100, 105, 306).

A primary impulse behind both *Specters* and the *Politics of Friendship* is the perceived need to apply the insights of deconstruction to the various geopolitical challenges of the 'new world order'; the order to enthusiastically proclaimed by Fukuyama as the triumph of liberal democracy (Fukuyama, 1992). 'The world', Derrida bluntly asserts in *Specters*, 'is going badly, the picture is bleak'. As Nietzsche prophesied, the pretences of Enlightenment have been laid bare; 'no degree of progress allows one to ignore that never before, in absolute figures, have so many men, women and children been subjugated, starved, or exterminated on earth' (Derrida, 1994, pp 78, 85). In his earlier essay on the European 'Question', *The Other Heading*, Derrida had already chastised the project of European integration as an apology for the rapacious exploitation of neo-liberal economic ideology. The great shame of the 'new' Europe, Derrida declared, was its 'active forgetting' of the 'other', a refusal to appreciate that the humanism that defines European public philosophy is a humanism of 'difference' and plurality (Derrida, 1992, pp 3–5, 24–25; cf Derrida, 1994, p 116).

The same essential thesis is applied to the broader challenges of the 'new world order' in *On Cosmopolitanism and Forgiveness*. Here Derrida has investigated further two particular aspects of friendship: the integration of the 'other' and the capacity to forgive. According to Derrida, the idea of 'cosmopolitanism' is definitive of humanism, and humanity; the willingness to include, to recognise the 'other'. Once again, his immediate political concern is with those perennial 'others', the refugees who are condemned to wander the 'new' world order, as they did the old, as the 'actively forgotten' (Derrida, 2001, pp 3–24). And alongside the need to integrate the 'other', comes a need to forgive another identifiable 'other', the oppressor. The essence of such an idea of forgiveness is its emotional drive, the triumph of sensibility over sense. A 'pure and unconditional forgiveness, in order to have its own meaning, must have no meaning, no finality, even no intelligibility'. Deploying an archetypically Nietzschean metaphor, Derrida suggests that it is located in the 'night of the unintelligible' (Derrida, 2001, pp 45, 49).

The idea bears all the hallmarks of postmodern playfulness, and is, as ever, rather opaque. But it does advance a genuinely original, and strikingly alternative, ethics. And the immediate context within which Derrida writes, that of globalisation and the 'new world order', does seem to invest the postmodern insight with a certain pressing relevance. The idea that this world order is definitively postmodern has been advanced elsewhere, perhaps most famously by Bonaventure de Sousa Santos (Santos, 1995). And the idea that a postmodern ethics might be defined, not just by its consciousness of the fate of the 'other', but by a particular interest in the idea of forgiveness enjoys considerable contemporary popularity. In this context, Derrida can be placed, perhaps rather incongruously, alongside the likes of Desmond Tutu, whose particular idea of justice, as we have already noted, owes much to more classical conceptions of natural law. Derrida has himself noted the incongruity, suggesting that the advance of these new jurisprudential concepts, such as forgiveness, opens up the way to an identifiably postmodern ethics that is itself indelibly modern (Derrida, 2001, pp 42–43).

It has been suggested that the kind of jurisprudence that haunts the writings of both Derrida and Tutu describes a new and revitalized 'legal humanism', a politics, not just of 'friendship', but of sensibility and compassion (Ward, 2001; cf Finkielraut, 2000, pp 91–93, 112). If true, then it would indeed represent the resurrection of a new humanism, as Derrida pressed in *Specters*. But it would also do rather more, as Nietzsche feared and Derrida appreciates. It returns postmodernism to the very heart of modernity, and to the idea that a postmodern ethics, and jurisprudence, can be traced to original classical conceptions of the good life. It is for this reason that there is such a sharp affinity between the kind of 'friendship' and 'forgiveness' espoused by Derrida and Tutu, and that which can be found lurking, as we have already seen, in the rather older texts of Erasmus or Leibniz.

Deconstruction and critical legal thought

Despite, or perhaps because of, its very obvious ethical injunction, deconstruction, it is often alleged, threatens the coherence of law, perhaps even the downfall of modern theories of law and society. Certainly the turn towards textuality and postmodernism has taken hold in contemporary critical legal thinking. Alan Hunt has presented postmodernism as a natural evolution from critical legal studies, founded on a shared 'profound disenchantment with modernity'. The deconstructive challenge is directed at the 'legitimacy of legal discourse as a mechanism of power disguised as the pursuit of interpretive truth'. Such truths are mere interpretive feints (Hunt, 1990). According to Peter Goodrich, law is a thoroughly aesthetic phenomenon. The legal text, he suggests:

> … circulates as an image and the power of its effect is largely resident in that aesthetic quality rather than in its supposed rational content, for few ever read the law, none ever read all of it (Goodrich, 1991, p 251).

Two fine examples of deconstruction and postmodern legal scholarship can be found in the work of Costas Douzinas and Drucilla Cornell. Both emphasise the ethical dimension of deconstruction. Douzinas, along with Ronnie Warrington, opened *Justice Miscarried* with the prescient observation that the 'crisis of law can be described as a crisis of legal form and a demand for an ethics'. Intriguingly, they suggested that the enterprise should be understood as an evolution, albeit a radical one, of CLS scholarship (Douzinas and Warrington, 1994, pp 1, 14). Equally perceptive was the suggestion that the postmodern interest in aesthetics and language could be traced back to the Kantian critique of judgment. A postmodern jurisprudence, they suggested, is founded on the appreciation that an 'aesthetic community is in a continuous state of formation and dissolution'. And it is this innate contingency that facilitates democracy, as well as liberty, in political communities (Douzinas and Warrington, 1994, pp 132–85).

More recently, in *The End of Human Rights*, Douzinas has again impressed the natural progression from the politics of critical legal studies to the aesthetics of postmodern legal thought. The particular focus of Douzinas's attention, the idea of human rights, is, of course, quintessentially modern. It represents, as Douzinas opines, the 'fulfilment of the Enlightenment promise'. According to Douzinas, the problem with jurisprudential conceptions of human rights, at least in the modernist tradition, is their over-zealous interest in 'rights' at the expense of the 'human' (Douzinas, 2000, pp 1, 17–19, 255–59, 268). And so the task for postmodernism is to revisit the very idea of humanity:

> The utopia projected by the human rights imaginary would be a social organisation which recognises and protects the existential integrity of people expressed in their imaginary domain. The postmodern utopian hope has ontological importance: it protects the integrity of unique beings in their existential otherness, by promoting the dynamic realisation of freedom with others. While the individual imaginary helps build an other-dependent identity, the social imaginary supports a social organisation in which human relationships will respect and promote the uniqueness of the participants (Douzinas, 2000, p 341).

The idea of a 'human rights imaginary' impresses the non-essential nature of rights. Rights are merely instruments, imaginary ones at that. What has essence is humanity, the mutually determining relation of self and 'other'. The Derridean resonance is obvious, perhaps never more so then when Douzinas acknowledges that such a humanism must focus once again on the nature of 'love and affection, pity and friendship' as political concepts (Douzinas, 2000, p 33).

In the second of our examples, Drucilla Cornell uses Derrida in her specific critique of Unger's theory of rights to undermine any notion that there can be a 'logic of identity'; in other words, that any particular or individual can be determined. It is upon such certainties of meaning and identity that modern law depends. A criminal is assumed to be an entire criminal, not part criminal and part not. Yet not all criminals are the same. Indeed no two criminals are the same, any more than two crimes are the same. Law creates a fiction that they are, and in doing so denies fundamental humanity. This critique has a particular edge for Cornell, because it necessitates a rethinking of feminist legal thought. Just as there are no two criminals the same, or two tortfeasors, or two contractors, so too there are no two women the same. Law which seeks to determine the situation of women, either to oppress or to support, creates a particular fiction of 'women', thereby immediately fashioning a 'normative' woman, and necessarily, an 'abnormal' or 'other' woman.

In these terms, the postmodern 'project' is irreducibly political. In *The Philosophy of the Limit*, Cornell suggests that the entire 'project' is 'driven by an ethical desire to enact the ethical relation', meaning the:

> ... aspiration to a non-violent relationship to the Other, and to otherness more generally, that assumes responsibility to guard the Other against the appropriation that would deny her difference and singularity (Cornell, 1992, p 62).

This 'ethical relation' is a 'dialogic', communicative relation. More precisely, it is an ethics specifically situated as an alternative to the internal Kantian moral self. As Cornell confirms, it is an ethical alternative attached to the aesthetic insights of Heidegger and Derrida. The jurisprudence of the 'limit' is defined as the unending 'search for a principle' of legal ethics. Following Derrida, postmodern jurisprudence 'calls us to interpretation through an appeal to justice'. Justice must be constituted by our active participation in its interpretation, or description. This is the 'call to judicial responsibility'. The world in which we live, our particular community, is produced by precisely this jurisprudential exercise. Moreover, as a dialogic process, it remains 'open' and fluid. Legal 'interpretation' becomes the premise for social and political 'transformation' (Cornell, 1992, pp 30–37, 107–15).

This is the most important Derridean insight of all: that we are responsible for our own laws, and that we must take that responsibility. Law is not the possession of lawyers, and neither should it be. The lawyer is a chimera, an illusion justified by a fiction of legal textuality; an actor whose success depends upon the continuing inability of the audience to distinguish fiction from reality. Legal interpretation is performative, always an 'act' for which 'we cannot escape responsibility' (Cornell, 1992, pp 147–49). Cornell's 'call' is directed most immediately towards women. Rather than acquiescing to legal reforms, written largely by men, in line with male perceptions of what women are and what women need, Cornell suggests that particular women must take responsibility for fashioning their own legal and political fates. More precisely, a feminist legal theory must be 'written' by different women. It is text which presents the 'transformative potential' which a postmodern legal feminism requires. Women are the designated 'other', and so must use the insight of the Derridean 'beyond' in order to seize the opportunity to articulate 'a' feminist voice, as opposed to 'the' feminist voice. Accordingly:

> ... the alliance of deconstruction and feminism is crucial if we are not to endorse a conception of justice that entraps us in what is as the only basis for a positive definition. We are constantly envisioning what cannot be seen or even imagined, a society in which human beings were not crippled by the hierarchical structure of gender identity ... But we must also recognise that as we articulate injustices against justice, we do not presume to define justice once and for all. We are called to work within the law but we should not conflate law with justice. As we work within the law we are also called to 'remember' the disjuncture between law and justice that deconstruction always insists upon (Cornell, 1991, pp 115–16).

The political import of Derrida, for Cornell, is that the world is a world of 'others', connected solely by language. All we have in 'common' is language, nothing else. Any political 'ethic of citizenship' must be founded on this appreciation of 'otherness'. Cornell's use of Derrida is, of course, only one use, albeit a particularly striking and influential one. The jurisprudence of deconstruction or postmodernism is of potential application to all, and of particular potential for all who wish to accommodate those who are 'other' in contemporary western society: women, black, disabled, old, indeed almost anyone who is not male, white, fit and wealthy. It can reinvest justice in all those who fail to live up to the Socratic model of the ideal citizen, and it does so because it recognises that, whilst this model enjoys a strong tradition, it is only a model, and only a rhetorical expression – nothing more. The society in which we live is a plurality of different relationships, all mediated by language, and it is the ability to participate in this discourse which provides the means by which justice can indeed become a reality for all. Justice, ultimately, is simply a matter of conversation.

PRAGMATISM AND POSTMODERNISM

Rorty's mirror

A related yet distinctive variant of postmodernism can be found in the work of the American philosopher, Richard Rorty. In his *Philosophy and the Mirror of Nature*, Rorty founded an essentially pragmatic 'postmodern liberalism' on the writings of three dominant figures in modern philosophy. The first of these is Martin Heidegger. The second is John Dewey, whom we encountered in the last chapter. At the root of Dewey's philosophical position was a fundamental denial of 'absolute' truth. It does not matter whether or not something is supposed to be true or not. That is simply a matter of some individual's opinion. What matters is whether something is functionally good or not. In other words, does it work? A third of these philosophers is Ludwig Wittgenstein. The early Wittgenstein tried to construct an analysis of language and linguistic interpretation which could be used to found understanding. Following the Swiss language philosopher, Ferdinand de Saussure, who presented an essentially scientific theory of interpretation of language as a system of 'signs', Wittgenstein suggested that a word should be seen, literally, as a 'sign' to a particular meaning. Sentences and texts then become simply a matter of interpreting accurately the meaning of these various constituent signs. His *Tractatus* was written in the spirit of an essentialist, or positivist, theory of interpretation. In such terms, all words have a purpose, and acquire meaning in this functional sense, and thus a collection of words can be wholly discrete and provide a certain determinable meaning in a functional context. Such a thesis, Wittgenstein suggested, provides 'an all embracing logic, which mirrors the world'. Language could provide a foundation for philosophy, even if it was a reflective or illusory one.

In *Philosophical Investigations*, the later Wittgenstein turned against this foundationalist ambition. Philosophy, he suggested, could not be turned into a positive science, because it has nothing to 'find out'. Language is self-referential, and thus language is all there is for philosophers to worry about. Moreover, language defines the limits of philosophical investigation. Accordingly:

> We never arrive at fundamental propositions in the course of our investigation; we get to the boundary of language which stops us from asking further questions. We don't get to the bottom of things, but reach a point where we can go no further, where we cannot ask further questions (Monk, 1991, p 301).

In these terms, positive or objective meaning cannot be ascertained from words, or even words in terms of their intended function. The author of a text, the articulator of words, cannot determine their meaning. Language only exists in ordinary discourse, and such discourse is created as much by the interpreter, reader or conversationalist. Because there is an infinity of such conversationalists, there is an infinity of particular meanings of words, quite distinct from their original intended usage. A system of language can never be discrete and, accordingly, cannot be said to provide any sort of foundation, even a reflected one. The contingency of the conversationalist defeats the possibility of positive or objective interpretation. As Wittgenstein emphasised, the 'sentence gets its significance' only 'from the language to which it belongs', and that language is itself a series of sentences. The argument is reductive, and there is no foundation. There are no universal rules of interpretation, just 'family resemblances' which can help to guide us towards the necessarily fluid meaning of particular sentences in particular contexts. In these terms, Wittgenstein famously suggested that we are all participators in 'language games', which are ongoing games that evolve as we evolve through real life experiences. The 'learning of a language' is not 'explained', but rather gained through our participation in it. It is acquired in the 'stream of life' (Wittgenstein, 1958).

The influence of Heidegger, Wittgenstein and Dewey underpinned Rorty's *Philosophy and the Mirror of Nature*, published in 1980. What connected the three philosophers, Rorty emphasised, was a fervent anti-foundationalism. None of them, he suggested, wasted their time worrying about 'truth'. In place of this anxiety, Rorty recommends a 'spirit of playfulness', which is better able to reconcile a world of 'contingent truths', a 'spirit' akin to the comedic attitude of Nietzsche and particularly the more optimistic version recommended by Camus. Mirrors furnish reflections. They may not be precise reflections, but they are reflections all the same. The reflection is not the same as the thing it reflects. The illusion which Rorty wants to break is that which assumes that our sensation or experience of something somehow describes that something precisely. Any attempt to describe 'how things are' unavoidably becomes a creative act of 'how things are' (Rorty, 1980, pp 114, 166–79). The most instructive part of *Mirror of Nature* is Rorty's introduction of an alternative hermeneutic theory of knowledge and understanding. Following the basic model articulated by Gadamer, Rorty suggests that interpretation is always bounded by these three factors, text, author and reader, which provide the textual and contextual 'constraints' of understanding or epistemology (Rorty, 1980, pp 357–64).

Obviously there is a degree of foundationalism in this idea of hermeneutics. However, at this stage Rorty is less troubled by a degree of textual foundation and sees hermeneutics as offering a constructive, non-foundational alternative to classical theories of understanding. It is not, he emphasises, some sort of replacement. Indeed, hermeneutics is the 'hope' that we can do without replacements, such that 'our culture should become one in which the demand for constraint and confrontation is no longer felt'. In these terms it is, above all, an anti-necessitarian concept:

> Hermeneutics sees the relations between various discourses as those of strands of a possible conversation, a conversation which presupposes no disciplinary matrix which unites the speakers, but where hope of agreement is never lost so long as the conversation lasts (Rorty, 1980, pp 315–18).

Any philosophical 'constraints' are merely the constraints of 'normal discourse', and instead of some purported 'way of knowing' there is merely a 'way of coping'. Hermeneutics, in its determination to describe our own self-expression, rather than attempting to construct it, is an 'edifying', as opposed to 'systematic', philosophy. In other words, hermeneutics, by recognising the role of the reader in constituting meaning, empowers us all as readers. Echoing Derrida's observations with regard to deconstructionism, Rorty suggests that hermeneutics is likewise an inherently ethical and political enterprise. The concentration on the politics of 'edification' through the constructive participation in 'conversations' emerges as the centrepiece of Rorty's subsequent writings. The most acute form of such edification, Rorty suggests, is 'poetry'. In its desire to refrain from prescribing precise meaning to texts, but rather inviting the reader to express individual interpretation, it is an intrinsically 'edifying' process, which 'opens' up meaning rather than 'closing' it. The three great edifying philosophers are, of course, Dewey, Wittgenstein and Heidegger. They recognised the exclusionary power of language, and sought to keep it open by writing a 'poethics' as an 'abnormal discourse'. As edifying philosophers, what united all three was a desire 'to keep space open for a sense of wonder which poets can sometimes cause' (Rorty, 1980, pp 320, 356–70).

Contingency and conversation

Rorty's ambition is to effect an accommodation between the anti-foundationalism of Dewey's pragmatism and Heidegger's textualism. A revitalised textualised pragmatism, a conjoining of Dewey with the Heidegger-Derrida 'line', can regenerate American philosophy. It can take the deconstructive tendencies of Heidegger-Derrida and meld them with the reconstructive impulses of pragmatic liberalism. Rorty suggested that the great value of pragmatic liberalism lies in its 'vocabulary of practice rather than of theory, of action rather than contemplation, in which one can say something useful about truth'; in other words, that it is contingent. Its other great value is that the only practical constraints it recognises are conversational. A reconstructed democratic liberalism will be a society of conversationalists, aware of the contingency of every truth. This is the spirit of 'democratic pluralism' (Rorty, 1982, pp 160–75). In *Contingency, Irony, and Solidarity*, Rorty suggests that the overriding ambition of any postmodern liberal vision is to achieve 'justice'. The essential distinction in postmodern thought lies between the optimistic and the pessimistic, between the Deweyan-pragmatist line of 'public hope' and 'solidarity', the pervasive sense of community, and the Heidegger-Derrida line of 'private irony', the similarly pervasive sense of self. The key intellectual switch lies in the transference of attention, from freedom or truth, to freedom and truth. Truth no longer constrains freedom of opinion. The marrying of these various dualities, freedom and truth, private and public, solidarity and irony, will realise a liberal utopia, which will be a narrative rather than theoretical utopia, meaning a utopia that is created by all the conversationalists who live within it, rather than discovered by some metaphysician tucked away in a university, monastery or TV station. Solidarity, or community, will be created by us, not by anyone else, and being created by us, need not challenge our sense of autonomy (Rorty, 1989, pp xiii–xvi).

The 'contingency' of three defining qualities of life, of 'language', of 'selfhood', and of 'community', preserves this autonomy, and the core of Rorty's anti-foundationalism lies in the refusal to recognise any particular truth, in ideas of language, of the self and of community. Language is always shared and intersubjective, fashioned by a never ending sequence of contingencies. In an eloquent passage he suggests:

> To say that truth is not out there is simply to say that where there are no sentences there is no truth, that sentences are elements of human languages, and that human languages are human creations ... The world does not speak. Only we do. The world can, once we have programmed ourselves with a language, cause us to hold beliefs. But it cannot prepare a language for us to speak. Only other human beings can do that (Rorty, 1989, pp 5–6).

The 'contingency of selfhood' is the complement to that of language, because the self is a conversationalist and is defined as such. Rorty invokes Nietzsche's idea of life being a 'mobile army of metaphors' to describe our narrative conversational existences. The liberal self, in these terms, is equipped to be 'ironic', in other words to be self-critical, and empowered to assert truths which are contingent and particular to the self. Life is itself a narrative, and we, as self-assertive liberals, are 'poets' of our own contingencies and indeterminacies. For Rorty it is this very fact that unlocks a postmodern conception of freedom and provides the conditions for 'social hope' (Rorty, 1989, pp 23–43).

The synthesis of language and self is effected by the 'contingency of community'. Freedom in the contingent community is the freedom to converse and to persuade. It is the freedom to access 'public space', the kind of freedom advocated by Arendt, Habermas or Unger. What distinguishes Rorty's notion of public space is that it is discursively constructive. Language is lived. It is not something we can stand outside of, and use merely in the public sphere. Language is, at once, private and public. The language of philosophy is thus the language of politics and literature. The liberal 'polity' is the community in which the 'strong poets' are the heroes. The echoes of Shelley's famous injunction are resonant. Poets describe and redescribe, aware that any truth is their truth, and a merely textual truth (Rorty, 1989, pp 50–54). A postmodern liberal politics must, then, pursue the poetic model:

A liberal society is one whose ideal can be fulfilled by persuasion rather than by force, by reform rather than revolution, by the free and open encounters of present linguistic and other practices with suggestions for new practices. But that is to say that an ideal liberal society is one which has no purpose except freedom, no goal except a willingness to see how such encounters go and to abide by the outcome. It has no purpose except to make life easier for poets and revolutionaries while seeing to it that they make life harder for others only by words, and not deeds. It is a society whose hero is the strong poet and the revolutionary because it recognises that it is what it is, has the morality it has, speaks the language it does, not because it approximates the will of God or the nature of man but because certain poets and revolutionaries of the past spoke as they did. To see one's language, one's conscience, one's morality, and one's highest hopes as contingent products, as literalisations of what once were accidentally produced metaphors, is to adopt a self-identity which suits one for citizenship in such an ideally liberal state (Rorty, 1989, pp 60–61).

The postmodern liberal utopia is described by two spheres, of 'private irony' and 'public solidarity'. The world of the postmodern ironist is the world of the self reconciled to fundamental political indeterminacy. This, he suggests, is the self described by the French Heideggerians, Derrida and Foucault. The ironist acknowledges the ever-openness of discourse, as the residuum of freedom both public and private, and Rorty has repeatedly suggested that Foucault in particular 'caught a glimpse' of the postmodern world as a world of 'contingency and chance'. It was Foucault, better than anyone, who appreciated the need rigorously to delimit the boundaries of public and private (Rorty, 1991a, pp 193–98). Derrida, in turn, has emphasised the extent to which there is always a 'beyond', another text which we must read, and in reading rewrite and reshape. Derrida, accordingly, empowers the private ironist, and makes him or her a public figure as well as a private one (Rorty, 1991a, pp 101–06). At the same time, despite their insights, Rorty rejects the fatalism of Foucault and Derrida. What he wants to do is to take this irony and 'yoke' it to a liberalism of 'solidarity', and in this way create a more optimistic postmodern politics. The theory of 'solidarity' is the theory of the postmodern liberal, a theory of belonging that does not presume some metaphysical idea of truth which legitimates, even demands, our political or emotional association.

The end of postmodernism?

Towards the end of *Contingency, Irony, and Solidarity*, Rorty sought to impress an overarching conclusion, and aspiration:

> I want to distinguish human solidarity as the identification with 'humanity as such' and as self-doubt which has gradually, over the last few centuries, been inculcated into inhabitants of the democratic States – doubt about their own sensitivity to the pain and humiliation of others, doubt that present institutional arrangements are adequate to deal with this pain and humiliation, curiosity about possible alternatives ... Distinguishing these questions makes it possible to distinguish public from private questions, questions about pain from questions about the point of human life, the domain of the liberal from the domain of the ironist. It thus makes it possible for a single person to be both (Rorty, 1989, p 198).

We can, Rorty implied, lead perfectly fulfilled lives, and perfectly just ones, without having to justify them in some grand metaphysical scheme. As Camus suggested, there does not need to be an absolute meaning to life, for human beings, even lawyers, to find something useful to do and some reason to live. The postmodern future will be one in which our idea of 'justice' will be reformed so as to reflect a world of 'small contingent facts' rather than an ephemeral illusion of 'large necessary truths' (Rorty, 1989, pp 187–88). Only Rorty is no longer prepared to term this a postmodern world. Admitting an increasing 'scepticism about the postmodern', in his most recent writings Rorty has, instead, preferred to concentrate on the pragmatic, and political, implications of his thesis. And here, he is particularly keen to avoid the potential hazards of pure relativism, or absolute contingency. Rorty's post-postmodern, or 'post-Nietzschean', world will not be quite so ironic or whimsical or playful as its postmodern precedessor. The stakes, in terms of human suffering, are too high and too immediate (Rorty, 1999, pp xiv–xvii, 168).

The problem, of course, is that the rejection of the kind of absolute contingency that Rorty ascribes to Nietzschean postmodernism, appears to leave the philosopher with either Kantian universalism, or some kind of rather murky middle ground. And the problems that can be encountered in this middle ground were vividly illustrated by a series of controversial essays Rorty produced during the early 1990s in which he used a model of 'ethnocentrism'. Here Rorty deployed the idea of 'ethnocentrism' as the privileging of localised group moralities and political values. In doing so, he cited Unger and Rawls as protagonists of ethnocentrism. Critics suggested that this model of ethnocentrism is dangerously anti-liberal, and liable to justify any number of undesirable and unliberal forms of exclusionary politics. Rorty countered by suggesting that such a danger can be avoided by employing strong liberal political institutions which can preserve procedural justice. The ethnocentric model, Rorty advises us, can prevent us slipping into the kind of classical modernist liberalism of such as Kant. Such a model will be historical, as opposed to ahistorical, and narrative as opposed to philosophical. It offers the best hope for a pragmatic liberalism because it redefines freedom as 'interdependence' and as a constituent of 'solidarity' (Rorty, 1991b, pp 175–202).

Rorty subsequently used this idea of pragmatic or relative 'solidarity' as a model with which to describe a non-foundational idea of human rights; one that bears a striking resemblance to that advocated by the likes of Douzinas. Here, like Douzinas, and of course jurists such as Dworkin and Twining, Rorty clearly felt the pull of contemporary anxieties regarding the need to devise some kind of philosophy for the emergent 'new world order' (Rorty, 1998, pp 84–85; 1999, pp 230–33). Such a non-foundational human rights, he suggested, is a human rights of consciousness, a response to hearing 'sad and sentimental stories', rather than a human rights founded on moral knowledge or any other such illusion. It is, Rorty adds, a human rights that might be Kantian in spirit, but which is Derridean in execution. Repeating an assertion at the centre of *Contingency, Irony, and Solidarity*, he affirmed that the energy of liberal anger is far better directed at refuting instances of 'cruelty' than composing erudite academic theses on human rights (Rorty, 1993, pp 111–34).

Whilst Rorty has been ever keener to impress the pragmatic, rather than ironic, nature of this political enterprise, the basic metaphysical critique remains consistent. Above all, there is no need for absolutes in our present 'post-Nietzschean' world:

> But to us pragamatists moral struggle is continuous with the struggle for existence, and no sharp break divides the unjust from the imprudent, the evil from the inexpedient. What matters for pragmatists is devising ways of diminishing human suffering and increasing human equality, increasing the ability of all human children to start life with an equal chance of happiness. This goal is not written in the stars, and is no more an expression of what Kant called 'pure practical reason' than it is the will of God. It is a cause worth dying for, but it does not require backup from supernatural forces (Rorty, 1999, p xxix).

It might be said that the rhetoric of the post-postmodern Rorty bears a striking resemblance to that of its postmodern predecessor. And it does. And the same political urgency is ever-present too. Increasingly, Rorty is convinced that an 'ideal community' is not one established in honour of any particular ideals at all, but simply one 'in which everybody thinks that it is human solidarity, rather than knowledge of something not merely human, that really matters'. Once again, the concentration on the 'human' is striking, as is the collateral focus on sentimentality. For the post-postmodern Rorty, the desire to reduce philosophy to a matter of 'increasing sensitivity' is just as pressing. It is for this reason, he continues to opine, that a progressive idea of 'justice' should be seen as a matter of sentiment rather than law, of 'poetry' rather than 'principles' (Rorty, 1999, pp 81–83, 99).

Above all, however, Rorty is determined to argue the case for a post-postmodern philosophy of hope. The most that a pragmatist can do, he repeatedly affirms, is to 'substitute hope for the sort of knowledge which philosophers have usually tried to attain' (Rorty, 1999, pp 20, 24, 31). It is this hope, Rorty now suggests, that describes the affinity between American pragmatists such as himself, and European postmodernists such as Derrida. The 'ultimate romantic hope' that Rorty sees in Derrida is no less attractive now than it was a decade ago. But the intellectual affinity is now compromised by Rorty's determination to engage the pragmatics of political 'solidarity'. What the 'new world order', and particularly the American bit of it, needs today is not metaphysical, or even post-metaphysical, whimsy, but 'just good old American pragmatism' (Rorty, 1999, pp 47, 211–16, 237). The parochial nature of this distinction is striking. Europeans, Rorty confirms in his paean to a 'progressive' American public philosophy, *Achieving Our Country*, must be left to their reductive 'obsession' with metaphysics and the search for truth, or its opposite (Rorty, 1998, p 22).

It is here that the real sense of urgency is most clearly felt. America, according to Rorty, should be the harbinger of liberal values of toleration and humanity. But it is, today, a 'country in decline', its original crusading spirit, the spirit of Dewey and Walt

Whitman, lost, crushed by decades of rampant intellectual neo-conservatism. America must, once again, take up the banner of humanity, and in order to do so its intellectuals must, once and for all, abandon 'futile attempts to philosophize one's way into political relevance' (Rorty, 1998, pp 14–19, 30–32, 86; 1999, pp 94, 234). Perhaps so. But even now, Rorty cannot quite abandon his own metaphysical and romantic yearnings, as the conclusion to *Philosophy and Social Hope* reveals:

> The reason this kind of philosophy is relevent to politics is simply that it encourages people to have a self-image in which their real or imagined citizenship in a democratic republic is central. This kind of anti-authoritarian philosophy helps people set aside religious and ethnic identities in favour of an image of themselves as part of a great human adventure, one carried out on a global scale. This kind of philosophy, so to speak, clears philosophy out of the way in order to let the imagination play upon the possibilities of utopian future (Rorty, 1999, pp 238–39).

The poetry can never really be clearly extricated from the pragmatism. And it remains a matter of conjecture as to whether it really needs to be.

The return to deconstruction

By way of a contrast to Rorty's more reconstructive political agenda, another American pragmatist, Stanley Fish, has consistently employed a more radical deconstructionist theory of language and interpretation against any hermeneutic attempt to 'constrain' possible meanings of texts. As he stated in *Is There a Text in this Class?*, any constraints are themselves texts and subject to the same process of textual deconstruction. According to Fish, there is no privileged position outside texts, from which principles of interpretation can be derived. His critique was primarily levelled against the Dworkinian idea of interpretive 'principles', and suggested that all such principles, Dworkinian or otherwise, are merely texts themselves. Because 'we are never not in a situation, we are never not in the act of interpreting', and because 'we are never not in the act of interpreting, there is no possibility of reaching a level of meaning beyond or below interpretation'. In sum, Fish continued, 'whatever' readers do, 'it will only be interpretation in another guise because, like it or not, interpretation is the only game in town' (Fish, 1980, pp 276–77, 355). The idea of the game is important, because it implies a process of participation. Like it or not, we are always participating in the construction of our language, and, although Fish has resisted too close an alignment, there is a clear similarity here with Rorty's deep pragmatism. In *Doing What Comes Naturally*, as the title of the book suggests, Fish is keen to describe legal and literary interpretation as being no different from the strategies anyway employed in ordinary discourse. Interpretation, he emphasises, is something done, rather than something thought about (Fish, 1989; 1994, pp 6–8).

Fish's particular engagement with Owen Fiss on the possibility of objective interpretation of texts is instructive. In a 1982 essay entitled 'Objectivity and interpretation', Fiss presented a classical hermeneutic theory of interpretation, directed primarily against the deconstructionism which he perceived in so much CLS and postmodern writing. Interpretation, he affirmed:

> … whether it be in the law or literary domains, is neither a wholly discretionary nor a wholly mechanical activity. Rather, it is a dynamic interaction between reader and text, and meaning is the product of that interaction.

Fiss denied the necessity for interpretive indeterminism. The interpreter, he suggested, is 'constrained' by 'disciplining rules' and by his existence in an 'interpretive community, which recognises these rules as authoritative'. Accordingly, the 'idea of an objective interpretation does not require that the interpretation be wholly determined by some source external to the judge, but only that it be constrained'. At the same time, echoing Dworkin, he emphasised that this 'idea of objective interpretation accommodates the creative role of the reader' by 'recognising that the meaning of the text does not reside in the text' alone. He concluded by suggesting that interpretive 'constraints' help to make the law moral because the creative reader interprets in accordance with moral rules. What always prevents a judge interpreting in an 'unconstrained' manner is the 'argument of necessity', that he should always interpret and judge in terms of 'integrity'. This thesis, he concluded, makes for a constitutional morality that is both 'rich and inspiring' (Fiss, 1982).

Fish was not particularly interested in theories that were rich or inspiring, and taking a more radical deconstructionist line refused to accept that any 'constraining' rules could be anything but texts themselves. Being 'texts', Fiss's 'constraints' are in precisely the same 'need of interpretation and cannot themselves serve as constraints on interpretation'. Fish denied the possibility of objectifying either the text or its meaning. Accordingly, 'rules, in law or anywhere else, do not stand in an independent relationship to a field of action on which they can simply be imposed'. Rather, Fiss's rules:

> ... have a circular or mutually interdependent relationship to the field of action in that they make sense only in reference to the very regularities they are thought to bring about (Fish, 1989, pp 120–41).

In essence, of course, the argument is radically reductive, and prevents any sort of textual determinacy. The reader is wholly empowered, even if he or she is interpreting in an environment constituted by other texts. This may or may not be desirable, but as Fish has repeatedly emphasised, it is simply a fact. Of course, the obvious counter to Fish's position here is that this particular fact, that interpretation is the 'only game in town', is itself foundational and seeks some sort of privileged theoretical status. More recently, discussing the alternative liberal textual and pragmatic textual positions, Fish has admitted the danger in the deconstructionist position of transforming the refusal to see anything but text into a foundational argument (Fish, 1994, pp 215–17).

Fish's arguments against Fiss can, of course, be employed equally against the hermeneutics to which Dworkin adheres, and which have tempted Rorty. Nothing can ground text, simply because there is nothing else but text. There is, as he has more recently affirmed, no 'privileged' position, no 'critical self-consciousness' that allows us to interpret from some position detached from the text itself (Fish, 1995, p 107). Equally, there is no such thing as a 'legal' reading, as opposed to any other sort of reading. In an acutely pragmatic gesture, Fish reaffirms that there is no 'hierarchy in which the reflective practitioner is superior, even morally superior, to the practitioner who just goes about his business'. Moreover, the 'theoretical component of practice' is 'nothing more exalted than the habits of being alert and paying attention' (Fish, 1994, pp 228–30). The idea of conversation as liberating and empowering in this way is immediately resonant of Rorty, a similarly reluctant postmodernist, as well, of course, as Derrida and Cornell.

It also strikes a chord with a number of CLS critics of a postmodern bent, such as Costas Douzinas and Allan Hutchinson, as Fish himself acknowledges (Fish, 1994, p 21). The debate between hermeneutic and deconstructionist alternative theories of interpretation has remained virulent within the CLS movement. Hutchinson, for example, has taken Fish's side against liberals such as Rorty and Dworkin, suggesting that the assertion of interpretive constraints is simply a ruse by which a postmodern liberalism hopes to reassert its political authority and power, following the demise of classical modern liberalism. It privileges the liberal reader, and thereby disadvantages the communitarian, critical or radical alternative. At root, it is a political theory of interpretation, and must be understood as such (Hutchinson, 1984, pp 273–92). Hutchinson concludes, as we have already noted, that we 'are never not in a story'. History and human action only take on meaning and intelligibility within their narrative context and dramatic settings. He continues, our:

> ... conversations about these narratives are themselves located and scripted in deeper stories which determine their moral force ... Most importantly, it is the stories themselves that come to comprise the reality of our experience. In this sense, legal stories mediate our engagement in the world and with others: they provide the possibilities and parameters for our self-definition and understanding (Hutchinson, 1989, pp 13–14).

Our particular story is now complete. We have certainly not explored each and every critical legal theory, still less each and every legal theory. What we have presented, perhaps, is a particular series of 'stories', of impressions and perspectives, each of which has served to emphasise the extent to which law and legal theory must be understood as a deeply interdisciplinary and contextual exercise. From the very first chapter, and Aristotle's revision of Plato, we have encountered critical legal theories which have each sought to establish foundations, either descriptive or prescriptive of law, and each of which have done so by revising received jurisprudential wisdom. As a narrative history, the evolution of legal theory is immanently critical. It is also rich and varied. Most importantly, it is not complete. No theory of law, or book which seeks to describe theories of law, can ever be complete. The most exciting, perhaps ever inspiring, conclusion that we can reach is that law and legal theory is active, forever in a process of change and revolution, either politically or intellectually. There will be new theories of law and new theorists, and each to some degree will be critical, for each to some degree will seek to re-present and to rewrite a theory of law. Indeed, as a reader of this particular story, you too have already participated in the critical legal enterprise and in the constructive process of rewriting and rethinking law.

BIBLIOGRAPHY

Althusius, J, *Politica*, 1995, Indianapolis: Liberty Press.

Ansell-Pearson, K, *An Introduction to Nietzsche as a Political Thinker*, 1994, Cambridge: CUP.

Aquinas, St T, *Summa Theologica*, 1991, London: Methuen.

Arendt, H, *The Origins of Totalitarianism*, 1951, New York: Harcourt Brace Jovanovich.

Arendt, H, *The Human Condition*, 1958, Chicago: Chicago UP.

Arendt, H, *Eichmann in Jerusalem: A Report on the Banality of Evil*, 1963, New York: Viking Press.

Arendt, H, *Crises of the Republic*, 1972, New York: Harcourt Brace Jovanovich.

Arendt, H, *The Life of the Mind*, 1978, New York: Harcourt Brace Jovanovich.

Arendt, H, *Lectures on Kant's Political Philosophy*, 1982, Chicago: Chicago UP.

Arendt, H, *On Revolution*, 1990, London: Penguin.

Aristodemou, M, *Law and Literature: Journeys from Here to Eternity*, 2000, Oxford: OUP.

Aristotle, *The Ethics*, 1976, London: Penguin.

Aristotle, *The Politics*, 1981, London: Penguin.

Atiyah, P, *The Rise and Fall of the Freedom of Contract*, 1979, Oxford: OUP.

Austin, J, *The Province of Jurisprudence Determined*, 1995 [1832], Cambridge: CUP.

Bacon, F, *The Advancement of Learning and New Atlantis*, 1974, Oxford: OUP.

Bacon, F, *The Essays*, 1985, London: Penguin.

Barron, A, 'Feminism, aestheticism and the limits of law' (2000) 8 Feminist Legal Studies 275.

Bartlett, K, 'Feminist legal methods', in Barlett, K and Kennedy, R (eds), *Feminist Legal Theory: Readings in Law and Gender*, 1991, Boulder: Westview Press.

Baxter, R, *A Holy Commonwealth*, 1994, Cambridge: CUP.

Becker, G, *The Economic Approach to Human Behaviour*, 1977, Chicago: Chicago UP.

Bendersky, J, *Carl Schmitt: Theorist for the Reich*, 1983, Princeton: Princeton UP.

Bennington, G, *Jacques Derrida*, 1993, Chicago: Chicago UP.

Bentham, J, *Of Laws in General*, 1980, London: Athlone.

Bentham, J, *An Introduction to the Principles of Morals and Legislation*, 1982, London: Methuen.

Berlin, I, *Karl Marx*, 1995, London: Fontana.

Bernstein, R, *The New Constellation*, 1991, Cambridge: Polity Press.

Beveridge, F et al, 'Mainstreaming and the engendering of policy-making: a means to an end?' (2000) 7 Journal of European Public Policy 385.

Bhaskar, R, *Philosophy and the Idea of Freedom*, 1991, Oxford: Blackwell.

Bretherton, C, 'Gender mainstreaming and EU enlargement: swimming against the tide?' (2001) 8 Journal of European Public Policy 60.

Burgess, G, *Absolute Monarchy and the Stuart Constitution*, 1996, New Haven: Yale UP.

Burke, E, *Reflections on the Revolution in France*, 1986, London: Penguin.

Butler, J, *Gender Trouble: Feminism and the Subversion of Identity*, 1990, London: Routledge.

Calabresi, G, *The Costs of Accidents: A Legal and Economic Analysis*, 1970, New Haven: Yale UP.

Camus, A, *The Myth of Sisyphus*, 1975, London: Penguin.

Camus, A, *The Outsider*, 1983, London: Penguin.

Canovan, M, *Hannah Arendt*, 1992, Cambridge: CUP.

Cass, R, 'Coping with life, law, and markets: a comment on Posner and the law and economics debate' (1987) 67 Boston University L Rev 73.

Cassirer, E, *The Myth of the State*, 1946, New York: Little, Brown.

Cassirer, E, *The Philosophy of the Enlightenment*, 1951, Princeton: Princeton UP.

Cassirer, E, *Language and Myth*, 1953, London: Dover.

Cassirer, E, *Kant's Life and Thought*, 1981, New Haven: Yale UP.

Cixous, H and Clement, C, *The Newly Born Woman*, 1975, Minneapolis: University of Minnesota Press.

Coase, R, 'The problem of social cost' (1960) 3 Journal of Law and Economics 1.

Cohen, J, 'Posnerism, pluralism, pessimism' (1987) 67 Boston University L Rev 105.

Conaghan, J, 'Reassessing the feminist theoretical project in law' (2000) 27 Journal of Law and Society 351.

Connolly, W, *Political Theory and Modernity*, 1988, Oxford: Blackwell.

Coplestone, F, *Aquinas*, 1955, London: Penguin.

Cornell, D, *Beyond Accommodation*, 1991, London: Routledge.

Cornell, D, *The Philosophy of the Limit*, 1992, London: Routledge.

Cornell, D, *At the Heart of Freedom: Feminism, Sex and Equality*, 1998, Princeton: Princeton UP.

Cowling, M, *Mill and Liberalism*, 1990, Cambridge: CUP.

Crossan, F, 'Religion and natural law' (1988) 33 American Journal of Jurisprudence 1.

Cummings, R, 'The odd couple: Heidegger and Derrida' (1981) 34 Review of Metaphysics 487.

de Grazia, S, *Machiavelli in Hell*, 1992, London: Macmillan.

de Tocqueville, A, *On Democracy, Revolution and Society*, 1980, Chicago: Chicago UP.

D'Entreves, A, *Aquinas: Selected Political Writings*, 1959, Oxford: Blackwell.

Derrida, J, 'Violence and metaphysics', in Bass, A (ed), *Writing and Difference*, 1978, Chicago: Chicago UP.

Derrida, J, 'But beyond ... ', in Gates, H (ed), *Race, Writing and Difference*, 1985, Chicago: Chicago UP.

Derrida, J, 'The laws of reflection: Nelson Mandela, in admiration', in Derrida, J and Tlili, M (eds), *For Nelson Mandela*, 1987, New York: Free Press.

Derrida, J, *Of Spirit: Heidegger and the Question*, 1989, Chicago: Chicago UP.

Derrida, J, 'The force of law: the mystical foundations of authority' (1990) 11 Cardozo L Rev 921.

Derrida, J, *The Other Heading: Reflections on Today's Europe*, 1992, Bloomington: Indian UP.

Derrida, J, *Specters of Marx*, 1994, London: Routledge.

Derrida, J, *Politics of Friendship*, 1997, London: Verso.

Derrida, J, *On Cosmopolitanism and Forgiveness*, 2001, London: Routledge.

de Tocqueville, A, *On Democracy, Revolution and Society*, 1980, Chicago: Chicago UP.

Devlin, P, *The Enforcement of Morals*, 1965, Oxford: OUP.

Dewey, J, 'Logical method and the law' (1924) 10 Cardozo LQ 17.

Dewey, J, *Philosophy and Civilization*, 1963, New York: Little, Brown.

Dicey, A, *An Introduction to the Study of the Law of the Constitution*, 1959, London: Macmillan.

Dickens, C, *Bleak House*, 1994, London: Dent.

Dossa, S, 'Hannah Arendt on Eichmann: the public, the private and evil' (1984) 46 Review of Politics 163.

Dostoevski, F, *Crime and Punishment*, 1991, London: Viking.

Douzinas, C, *The End of Human Rights: Critical Legal Thought at the Turn of the Century*, 2000, Oxford: Hart.

Douzinas, C and Warrington, R, *Justice Miscarried: Ethics, Aesthetics and the Law*, 1994, London: Harvester Wheatsheaf.

Dunn, J, *The Political Thought of John Locke: An Historical Account of the Argument of the Two Treatises of Government*, 1969, Cambridge: CUP.

Duxbury, N, *Patterns of American Jurisprudence*, 1995, Oxford: OUP.

Dworkin, R, *Taking Rights Seriously*, 1977, London: Duckworth.

Dworkin, R, 'Law as interpretation' (1982) Texas Law Review 527.

Dworkin, R, *A Matter of Principle*, 1985, Oxford: OUP.

Dworkin, R, *Law's Empire*, 1986, Cambridge, Mass: Harvard UP.

Dworkin, R, *Life's Dominion: An Argument About Abortion and Euthanasia*, 1993, London: HarperCollins.

Dworkin, R, *Freedom's Law: The Moral Reading of the American Constitution*, 1996, Oxford: OUP.

Dworkin, R, *Sovereign Virtue: The Theory and Practice of Equality*, 2000, Cambridge, Mass: Harvard UP.

Dyzenhaus, D, *Judging Judges, Judging Ourselves: Truth, Reconciliation and the Apartheid Legal Order*, 1998, Oxford: Hart.

Eksteins, M, *The Rites of Spring*, 1989, Toronto: Lester and Orpen Dennys.

Eliot, G, *Selected Essays, Poems and Other Writings*, 1990, London: Penguin.

Erasmus, D, *The Education of a Christian Prince*, 1997, Cambridge: CUP.

Etzioni, A, *The Spirit of Community: Rights, Responsibilities and the Communitarian Agenda*, 1995, London: Fontana.

Ferguson, A, *An Essay on the History of Civil Society*, 1995, Cambridge: CUP.

Filmer, R, *Patriarcha and Other Writings*, 1991, Cambridge: CUP.

Finkielraut, A, *In the Name of Humanity: Reflections on the Twentieth Century*, 2000, London: Pimlico.

Finnis, J, *Natural Law and Natural Rights*, 1980, Oxford: Clarendon.

Fish, S, *Is There a Text in This Class? The Authority of Interpretive Communities*, 1980, Cambridge, Mass: Harvard UP.

Fish, S, *Doing What Comes Naturally: Change, Rhetoric, and the Practice of Theory in Literary and Legal Studies*, 1989, Oxford: OUP.

Fish, S, *There's No Such Thing as Free Speech ... and It's a Good Thing Too*, 1994, Oxford: OUP.

Fish, S, *Professional Correctness: Literary Studies and Political Change*, 1995, Oxford: OUP.

Fiss, O, 'Objectivity and interpretation' (1982) 34 Stanford L Rev 739.

Foucault, M, *The Archaeology of Knowledge*, 1974, London: Tavistock.

Foucault, M, 'Nietzsche, geneology, history', in Bouchard, D (ed), *Michel Foucault: Language, Counter-Memory, Practice*, 1977, Ithaca: Cornell UP.

Foucault, M, *Discipline and Punish: The Birth of the Prison*, 1979, London: Peregrine.

Foucault, M, 'Truth and power', in Gordon, C (ed), *Power/Knowledge: Selected Interviews and Other Writings 1972–1977*, 1980a, Brighton: Harvester Press.

Foucault, M, 'Two lectures', in Gordon, C (ed), *Power/Knowledge: Selected Interviews and Other Writings 1972–1977*, 1980b, Brighton: Harvester Press.

Foucault, M, 'Debate with Chomsky', in Rabinow, P (ed), *The Foucault Reader*, 1984, New York: Pantheon.

Foucault, M, *Madness and Civilization*, 1989, London: Routledge.

Foucault, M, 'The art of telling the truth', in Kritzman, L (ed), *Foucault: Politics, Philosophy, Culture*, 1990a, London: Routledge.

Foucault, M, *The History of Sexuality*, vols 1–3, 1990b, London: Penguin.

Foucault, M, 'Politics and the study of discourse', in Burchell, G, Gordon, C and Miller, P (eds), *The Foucault Effect: Studies in Governmentality*, 1991, Brighton: Harvester.

Franck, T, 'The emerging right to democratic governance' (1992) 86 American Journal of International Law 46.

Frankel, T and Miller, F, 'The inapplicability of market theory to adoptions' (1987) 67 Boston University L Rev 99.

Frug, G, 'The city as a legal concept' (1980) 93 Harv L Rev 1057.

Frug, J, 'Argument as character' (1988) 40 Stanford Law Review 867.

Frug, M, *Postmodern Legal Feminism*, 1992, London: Routledge.

Fukuyama, F, *The End of History and the Last Man*, 1992, London: Penguin.

Fuller, L, 'Positivism and fidelity to law – a reply to Professor Hart' (1958) 71 Harv L Rev 630.

Fuller, L, *The Morality of Law*, 1969, New Haven: Yale UP.

Gabel, P and Kennedy, D, 'Roll over Beethoven' (1984) 36 Stanford L Rev 1.

Gadamer, H-G, *Truth and Method*, 1975, London: Sheed and Ward.

Gaita, R, *A Common Humanity: Thinking About Love and Truth and Justice*, 2000, London: Routledge.

Galbraith, J, *The Affluent Society*, 1987, London: Penguin.

Galbraith, J, *A History of Economics: The Past as the Present*, 1991, London: Penguin.

Galbraith, J, *The Good Society*, 1996, London: Sinclair-Stevenson.

Gamble, A, *Hayek: The Iron Cage of Liberty*, 1996, Cambridge: Polity Press.

Gasche, R, *The Tain of the Mirror: Derrida and the Philosophy of Reflection*, 1986, Cambridge, Mass: Harvard UP.

Gauthier, D, 'Hobbes's social contract', in Rogers, G and Ryan, A (eds), *Perspectives of Thomas Hobbes*, 1988, Oxford: OUP.

Getman, J, 'Voices' (1988) 66 Texas L Rev 577.

Giddens, A and Hutton, W, 'In conversation', in Giddens, A and Hutton, W (eds), *On the Edge: Living with Global Capitalism*, 2000, London: Jonathan Cape.

Gilligan, C, *In a Different Voice*, 1982, Cambridge, Mass: Harvard UP.

Godwin, W, 'An enquiry concerning political justice', in Philp, M (ed), *Political and Philosophical Writings of William Godwin*, vol 3, 1993, London: William Pickering.

Golding, M, 'Realism and functionalism in the legal thought of Felix S Cohen' (1981) 66 Cornell L Rev 1032.

Goodrich, P, 'Specula laws: image, aesthetics and common law' (1991) 2 Law and Critique 233.

Goodrich, P, 'Duncan Kennedy as I imagine him: the man, the work, his scholarship and the polity' (2001) 22 Cardozo LR 971.

Goodrich, P and Mills, L, 'The law of white spaces: race, culture, and legal education', (2001) 51 Journal of Legal Education 15.

Gordon, R, 'Historicism in legal scholarship' (1982) 90 Yale LJ 1017.

Gray, J, *Essays in Political Philosophy*, 1989, London: Routledge.

Grayling, A, *What is Good?: The Search for the Best Way to Live*, 2003, London: Weidenfeld & Nicolson.

Guardiola-Rivera, O, 'The question concerning law' (2003) 66 MLR 792.

Guest, S, *Ronald Dworkin*, 1992, Edinburgh: Edinburgh UP.

Habermas, J, *The Philosophical Discourse of Modernity*, 1987, Cambridge: Polity Press.

Habermas, J, *Between Facts and Norms: Contributions to a Discourse Theory of Law and Philosophy*, 1996, Cambridge: Polity Press.

Habermas, J, *The Postnational Constellation*, 2001, Cambridge: Polity Press.

Hansen, P, *Hannah Arendt: Politics, History and Citizenship*, 1993, Cambridge: Polity Press.

Harrington, J, *The Commonwealth of Oceana*, 1992, Cambridge: CUP.

Hart, G, *Restoration of the Republic: The Jeffersonian Ideal in Twenty-First Century America*, 2002, Oxford: OUP.

Hart, H, 'Positivism and the separation of law and morals' (1958) 71 Harv L Rev 593.

Hart, H, *The Concept of Law*, 1961, Oxford: Clarendon.

Hart, H, *Law, Liberty and Morality*, 1968, Oxford: OUP.

Havel, V, *The Art of the Impossible: Politics as Morality in Practice*, 1998, New York: Fromm International.

Hayek, F, *The Road to Serfdom*, 1962 [1944], London: Routledge.

Hayek, F, *Law, Legislation and Liberty: Liberal Principles of Justice and Political Economy*, 1992, London: Routledge.

Hayman, R, *Nietzsche: A Critical Life*, 1995, London: Phoenix.

Hegel, G, *Phenomenology of Spirit*, 1977, Oxford: OUP.

Heidegger, M, *Being and Time*, 1962, Oxford: Blackwell.

Heidegger, M, 'Building, dwelling, thinking', in *Basic Writings*, 1977a, New York: Harper and Row.

Heidegger, M, 'The end of philosophy and the task of thinking', in *Basic Writings*, 1977b, New York: Harper and Row.

Heidegger, M, 'The self-assertion of the German university' (1985) 38 Review of Metaphysics 470.

Held, D, *Models of Democracy*, 1976, Cambridge: Polity Press.

Held, D, *Democracy and Global Order: From the Modern State to Cosmopolitan Governance*, 1995, Cambridge: Polity Press.

Henry, Y, 'Where healing begins', in Villa-Vicencio, C and Verwoerd, W (eds), *Looking Back, Reaching Forward: Reflections on the Truth and Reconciliation Commission of South Africa*, 2000, Cape Town: University of Cape Town Press.

Hill, C, *Liberty Against the Law*, 1996, London: Penguin.

Hobbes, T, *Leviathan*, 1985, London: Penguin.

Hobbes, T, *Behemoth*, 1990, Chicago: Chicago UP.

Hobbes, T, *De Cive*, 1998, Cambridge: CUP.

Holmes, O, *The Common Law*, 1963, Cambridge, Mass: Harvard UP.

Hooker, R, *Of the Laws of Ecclesiastical Polity*, 1989, Cambridge: CUP.

Hume, D, *An Enquiry Concerning the Principles of Morals*, 1966, La Salle: Open Court.

Hume, D, *Treatise*, 1978, Oxford: OUP.

Hume, D, *Political Essays*, 1994, Cambridge: CUP.

Hunt, A, 'The big fear: law confronts postmodernism' (1990) 35 McGill LJ 508.

Hunt, A and Wickham, G, *Foucault and the Law: Towards a Sociology of Law as Governance*, 1994, London: Pluto.

Hutchinson, A, 'Of kings and dirty rascals: the struggle for democracy' (1984) 17 Queens LJ 273.

Hutchinson, A, *Dwelling on the Threshold*, 1988, Toronto: Carswell.

Hutchinson, A, 'The three "Rs": reading/rorty/radically' (1989) 103 Harv L Rev 555.

Isaac, J, *Arendt, Camus, and Modern Rebellion*, 1992, New Haven: Yale UP.

Johnston, D, *The Rhetoric of Leviathan*, 1986, Princeton: Princeton UP.

Kafka, F, *The Trial*, 1953, London: Penguin.

Kant, I, *Critique of Pure Reason*, 1934, London: Dent.

Kant, I, *Critique of Practical Reason*, 1949, Chicago: Chicago UP.

Kant, I, *Groundwork to the Metaphysics of Morals*, 1964, London: Routledge.

Kant, I, *The Critique of Judgment*, 1991a [1790], Oxford: OUP.

Kant, I, *The Metaphysics of Morals*, 1991b [1797], Cambridge: CUP.

Keane, J, *Tom Paine: A Political Life*, 1995, London: Bloomsbury.

Kelly, J, *A Short History of Western Legal Thought*, 1992, Oxford: OUP.

Kelman, M, 'Trashing' (1984) 36 Stanford L Rev 321.

Kelman, M, *A Guide to Critical Legal Studies*, 1987, Cambridge, Mass: Harvard UP.

Kennedy, D, 'Legal education as training for hierarchy', in Kairys, D (ed), *The Politics of Law*, 1990, New York: Pantheon.

Kennedy, D, *Sexy Dressing etc*, 1993, Cambridge, Mass: Harvard UP.

Kennedy, D, *A Critique of Adjudication: Fin-de-Siecle*, 1997, Cambridge, Mass: Harvard UP.

Klare, K, 'Law-making as praxis' (1979) 40 Telos 123.

Klare, K, 'Labour law as ideology: toward a new historiography of collective bargaining law' (1981) 4 Industrial Relations LJ 479.

Klare, K, 'The quest for industrial democracy and the struggle against racism: perspectives from labour law and civil rights law' (1982) 61 Oregon L Rev 157.

Krog, A, *Country of My Skull*, 1999, London: Vintage.

Landes, E and Posner, R, 'The economics of the baby shortage' (1978) 7 Journal of Legal Studies 323.

Leibniz, G, *Political Writings*, 1988, Cambridge: CUP.

Lessnoff, M, *Social Contract*, 1986, London: Macmillan.

Llewellyn, K, *The Bramble Bush: On Our Law and Its Study*, 1960a, New York: Little, Brown.

Llewellyn, K, *The Common Law Tradition*, 1960b, New York: Little, Brown.

Llewellyn, K, *Jurisprudence*, 1962, Chicago: Chicago UP.

Llewellyn, K and Hoebel, F, *The Cheyenne Way*, 1941, Norman: University of Oklahoma Press.

Locke, J, *An Essay Concerning Human Understanding*, 1961, London: Dent.

Locke, J, *An Essay Concerning Toleration*, 1968, Oxford: OUP.

Locke, J, *Two Treatises of Government*, 1989 [1690], London: Dent.

Lyotard, J-F, *The Postmodern Condition: A Report on Knowledge*, 1984, Manchester: Manchester UP.

Lyotard, J-F, *The Differend*, 1988, Manchester: Manchester UP.

Lyotard, J-F, *Heidegger and the 'Jews'*, 1990, Minneapolis: Minnesota UP.

Lyotard, J-F, '*Sensus communis*', in Benjamin, A (ed), *Judging Lyotard*, 1992, London: Routledge.

Machiavelli, N, *The Prince*, 1961, London: Penguin.

Machiavelli, N, *The Discourses*, 1983, London: Penguin.

MacIntyre, A, *A Short History of Ethics*, 1967, London: Routledge.

MacIntyre, A, *After Virtue*, 1985, London: Duckworth.

MacIntyre, A, *Whose Justice? Which Rationality?*, 1988, London: Duckworth.

MacKinnon, C, *Towards a Feminist Theory of State*, 1989, Cambridge, Mass: Harvard UP.

Macpherson, C, *The Political Theory of Possessive Individualism*, 1962, Oxford: OUP.

Macpherson, C, 'Introduction', in *Leviathan*, 1985, London: Penguin.

Majury, D, 'Strategizing in equality', in Fineman, M and Thomadsen, N (eds), *At the Boundaries of Law: Feminism and Legal Theory*, 1991, London: Routledge.

Malloy, R, 'Invisible hand or sleight of hand? Adam Smith, Richard Posner and the philosophy of law and economics' (1988) 36 University of Kansas L Rev 209.

Malloy, R, 'Is law and economics moral? – Humanistic economics and a classical liberal critique of Posner's economic analysis' (1990) 24 Valparaiso University L Rev 147.

Marcuse, H, *From Luther to Popper*, 1972, London: Verso.

Marenbon, J, *Later Medieval Philosophy*, 1991, London: Routledge.

Marshall, J, *John Locke: Resistance, Religion and Responsibility*, 1994, Cambridge: CUP.

Marx, K, *Capital*, 1975, London: Lawrence and Wishart.

Marx, K and Engels, F, *The Communist Manifesto*, 1985, London: Penguin.

McBride, W, *Albert Camus: Philosopher and Litteratur*, 1992, New York: St Martin's Press.

McLellan, D, *Karl Marx*, 1995a, London: Macmillan.

McLellan, D, *The Thought of Karl Marx*, 1995b, London: Macmillan.

Meier, H, *Carl Schmitt and Leo Strauss: The Hidden Dialogue*, 1995, Chicago: Chicago UP.

Melville, H, *Billy Budd, Sailor*, 1967, London: Penguin.

Michelfelder, D and Palmer, R (eds), *Dialogue and Deconstruction*, 1989, New York: SUNY Press.

Miliband, R, *Marxism and Politics*, 1977, Oxford: OUP.

Mill, J, *On Liberty*, 1985 [1861], London: Penguin.

Mill, J, *Autobiography*, 1989, London: Penguin.

Mill, J, *Principles of Political Economy*, 1994, Oxford: OUP.

Mill, J, *The Subjection of Women*, 2000, London: Broadview.

Mill, J and Bentham, J, *Utilitarianism and Other Essays*, 1987, London: Penguin.

Miller, J, *The Passion of Michel Foucault*, 1993, London: HarperCollins.

Milton, J, *Political Writings*, 1991, Cambridge: CUP.

Monk, R, *Wittgenstein: The Duty of Genius*, 1991, London: Vintage.

Montaigne, M, *Essays*, 1993, London: Penguin.

More, T, *Utopia*, 1965, London: Penguin.

Morris, W, *News From Nowhere*, 1995, Cambridge: CUP.

Mortley, R, *French Philosophers in Conversation*, 1991, London: Routledge.

Mouffe, C, *The Democratic Paradox*, 2000, London: Verso.

Murdoch, I, *Metaphysics as a Guide to Morals*, 1992, London: Penguin.

Murphy, T, 'Feminism on flesh' (1997) 8 Law and Critique 37.

Naffine, N, 'In praise of legal feminism' (2002) 22 Legal Studies 71.

Nietzsche, F, *The Will to Power*, 1968, New York: Vintage.

Nietzsche, F, *Thus Spoke Zarathustra*, 1969, London: Penguin.

Nietzsche, F, *Ecce Homo*, 1979, London: Penguin.

Nietzsche, F, *The Birth of Tragedy*, 1993 [1872], London: Penguin.

Nozick, R, *Anarchy, State and Utopia*, 1974, Oxford: Blackwell.

Nussbaum, M, *Love's Knowledge*, 1990, Oxford: OUP.

Nussbaum, M, *Cultivating Humanity: A Classical Defence of Reform in Liberal Education*, 1997, Cambridge, Mass: Harvard UP.

Nussbaum, M, *Sex and Social Justice*, 1999, Oxford: OUP.

Nussbaum, M, *Women and Human Development: The Capabilities Approach*, 2000, Cambridge: CUP.

O'Neill, O, 'The public use of reason' (1986) 14 Political Theory 523.

Ott, H, *Martin Heidegger: A Political Life*, 1994, London: Fontana.

Paine, T, *Rights of Man*, 1985 [1791], London: Penguin.

Paine, T, 'Common sense', in *The Thomas Paine Reader*, 1987, London: Penguin.

Plato, *The Last Days of Socrates*, 1969, London: Penguin.

Plato, *The Laws*, 1970, London: Penguin.

Plato, *Republic*, 1987, London: Penguin.

Pollack, M and Hafner-Burton, E, 'Mainstreaming gender in the European Union' (2000) 7 Journal of European Public Policy 432.

Popper, K, *The Open Society and its Enemies*, 1966, London: Routledge.

Posner, R, *Economic Analysis of Law*, 1986, Boston: Little, Brown.

Posner, R, 'The regulation of the market in adoptions' (1987) 67 Boston University L Rev 59.

Posner, R, *The Problems of Jurisprudence*, 1990, Cambridge, Mass: Harvard UP.

Posner, R, *Sex and Reason*, 1992, Cambridge, Mass: Harvard UP.

Posner, R, *Overcoming Law*, 1995, Cambridge, Mass: Harvard UP.

Postema, G, *Bentham and the Common Law Tradition*, 1986, Oxford: Clarendon.

Proudhon, P, *What is Property?*, 1994, Cambridge: CUP.

Radbruch, G, 'Legal philosophy', in Patterson, E (ed), *The Legal Philosophies of Lask, Radbruch and Drabin*, 1950, Cambridge, Mass: Harvard UP.

Rawls, J, *A Theory of Justice*, 1971, Oxford: OUP.

Rawls, J, 'Kantian constructivism in moral theory' (1980) 77 Journal of Philosophy 515.

Rawls, J, 'Justice not fairness: political not metaphysical' (1985) Philosophy and Public Affairs 223.

Rawls, J, 'The idea of an overlapping consensus' (1987) 7 OJLS 1.

Rawls, J, *Political Liberalism*, 1993, New York: Columbia UP.

Rawls, J, *The Law of Peoples*, 2001, Cambridge, Mass: Harvard UP.

Reiss, H (ed), *Kant: Political Writings*, 1991, Cambridge: CUP.

Rhode, D, 'Feminist critical theories' (1990) 42 Stanford L Rev 617.

Riley, P, *Leibniz's Universal Jurisprudence: Justice as the Charity of the Wise*, 1996, Cambridge, Mass: Harvard UP.

Roberts, D, *A Philosophical Introduction to Theology*, 1991, London: SCM Press.

Rogow, A, *Thomas Hobbes*, 1986, New York: Norton.

Rorty, R, *Philosophy and the Mirror of Nature*, 1980, Princeton: Princeton UP.

Rorty, R, *The Consequences of Pragmatism*, 1982, Minneapolis: Minnesota UP.

Rorty, R, *Contingency, Irony, and Solidarity*, 1989, Cambridge: CUP.

Rorty, R, *Essays on Heidegger and Others*, 1991a, Cambridge: CUP.

Rorty, R, *Objectivity, Relativism, and Truth*, 1991b, Cambridge: CUP.

Rorty, R, 'Trotsky and the wild orchids' (1992) 2 Common Knowledge 140.

Rorty, R, 'Human rights, rationality and sentimentality', in Shute, S and Hurley, S (eds), *On Human Rights: The Oxford Amnesty Lectures 1993*, 1993, New York: Basic Books.

Rorty, R, *Achieving Our Country: Letfist Thought in Twentieth-Century America*, 1998, Cambridge, Mass: Harvard UP.

Rorty, R, *Philosophy and Social Hope*, 1999, London: Penguin.

Ross, I, *The Life of Adam Smith*, 1995, Oxford: OUP.

Russell, B, *History of Western Philosophy*, 1961, London: Routledge.

Sandel, M, *Democracy's Discontent: America in Search of a Public Philosophy*, 1996, Cambridge, Mass: Harvard UP.

Santos, B, *Towards a New Common Sense: Law, Science and Politics in Paradigmatic Transition*, 1995, London: Routledge.

Sartre, J-P, *What is Literature?*, 1967, London: Methuen.

Sartre, J-P, *Being and Nothingness*, 2003, London: Routledge.

Schmitt, C, *The Concept of the Political*, 1976, Newark: Rutgers UP.

Schmitt, C, *Political Theology*, 1985, Boston: MIT Press.

Schmitt, C, *Political Romanticism*, 1986, Boston: MIT Press.

Schmitt, C, *The Crisis of Parliamentary Democracy*, 1988, Boston: MIT Press.

Sen, A, *On Ethics and Economics*, 1987, Oxford: Blackwell.

Shelley, P, 'A philosophical view of reform', in Foot, P (ed), *Shelley's Revolutionary Year*, 1990, London: Redwords.

Sheridan, A, *Michel Foucault: The Will to Truth*, 1980, London: Tavistock.

Sidney, A, *Discourses Concerning Government*, 1996, Indianapolis: Liberty Fund.

Singer, J, 'The player and the cards: nihilism and legal theory' (1984) 94 Yale LJ 60.

Smart, C, *Law, Crime and Sexuality: Essays in Feminism*, 1995, London: Sage.

Smith, A, *An Inquiry into the Nature and Causes of the Wealth of Nations*, 1976a, Oxford: OUP.

Smith, A, *A Theory of Moral Sentiments*, 1976b, Oxford: OUP.

Steiner, G, *In Bluebeard's Castle*, 1971, London: Faber.

Strauss, L, *Natural Right and History*, 1953, Chicago: Chicago UP.

Strauss, L, *The Political Philosophy of Thomas Hobbes*, 1963, Chicago: Chicago UP.

Strauss, L, 'Review', in Schmitt, C, *The Concept of the Political*, 1976, Newark: Rutgers UP.

Tamanaha, B, *A General Jurisprudence of Law and Society*, 2001, Oxford: OUP.

Tawney, R, *Religion and the Rise of Capitalism*, 1990, London: Penguin.

Taylor, C, *Sources of the Self*, 1989, Cambridge: CUP.

Thomas, D, *Locke on Government*, 1995, London: Routledge.

Thompson, E, *Whigs and Hunters*, 1990, London: Penguin.

Thompson, E, *The Making of the English Working Class*, 1991, London: Penguin.

Thompson, E, *Customs in Common*, 1993, London: Penguin.

Thoreau, H, *Walden and Civil Disobedience*, 1986, London: Penguin.

Trubek, D, 'Toward a social theory of law: an essay on the study of law and development' (1972) 82 Yale LJ 1.

Tuck, R, 'Thomas Hobbes', in *Great Political Thinkers*, 1992, Oxford: OUP.

Tushnet, M, 'An essay on rights' (1984) 62 Texas L Rev 1363.

Tushnet, M, 'Critical legal studies: a political history' (1991) 100 Yale LJ 1515.

Tutu, D, *No Future Without Forgiveness*, 1999, London: Ebury Press.

Twining, W, *Globalisation and Legal Theory*, 2000, London: Butterworths.

Twining, W, 'Cosmopolitan legal studies' (2002) 9 International Journal of the Legal Profession 99.

Twining, W, 'A post-Westphalian conception of law' (2003) 37 Law and Society Review 199.

Unger, R, *Knowledge and Politics*, 1975, New York: Free Press.

Unger, R, *Law in Modern Society*, 1976, New York: Free Press.

Unger, R, *Passion: An Essay on Personality*, 1984, New York: Free Press.

Unger, R, *The Critical Legal Studies Movement*, 1986, Cambridge, Mass: Harvard UP.

Unger, R, *Politics, a Work in Constructive Social Theory*, 1987, Cambridge: CUP.

Unger, R, *What Should Legal Analysis Become?*, 1996, London: Verso.

Ward, I, 'Natural law and reason in the philosophies of Maimonides and St Thomas Aquinas' (1992) 86 Durham University Journal 21.

Ward, I, 'Thomas Hobbes and the nature of contract' (1993) 25 Studia Leibnitiana 90.

Ward, I, *Law and Literature: Possibilities and Perspectives*, 1996, Cambridge: CUP.

Ward, I, *Kantianism, Postmodernism and Critical Legal Thought*, 1997, Dordrecht: Kluwer.

Ward, I, 'Universal jurisprudence and the case for legal humanism' (2001) 38 Alberta Law Review 941.

Ward, I, *Justice, Humanity and the New World Order*, 2003, Aldershot: Ashgate.

Weinrib, E, 'Law as a Kantian idea of reason' (1987a) 87 Columbia L Rev 471.

Weinrib, E, 'The intelligibility of the rule of law', in Hutchinson, A and Monahan, P (eds), *The Rule of Law: Ideal or Ideology?*, 1987b, Toronto: Carswell.

Weinrib, E, 'Legal formalism: on the immanent rationality of law' (1988) 97 Yale LJ 949.

Weisberg, R, *Poethics: and Other Strategies of Law and Literature*, 1992, New York: Columbia UP.

West, R, *Narrative, Authority and Law*, 1993, Ann Arbor: University of Michigan Press.

White, J, *When Words Lose Their Meaning: Constitutions and Reconstitutions of Language, Character, and Community*, 1984, Chicago: Chicago UP.

White, J, *Justice as Translation: An Essay in Cultural and Legal Criticism*, 1990, Chicago: Chicago UP.

Williams, P, *The Alchemy of Race and Rights*, 1991, Cambridge, Mass: Harvard UP.

Williams, P, *The Rooster's Egg: On the Persistence of Prejudice*, 1995, Cambridge, Mass: Harvard UP.

Wittgenstein, L, *Philosophical Investigations*, 1958, Oxford: Blackwell.

Wollstonecraft, M, *A Vindication of the Rights of Women*, 1995, London: Dent.

Wordsworth, W, 'The prelude', in *Complete Poetical Works*, 1936, Oxford: OUP.

Young-Breuhl, *Hannah Arendt: For Love of the World*, 1982, New Haven: Yale UP.

INDEX